GREAT COURTROOM BATTLES

Other books by
Richard Rubenstein:

REBELS IN EDEN
Mass Political Violence
in the United States

LEFT TURN
Origins And Next
American Revolution

GREAT COURTROOM BATTLES

Edited by

RICHARD E. RUBENSTEIN

PP

A PLAYBOY PRESS BOOK

Published simultaneously in the United States and Canada by Playboy Press, Chicago, Illinois. Printed in the United States of America. Library of Congress Catalog Card Number: 73-84923. First edition.

To
ALEC *and* MATTHEW

Acknowledgments

"The Lizzie Borden 'Axe Murder' Case." Adaptation of "Lizzie Borden" from VERDICT IN DISPUTE by Edgar Lustgarten is used by permission of Charles Scribner's Sons. Copyright © 1950 Charles Scribner's Sons.

"The 'Torso Murder' Case." Copyright © 1971 by F. Lee Bailey and Harvey Aronson from the book THE DEFENSE NEVER RESTS reprinted with permission of Stein and Day Publishers.

"The Cutter Labs 'Poison Vaccine' Case." Adaptation of "A Case of Warranty." Copyright © 1966 by The Lawyers Co-operative Publishing Company. From the book THE VERDICTS WERE JUST, edited by Albert Averbach and Charles Price, published by the David McKay Company, Inc. Reprinted by permission of the publishers.

"*Fanny Hill* In Hackensack." Adaptation of "*Fanny Hill* In Hackensack" condensed from THE END OF OBSCENITY by Charles Rembar, published by Random House, Inc. Copyright © 1968 by Charles Rembar. Reprinted by permission of Random House, Inc.

"The Al Capone Tax Case." Originally titled "The Trial of Alphonse Capone" from ENEMIES OF THE STATE by Francis X. Busch. Copyright © 1954 by The Bobbs-Merrill Company, Inc. Reprinted by permission of the publisher.

"The Alger Hiss Perjury Case." Adapted from Chapter 7, "A Traitor from Harvard," of . . .*And Justice For All* by William M. Kunstler. Published by Oceana Publications, Inc. Copyright © 1963 by William M. Kunstler. Adapted by permission of the publisher.

"The Trial of Reies Lopez Tijerina." From POLITICAL TRIALS, edited by Theodore L. Becker, Copyright © 1971 by The Bobbs-Merrill Company, Inc. Reprinted by permission of the publisher.

"The Court-Martial of Billy Mitchell" and "Mylai: The Court-Martial of Lt. Calley." From GREAT COURT-MARTIAL CASES by Joseph Di Mona. Copyright © 1972 by Joseph Di Mona. Published by Grosset & Dunlap, Inc.

"The Trial of Adolf Eichmann." Adaptation of "Witness Against Eichmann" by Justice Michael A. Musmanno. Copyright © 1966 by the Lawyers Cooperative Publishing Company. From the book THE VERDICTS WERE JUST, edited by Albert Averbach and Charles Price. Published by the David McKay Company, Inc. Reprinted by permission of the publishers.

TABLE OF CONTENTS

INTRODUCTION

People everywhere are fascinated by trials. Perhaps this is because a great courtroom battle, like those presented in this anthology, is a unique fusion of art and reality, combining all the elements of theatrical drama with the seriousness of real life in society. The performances of the brilliant trial lawyers represented in this volume *are* "performances" in the theatrical sense, but the result of a triumph is not merely critical acclaim; it is a life saved, a law reinterpreted, a reputation vindicated, a wrong righted.

In another sense, a courtroom confrontation resembles the competition between skilled athletes. We can hardly avoid identifying with one "team" or the other, and pulling for "our side" to win. The cases included in this book demonstrate what happens when two (or more) well-trained and talented trial lawyers meet head-to-head in legal combat before judge and jury. They are reminders that our civilized trials in decorous surroundings bear strong traces of their origin in armed "trial by combat" between sword-wielding champions.

For Americans, courtroom battles have a particularly strong fascination. Just think about the real and fictional trials embodied in our literature (from Melville's *Billy Budd* to Wouk's *Caine Mutiny*), our theater *(Inherit the Wind, The Crucible),* movies *(Compulsion, Anatomy of a Murder, To Kill a Mockingbird)* and television shows ("Perry Mason," "The Defenders," and so forth). In part, I think, this is because the American courtroom is so often the forum in which momentous issues of morality, politics and even religion are thrashed out. From the Salem witch trials and the conspiracy trial of Aaron Burr, through the Scopes "monkey trial," the Leopold-Loeb murder case and the trial of Sacco and Vanzetti, down to the Chicago conspiracy case and the Calley court-martial of our own time, matters of greatest importance to all Americans have been decided by lawyers, judges and juries. No wonder we look upon outstanding trial lawyers as champions.

The cases collected here, with few exceptions, are not those which are well known to every American schoolchild. In these pages the reader will discover great murder and obscenity cases, libel suits and negligence actions, political trials and military courts-martial. Although they all raise serious questions of law and morality, it is in no small part the quality of the lawyers' performances—and the excitement of equal combat—that makes them additionally memorable.

Aside from the sheer fascination their reading affords, these cases serve another purpose. Our strong interest in courtroom combat has produced a popular and vastly oversimplified version of trial procedures in which "good guys" and "bad guys" fight it out like old-time cowboys and Indians, with the bad guys naturally losing in the end. (On the *Perry Mason* television series, they not only lose, they confess!) This simplification demeans the whole process and its skills. For example, many people assume that the purpose of cross-examination is to discover the guilty party, Perry Mason style, when its real purposes are more subtle and complex (and, to the knowing observer, much more exciting) than this. Such popular fiction actually underrates the ingeniousness and underestimates the fighting qualities of the real "champions" of the courtroom. I would rather try a case against Perry Mason than against Mel Belli any day!

But I need say no more about this. These cases, as described by expert reporters, speak for themselves.

Richard E. Rubenstein
Chicago
February 1972

GREAT COURTROOM BATTLES

THE LIZZIE BORDEN "AXE MURDER" CASE

Hosea Knowlton
for the prosecution

vs.

George D. Robinson
for the defense

by Edgar Lustgarten

The trial of Lizzie Borden, daughter of a distinguished New England family, for the murder of her mother and father was the most sensational murder trial of the 19th Century in America. Some 80 years later, children skipping rope in Los Angeles or New York may still be heard chanting, "Lizzie Borden took an axe, gave her mother forty whacks . . ." The trial itself was remarkable—but so is this description by Edgar Lustgarten, a contemporary British writer who has no equal in retelling trial stories. Lustgarten's forte is his understanding of the intricacies of trial practice and his respect for the art of the great practitioners. His commentary on the technique of cross-examination is a small masterpiece of its kind. Read on!

The charge against Lizzie Borden was inconceivable. That was the enduring strength of her defense. No matter how cogent the evidence, no matter how honest the witness, how could anyone credit the prosecution's case? That a woman, gently bred and delicately nurtured, should plan a murderous assault upon her stepmother; that she should execute it in the family home with such ferocious and demoniac force that the victim's head was smashed almost to pulp; that, having gazed upon her sickening handiwork, she should calmly wait an hour or more for her father to return; that she should then slaughter him with even greater violence so that hardened physicians shuddered at the sight; that neither loss of nerve nor pricking of remorse seemed to follow in the wake of such unnatural butchery—this was a tale that not merely challenged but defied belief. It was like asking one to accept the testimony of others that a horse recited Shakespeare or a dog had solved an anagram.

Everything combined to make this strain upon credence almost insupportable. At the eighteenth century's lowest moral ebb, some slatternly wanton such as Hogarth drew might have done these murders in a fetid slum, and still relied on incredulity giving the most unthinking jury pause. But this was not the eighteenth century; it was 1892. It was no strumpet of the streets who faced her trial, but the well-respected daughter of a well-respected man. And the setting of the scene was not Gin Lane or Seven Dials but Fall River, Massachusetts, deep in the heart of puritan New England.

Fall River at that time was a pleasant enough place, about

the size of modern Cambridge, and not unlike a university town in its strong sense of community. People took close interest in other people's business. The leading citizens and chief officials were known by sight to all. Town matters wagged more tongues than national politics, and Fall River natives recognized as aristocracy, not the remote Four Hundred of New York, but the old Yankee families dwelling in their midst.

To this local elite belonged the Bordens, with Andrew Jackson Borden at their head. He was a prosperous businessman and banker who, through a union of acumen and avarice, steadily increased his considerable wealth. He chose to live, however, in rather modest style. His first wife having died when he was forty, he presently wedded one Miss Abby Gray and, with her and the two daughters of his former marriage, took up residence in a house on Second Street. It was a narrow house standing in a narrow garden, hemmed in by other houses on almost every side, with its front door only a few feet from the traffic and bustle of a much frequented thoroughfare. In a sense, nothing was lacking: downstairs had a sitting room, a dining room, and a parlor; upstairs had a guest room and a dressing room for Mrs. Borden besides a separate bedroom for each of the two girls. But there was space without spaciousness, convenience without luxury, and both inside and out the house was unimposing if one remembered that this was the abode of a rich man.

In August 1892 the Bordens had been living there for about twenty years. Andrew was almost seventy. His wife was sixty-four. Miss Emma was forty-one. Miss Lizzie was thirty-two.

Before Miss Lizzie reached the age of thirty-three, this sedate and unexciting gentlewoman had made her name a lasting household word.

To all outward appearance the Borden house harbored a tranquil and contented household. But the facade was deceptive.

Behind its look of blank correctitude lay deep antipathies and painful tensions.

The causes, though various, were intimately allied. There was the unattractive nature of the master; with his niggardly ways of autocratic temper, old Andrew inspired dread rather than affection. There was the classical aversion to the presence of a stepmother; the second Mrs. Borden, though amiable and harmless, could not engage the goodwill of Andrew's daughters. And as the latter grew up, their bitterness developed in the shape of jealousy and squabbling over property—jealousy that sprang from already strained relationships, squabbling that shadowed those relationships still more. The time came when Miss Lizzie, sharper-spoken of the sisters, pointedly dropped the appellation "Mother" and adopted the formal "Mrs. Borden" in its stead.

The division in the family intensified and hardened. As years went by, Miss Emma and Miss Lizzie evolved a technique to avoid their parents' company. Downstairs in the common rooms some contact was inevitable, but they contrived to reduce this to a satisfactory minimum by altering the times at which they took their meals. Upstairs it was much simpler. By bolting a single communicating door, the first floor could be split up into independent parts, one served by the front stairs, the other by the back.

On both sides of this door the bolts were permanently drawn.

The Massachusetts summer is uncomfortably hot. That of 1892 was no exception to the rule, and Fall River sweltered through those long July days during which dogs are reputed to go mad.

Late in the month Miss Emma left for Fairhaven, where she had arranged to spend a holiday with friends. At the same time Miss Lizzie paid a visit to New Bedford, but was back again at home before the week was out. In the sultry, stifling nights that followed her return, four people slept at the house on Second Street: Miss Lizzie, the old couple, and the servant, Bridget Sullivan, who occupied a room on the attic floor above.

On Wednesday, August 3rd, the four increased to five. Uncle Morse, a brother of the late Mrs. Borden, arrived unexpectedly to stay a night or two. He found Andrew and his wife a little out of sorts; whether through the heat, or through some less obvious cause, in the previous night both had been seized with vomiting, and, though better, were still not free from physical malaise. Lizzie, too, they told him, had been similarly affected, but, in that divided and dissevered house, Uncle Morse was not to see his niece till nearly noon next day.

By then any thought of this mild indisposition had vanished in the stress of far more terrible events.

August 4th, 1892, is a memorable date in the history of crime.

At the Borden home, where the grisly drama was to be enacted, the morning opened normally enough. The older people were all early risers, and seven o'clock found them sitting down to breakfast, prepared and served by the young Irish maid. The sun climbed swiftly into a clear sky; the air was heavy with the heat of many weeks; all signs portended, rightly as it proved, that they were in for another scorching day. All the more reason to perform one's chores before the torrid blaze of afternoon.

By nine o'clock Uncle Morse had left the house to visit relatives elsewhere in the town. By nine fifteen Mr. Borden had set out on his round of business calls. Mrs. Borden had got a feather duster and was occupying herself with her household duties.

Meanwhile Miss Lizzie had made her first appearance. At nine o'clock she came into the kitchen where the servant Bridget was washing up the dishes. Bridget asked her what she fancied for her breakfast, but Miss Lizzie didn't seem to fancy very much. Having helped herself to a cup of coffee, she sat down to drink it at the kitchen table.

When the dishes were finished, Bridget took them to the dining room. There Mrs. Borden was assiduously dusting. She had noticed that the windows had got dirty and asked Bridget to wash them as her next domestic task.

Bridget decided to wash the outsides first. She got a brush and some clothes, filled a pail with water, and went out through the side door, which she left unlocked.

Mrs. Borden stayed inside. So did Miss Lizzie. The sun beat down with pitiless persistence and a drowsy silence fell upon the house.

At the partition fence Bridget stopped for a gossip with the maid next door. Then she started on the window-cleaning, working her way methodically round the house. She naturally looked into each ground-floor room in turn. She saw nobody in any.

The outside washing took perhaps an hour. Bridget then went back into the house, carefully locking the side door behind her. The Bordens were fussy about things like that, being morbidly fearful of robbers and intruders.

Everything was quiet; no one was about. Upstairs, taking it easy, Bridget enviously thought; best thing to do, on a broiler such as this. Conscientiously she started on the inside of the windows. . . .

At a quarter to eleven there was a noise at the front door; fumbling with a key and rattling of the lock. Must be Mr. Borden. Bridget dropped her cloths and ran to let him in.

She found the front door not only locked but bolted. As she struggled to get it open so as not to keep the master waiting, somebody behind her laughed out loud.

Bridget glanced over her shoulder. Miss Lizzie was standing

at the top of the staircase, a few feet from the open door of the guest room. What moved her to mirth at that particular moment must ever be a theme for speculation; whether it was the spectacle of a flustered Bridget, or whether it was some hilarious secret of her own. . . .

When Mr. Borden was finally admitted, Miss Lizzie came downstairs.

"Mrs. Borden has gone out," she volunteered. "She had a note from someone who is sick."

Her father made no comment. It was hotter than ever, and he had still not shaken off the after-effects of that mysterious illness. His walk round town had tired him more than usual. He went into the sitting room to rest.

Bridget was now doing the windows in the dining room. Miss Lizzie joined her there. She brought in an ironing board, put it on the table, produced some handkerchiefs, and commenced to iron.

For a space the two women worked away in silence. Then Miss Lizzie asked a casual-sounding question.

"Are you going out?"

"I don't know," Bridget said, energetically polishing. "I might and I might not."

"If you go out," said Miss Lizzie, "be sure and lock the door, for Mrs. Borden has gone out on a sick call and I might go out too."

"Miss Lizzie, who is sick?" the maid inquired.

"I don't know. She had a note this morning; it must be in town."

The windows were finished. Bridget withdrew into the kitchen, where she washed out the cloths. Presently Miss Lizzie followed her.

"There's a cheap sale of dress goods on downtown," she remarked. "They are selling some kind of cloth at eight cents a yard."

"Well," Bridget said, "I guess I'll have some."

But at the moment Bridget did not feel inclined for out-of-doors. She had been up since six and kept hard at it ever since. A lie on the bed would make a nice mid-morning break. . . .

In her attic box, Bridget yawned, stretched herself, and relaxed. On the sitting-room couch old Andrew, spent by his exertions, fell asleep. Once again the house lay in the stillness of that drowsy quiet.

The alarm was given fifteen minutes later.

Bridget, day-dreaming beneath the baking roof, heard her name called somewhere far below. Even at that distance, though, she caught the note of urgency. She jumped up at once and called out to know what was the matter.

"Come down quick," Miss Lizzie's voice floated up through the house. "Come down quick; Father's dead; somebody came in and killed him."

Dumbfounded and mistrusting her own ears, Bridget ran down the back stairs as fast as she could go.

Miss Lizzie was standing close to the side door. Bridget made as if to go into the sitting room, but Miss Lizzie checked her—perhaps to spare her feelings.

"Don't go in. I've got to have a doctor quick."

Doctor Bowen lived opposite. Bridget flew across the road, leaving Miss Lizzie sole guardian of the dead.

The doctor arrived and went straight into the sitting room. He was to describe what he saw there later on the witness stand. "Mr. Borden was lying on the lounge. His face was very badly cut, apparently with a sharp instrument; it was covered with blood. I felt of his pulse and satisfied myself that he was dead. I glanced about the room and saw there was nothing disturbed; neither the furniture nor anything at all. Mr. Borden was lying on his right side, apparently at ease, as if asleep. His face was hardly to be recognized by one who knew him."

The news spread like wildfire. As police and officials hurried to the house, a crowd of gapers packed the street outside, eager for any sight or sound connected with calamity.

Dr. Bowen had to force a passage through this throng when he came out of the gate. He had covered Andrew Borden's body with a sheet; there was no other service he could usefully perform; now, at Miss Lizzie's personal request, he was going to the post office to telegraph Miss Emma. Mrs. Borden, he had gathered, had gone upon some errand, and all they could do was wait for her return. Poor woman, Dr. Bowen thought, as he watched the gathering thicken; wherever she is, she'll hear the tidings soon enough.

He dispatched the telegram and gloomily made his way back towards the house. As he entered, a neighbor of the Bordens caught his arm. Her face was grey and her hands shook uncontrollably.

"They have found Mrs. Borden," she said huskily.

"Where?" asked the doctor.

"Upstairs," said the neighbor. "In the front room."

It was Miss Lizzie's suggestion that had prompted them to search; "I'm almost positive," she said, "I heard her coming in." It was Bridget and the neighbor who discovered Mrs. Borden, lying lifeless and mangled on the guest-room floor. Her body was growing cold, and the blood which enveloped her mutilated head had already become matted and practically dry.

The doctors concluded that when Andrew Borden died his wife had already been dead more than an hour.

If the case had stopped short there, if no charge against anyone had ever been preferred, Massachusetts would still have gone through weeks of ferment. If some hobo, some outcast, had been taxed with the crimes, his trial and the verdict determining his fate would have furnished all America with months of keen discussion. But when, after seven days of correlating evidence, during which the incredible gradually took shape, Fall River police arrested Lizzie Borden, the case at once acquired an entirely different stamp. It transcended the limits of geography and fashion; its range in time was perpetuity, in space the globe.

The trial of Lizzie Borden, delayed by various formalities of the law, took place at New Bedford in June 1893. It lasted thirteen days. . . .

Three judges sat upon the bench: Chief Justice Mason, Mr. Justice Blodgett, and Mr. Justice Dewey. For the Commonwealth (equivalent of the Crown) was Hosea Knowlton, the District Attorney, aided and partnered by William Moody, a colleague imported from an adjacent area. George D. Robinson, a former Congressman and ex-Governor of the State, with Andrew Jennings and Melvin Adams made up the team engaged for the defense.

To the modern eye, which finds a whiskered barrister hardly less freakish than a bald musician, there would have been something richly comic in the fine display of fringe, moustache, and beard visible on counsels' row at Lizzie Borden's trial. But the advocates who sported these adornments were far from comic figures. They were masters of their complicated craft: shrewd in tactics, dexterous in argument, keen in cross-questioning, eloquent in speech. The defense, while energetically contesting every point and seizing every benefit admitted by the rules, took care in doing so never to depart from the highest standard of forensic practice. The prosecution, while making no effort to conceal the reluctance and distaste with which they entered on the case, did not suffer this to influence or impede the effective discharge of their melancholy duty. . . .

Moody's speech was diffidently phrased, as befitted a naturally modest second string. He had frequent recourse to the protective "I believe" and to the half-apologetic "We fix that as well as we can." But there was no cause for diffidence in the evidence he outlined. Before he had finished, it was clear to demonstration that the Commonwealth had only moved on very solid ground. Their case was widely as well as firmly based—on proof of motive, indications of design, circumstances pointing to exclusive opportunity, and acts by Miss Lizzie which (it could be argued) were only reconcilable with consciousness of guilt.

The motive broached, of course, was hatred of the stepmother, and concern for the destination of the father's substance. Counsel crystallized the bitterness that had inspired the former by referring to a slight but illuminating incident. It had occured in the house on the morning of the murders while the bodies were still lying there in piteous quiescence. The Assistant City Marshall had arrived upon the scene, and in fulfillment of his office was questioning Miss Lizzie. "When did you last see your mother?" he had asked. "She is not my mother, sir," Miss Lizzie had replied. "She is my stepmother. My mother died when I was a child. . . ."

The prisoner's opportunity of accomplishing both murders was plain and incontestable on the admitted facts. But the Commonwealth was able to take this a step further. It was not only that Miss Lizzie had had ample opportunity; was there any opportunity for anybody else? The other members of the household were ruled out; Emma was in Fairhaven, Uncle Morse was with a niece more than a mile away, Bridget at the time of the second murder was upstairs. If it was not Miss Lizzie, then it must have been an intruder. There had been no entry by force. And, assuming for the moment that someone could get in and out completely unobserved, where were the signs that anyone had done so? Nothing was disturbed. No property was taken. No drawers had been ransacked. Mr. Borden's watch and money—more than eighty dollars—were left upon his person. What then was the motive prompting someone from outside? Was he perhaps one of those men Miss Lizzie spoke of to Miss Russell who had come to pay old Borden out after some angry clash? Then how came it that there was not the slightest evidence of a struggle? Old Andrew may have been asleep upon the sitting-room couch, but his wife would hardly go to sleep upon the guest-room floor. And yet, said Moody, "the assailant, whoever he or she may have been, was able to approach each victim, in broad daylight, and, without a struggle or a murmur, to lay them low."

Motive fixed; design set forth; opportunity established. But there still remains the weightiest part of the prosecution's case: the *behavior* of Miss Lizzie that day and the days after. Upon three matters especially the Commonwealth pressed hard: one, the note from the unidentified sick person; two, the variations in Miss Lizzie's story; three, the burning of the light-blue figured dress.

The business of the note is perhaps the most damning single point against the prisoner. "Mrs. Borden has gone out," says Miss Lizzie to her father, at the moment when he may go looking for her round the house. "She had a note from someone who is sick." There can be no denying that was what Miss Lizzie said; she admitted it herself when examined at the inquest. She had not, she deposed, seen the note with her own eyes, but Mrs. Borden told her of it, without naming the sender. Hence her own statement when her father returned home—a natural passing-on of domestic information. But the Commonwealth would have none of it. "That statement," declared Moody, "we put forward as a lie; it was intended for no purpose except to stifle inquiry into the whereabouts of Mrs. Borden."

It is the grave and awful fact that neither note nor sick person ever came to light. The implications for the prisoner are appalling, and, try as they would, the defense could not avoid them. The Commonwealth, not surprisingly, came to elevate the note to the most vital place of all, and it formed the subject matter of a powerful passage in the long speech which constituted Knowlton's winding up. "My learned associate said in opening that that statement was a lie. I reaffirm that serious charge. No note came; no note was written; nobody brought a note; nobody was sick. Mrs. Borden had not had a note. *I will stake the case,"* said the District Attorney, *"on your belief in the truth of that proposition. . . .*

"Little did it occur to Lizzie Borden when she told that lie to her father that there would be eighty thousand witnesses of its falsity. My distinguished friend has had the hardihood to suggest that somebody may have written that note and not come forward to say so. Why, Mr. Foreman, do you believe there exists in Fall River anybody so lost to all sense of humanity who would not have rushed forward without anything being said? But they have advertised for the writer of the note which was never written and which never came. . . . The whole falsehood of that note came from the woman in whose keeping Mrs. Borden was left by Andrew Borden, and it was false as the answer Cain gave to his Maker when He said to him, 'Where is thy brother Abel?' "

Cain had answered, "Am I my brother's keeper?" Lizzie Borden had not waited to be asked. "Mrs. Borden has gone out. She had a note from someone who is sick."

Maybe she was more free from sin than Cain. Maybe she was just smarter. . . .

The murders were committed on a Thursday. It was not till the next Sunday that Miss Lizzie burnt the dress.

There was no attempt at concealment or deception; no surreptitious happenings beneath the cloak of night. She acted quite openly, in daylight, before witnesses. For an innocent woman, her behavior was extraordinarily naïve; for a guilty one, it was extraordinarily stupid—or, as in the tales of G.K. Chesterton and Poe, extraordinarily clever in its very ostentation. For Miss Lizzie had been warned to pick her steps with care. On the Saturday evening the Mayor of Fall River had expressly informed her that she was now under suspicion.

It was the following day, a little before noon. Alice Russell, who at this time was staying in the house, came down from the upper floor and went into the kitchen. There she found both Miss Lizzie and Miss Emma. The latter was busy washing dishes at the sink. Miss Lizzie was standing at the far end by the stove. She had a dress over her arm.

As Miss Russell came in Miss Emma turned her head and said to her sister: "What are you going to do?" "I'm going to burn this old thing up," replied Miss Lizzie. "It's all covered with paint."

She proceeded forthwith to tear it into strips.

There were several policemen on duty in the yard who could easily see in any time they chose to look. Miss Russell was so conscious of the equivocal effect created by this scene that she urged her friend at least to stand back from the window. "I wouldn't do that," she said, "where people can see you." Perhaps this remark took Miss Lizzie by surprise. At any rate, she did step a little out of vision—and placidly went on with the destruction of the dress.

The police, as Moody pointed out, had already searched the house and examined every garment to see if it was stained. They had found none marked with paint.

If the Commonwealth could have proved beyond a peradventure that the dress Miss Lizzie burnt upon the stove was the dress she had worn on the morning of the murders, they would have pried loose the chief plank in her defense. *Not one who saw her on that convulsive morning had observed any blood upon her person or her clothes,* though—out of convention rather than necessity—neighbors had unhooked her dress, fanned her face and rubbed her hands. . . . If Miss Lizzie committed these two sanguinary crimes ("the assailant would be spattered," said the prosecution expert) she would . . . presumably be bound to wash and change. But she must have done it *twice* —and each time at the risk of being come upon by Bridget before all the traces of blood had been removed. And even if she ran that risk and, by the yardstick of success, justified her daring, how did she dispose of the incriminating clothes? After the second death, when the time margin was so narrow, they could only have been hidden somewhere in the house.

There lay the significance of the light-blue figured dress which the prosecution sought to prove was the robe of homicide. But this was precisely what they could not do. Their witnesses disagreed among themselves about the dress Miss Lizzie wore upon the crucial day. Mrs. Churchill said one thing, Doctor Gowen said another, and neither Bridget nor Miss Russell could recall the dress at all.

Nonetheless, and notwithstanding its contradictory features, the Sunday-morning episode in the kitchen was not one calculated to allay suspicion.

If, upon purely circumstantial evidence, you invite a jury to convict someone of murder, you must be ready with the answers to all their unspoken questions. Moody had dealt with "What for?" There still remained "What with?"

Murders like these are not done with the bare hands, nor with any light and pocketable weapon. From some of the wounds on Andrew Borden's head the length of the inflicting blade could be accurately fixed. It was three and a half inches, and it had fallen with the weight of a hatchet or an axe.

Where was this fearsome and death-dealing instrument?

It had not been abandoned at the scene of the crime. The murderer, therefore, had taken it away. Was it likely, Moody asked, that an intruder would have done so—that he would have run out with his bloodstained weapon into the sunlit street? Or did probability point to an inmate of the house, acquainted with its resources for concealment and disposal?

In the cellar, in a box upon the chimney shelf, the police had discovered a hatchet's head. The handle had been broken off, and the fragment that remained was covered with a coarse white dust of ashes. The blade of this hatchet had been measured. It was exactly three and a half inches long. . . .

Here once again was deep suspicion that fell short of proof. The Commonwealth was appropriately reserved. "We do not insist," said Moody, "that these homicides were committed with this hatchet. *It may* have been the weapon." He paused. "It may *well* have been the weapon." . . .

Next day the witnesses got into their stride, and defender Robinson got into his.

The ex-Governor was a jury advocate of natural talent and mature experience. He knew the world; he gauged people astutely; he had a flair for methods of approach. His mind was subtle, his expressions simple; he not merely understood others, he could make others understand.

In the Borden trial, his most important cross-examination was that of Bridget Sullivan, the Irish maid. It could hardly have been bettered.

Bridget was not by any means a vulnerable witness. She was neither fool nor knave. But, like most human beings, she was susceptible to suggestion and subject to mistake. Discreetly

Robinson made his own suggestions; relentlessly he exploited her mistakes.

He began by seeking Bridget's help in challenging the idea that the Borden family was rent asunder by ill feeling. How far he could go with this could hardly be foreseen, and it is worth observing how every question tests or prepares a foothold for the next.

"Did *you* have any trouble there?" he asked.

"I?" said Bridget. "No, sir."

"A pleasant *place* to live?"

"Yes, sir."

"A pleasant *family* to be in?"

"I don't know how the family was," said Bridget, "I got along all right."

This was a slight setback. It might even be a warning. Robinson explored with a sure but gentle touch, like a surgeon who comes upon some dubious obstruction.

"You never saw anything *out of the way?"*

"No, sir."

Good; if she never saw anything "out of the way" one might be a little bolder and more definite.

"You never saw any *conflict* in the family?"

"No, sir."

Excellent; one could go the whole hog now, and put it into terms the jury couldn't fail to grasp.

"Never saw any *quarrelling,* or anything of that kind?"

"No, sir," answered Bridget, "I did not see."[1]

So far so good. The girl had seen no open wrangles. But Robinson wished to take it a stage further, and dispel any belief in a purely passive feud. He tackled Bridget about the allegation that Miss Emma and Miss Lizzie held aloof from family meals.

---

[1]Those interested in the technique of cross-examination will find a detailed analysis of this passage in the Appendix.

"Didn't they eat with the family?" he asked.

"Not all the time."

Robinson took this reply and turned it upside down.

"But they did from time to time, did they not?"

The meaning was the same but the effect had been changed. It was like substituting "half-full" for "half-empty."

"Yes, sir," Bridget said, somewhat doubtfully, and added, "Most of the time they didn't eat with their father and mother."

Counsel met her insistence with the utmost ingenuity.

"Did they get up as early as the father and mother?"

"No, sir."

"So they had their breakfast later?"

A logician would have jibbed at the word "so." But George D. Robinson had the measure of his audience. The Borden jurymen would not be conversant with the fallacy of *post hoc propter hoc.* Absences from breakfast were credibly accounted for.

"And how was it at dinner?"

"They were sometimes at dinner," Bridget said. "But a good many more times they were not."

"Sometimes they were out?" Robinson suggested.

"I don't know where they were; I could not tell."

Bridget was digging in her heels. A whole string of gains may be sacrificed by ill-timed importunity. Smoothly the advocate altered his direction.

"Did you ever hear Miss Lizzie talk with Mrs. Borden?"

"Yes, sir; she always spoke to Mrs. Borden when Mrs. Borden talked to her."

"Always did?" repeated Robinson, making certain they had caught it in the recesses of the jury box.

"Yes, sir."

"The conversation went on in the ordinary way, did it?"

"Yes, sir."

"How was it this Thursday morning after they came downstairs?"

Bridget wrinkled her forehead.

"I don't remember."

"Didn't they talk in the sitting room?"

"Yes."

"Who spoke?"

"Miss Lizzie and Mrs. Borden."

"Talking calmly, the same as anybody else?"

"Yes, sir."

This enabled Robinson to make a bigger throw.

"There was not, as far as you know, any trouble that morning?"

"No, sir," said Bridget. "I did not see any."

In this phase of the questioning relations were quite amicable. It would not have suited Robinson if they had been otherwise. But now a more acrimonious passage was impending.

The conception of a murderous intruder constituted a vital part of Robinson's defense. To account for the fact that between crimes One and Two an intruder must have remained upon the premises more than an hour, experiments had been carried out with the object of establishing that he could have concealed himself in a closet in the hall. But primarily he would have had to obtain access to the house; and this in practice was limited to periods during which the side door had been left unlocked. The more they were, and the longer, the better for Miss Lizzie.

Bridget, in direct examination, had fixed one; she owned to leaving the side door "off the hook" while she was cleaning the outside of the windows. She agreed, too, with Robinson that, while she was engaged upon the windows in the front and while she was chatting to the next door neighbors' maid, the side door would be hidden from her view and—Robinson's words—"the field pretty clear for a person to walk in."

All that was very well, but it was not enough. Robinson knew that a useful piece was missing. Earlier on the morning of the murders, Bridget had gone out, not to the front but to the yard; it would widen the scope for the conjectural intruder if she had left the door unhooked when she returned on that occasion. Many months before, at the inquest at Fall River, she had said she couldn't tell whether she did or not. With Miss Lizzie on trial for her life, Bridget had somehow recollected, "When I came back from the yard," she had asserted, "I hooked up the side door."

Robinson did not propose to let the matter pass. Every minute that the side door might have been unhooked was precious. Before she left the stand the girl was going to retract.

He picked up a bulky set of papers. It was a transcript of the evidence at the inquest.

"Do you think," he said, "and there was the faintest undertone of menace in his drawl, "do you think you have told us today just as you told us before?"

"I have told all I know," said Bridget.

"I don't ask you that." The tone suddenly sharpened. "What I want to know is whether you have told it today just as you did before?"

"Well, I think I did," said Bridget, a shade taken aback. Mr. Robinson had seemed such an easy, pleasant man. "I think I did, as far as I remember."

"What did you do as to the side door when you came in from the yard?"

"I hooked it."

"Did you say so before at the other examination?"

"I think so."

"Do you *know* so?"

Bridget wavered.

"I'm not sure," she said.

"Let me read and see if you said this." He read aloud, very

slowly and distinctly. " 'Question: When you came in from the yard did you hook the side door? Answer: I don't know whether I did or not.' Did you say so?"

"Well, I *must* have hooked it because—"

"That isn't it," Robinson cut in without ceremony. "Was that the way you testified?"

"I testified the truth."

"I don't imply that you didn't." It was indeed Robinson's whole point that she did; that the truth about the hooking of the door had been given at the inquest and not at the trial. "I merely want to know if you recall testifying over there at Fall River that you couldn't tell whether you hooked the door or not?"

But it stuck in Bridget's gullet.

"It is *likely* I did hook it, for it was always kept hooked."

Robinson's face was very stern.

"Do you positively recollect one way or the other?"

"Well," said Bridget, scared but obstinate, "I *generally* hook the side door."

"That isn't what I asked." The ex-Governor was peremptory. "Did you hook it or did you not?"

"I know I *must* have hooked the door for I always—"

"That isn't it. Did you hook it or did you not?'

Bridget gave up.

"I don't know," she said. "I don't know whether I did or not."

The spectators took a deep breath. Ex-Governor Robinson's frown relaxed. He looked almost affable again as he passed on to the next question. . . .

With the acknowledged leading lady unwilling to perform, Miss Emma Borden became the star of the defense.

Here was indeed a most serviceable deputy. She could give much of Lizzie's story without running Lizzie's risk. She could tell the jury almost all her sister could have told about the prelude, the background, and the sequel to the crimes; but because on August 4th she had been away at Fairhaven, she could not be cross-questioned about the day itself. The substitution of the elder sister for the younger was a neat and effective tactical device.

According to the best theatrical tradition, Miss Emma's entrance was deliberately delayed. When at long last the Commonwealth rested (on the tenth day, in defiance of the scriptures), the defenders first released a little swarm of witnesses each of whom contributed some item of his own. One, who lived just behind the Borden home, had heard a curious "pounding" on the night of August 3rd. Another, who had passed the house early on the 4th, had seen a young fellow hanging around; he was pale and "acting strangely." A third, walking by a little later in the morning, observed an unknown man leaning up against the gate. Such evidence was flimsy, not to say remote, but shrewd George Robinson perceived a latent value in composing this sketch of an alternative assassin.

The jury spent some hours among these fanciful conjectures. When the big moment arrived, though, and Miss Emma took the stand, they were instantly plunged back into the cold, harsh world of fact.

Miss Emma, whatever nervousness she felt, rose to the requirements of her exacting role. Her timing was precise. She described how her father always wore a single ring; how it had been given to him years ago by Lizzie; how it was the only jewelry he ever wore; how it was on his finger at the moment of his death and how it was still upon his finger in the grave. She described how thoroughly the police had searched the house and how Miss Lizzie never made the least objection. She described how her sister burnt the dress on Sunday morning, and said that *she, Miss Emma, had prompted her to do it.* "The dress got paint on it in May when the men painted the house.

. . . On Saturday the day of the search, I went to the clothes press to hang up my own dress. There was no vacant nail. I searched round to find a nail and noticed this dress. "You've not destroyed that old dress yet," I said to Lizzie. She said: "I think I will," and I said: "I would if I were you."

Miss Lizzie would certainly have done it far less well. George Robinson himself could not have done it better. The telegraph systems tapped it out across the world; the sister has come out strongly on Lizzie Borden's side. . . .

Other things being equal, recent impressions are bound to be the strongest. That is why advocates contend for the last word. In the Borden trial the last word lay with Knowlton, because of the evidence that had been called for the defense. Robinson had to precede his opponent, with all the disadvantages attached to that position.

In his introduction to the transcript of the trial—an essay that stands high in the literature of crime—Mr. Edmund Pearson compares Robinson with Knowlton, and does not conceal his preference for the latter. It is true that Knowlton was animated by the loftiest sentiments and the noblest ideals. It is true that he spoke majestic prose with a splendid rhythm and an almost biblical ring. It is true that Robinson, by contrast, was homespun and colloquial, with both feet firmly planted on the Massachusetts earth. None the less, I am convinced, he was the better advocate and had the astuter mind. He possessed what, for want of a better word, one may call courtcraft; he attuned himself exactly to the mental pitch prevailing; he neither preached to nor lectured nor apostrophized the jury, but *talked* to them about the case as a neighbor might at home.

Along these lines and within these limits, his final speech was a real forensic feat.

It is evident that throughout he kept in mind not only the logic of facts and of events, but the way the jury could be relied upon to *feel.* He began by playing on their natural reluctance to believe that a woman could have carried out these crimes; "It is physically and morally impossible." He traded on the human love of jeering at the police: "They make themselves ridiculous, insisting that a defendant shall know everything that was done on a particular time, shall account for every moment of that time, shall tell it three or four times alike, shall never waver or quiver, shall have tears or not have tears, shall make no mistakes."

Beside these matters of emotional propensity, he swept into place the one solid piece of evidence that told heavily and positively in favor of his client. "Blood speaks out, though it is voiceless. It speaks out against the criminal. Not a spot on her, from her hair to her feet, on dress or person anywhere. Think of it! Think of it for an instant."

Having laid this foundation of artistically commingled hypothesis and fact, Robinson turned to the prosecution's case. He took the points against him one by one, and in plain, familiar words, with nicely managed raillery, made all—or nearly all—appear paltry or fallacious.

"Why do they say she did it?" he inquired. "Well, in the first place, they say she was in the house." Already it sounded far less good a point than when it had been termed "exclusive opportunity." Robinson added to the ground so quickly gained. "She was in the house. Well, that may look to you like a very wrong place for her to be in. But . . . it is her own home. I don't know where I would want my daughter to be than at home, attending to the ordinary vocations of life, as a dutiful member of the household."

The jury pouted their lips sagely. No doubt about that; she had a right to be at home. No, sir; couldn't say she was to blame for being at home.

Next, the Commonwealth had talked about a motive. Why, Robinson demanded, did they set great store on this? "If a person commits a murder and we know it, there is no reason to inquire for what reason he did it. If he did it, then it does not make any difference whether he had any motive or not. . . . In this case the motive is only introduced to explain the evidence, and to bind her to the crimes." And what sort of motive had they ultimately proved? They had shown that, from five to six years ago, Lizzie did not call Mrs. Borden "Mother"—Lizzie, who was indeed her stepdaughter, and was now a woman thirty-two years old. They had stressed her correction of the Assistant City Marshall; "She is not my mother, sir; she is my stepmother." Robinson's comment on this was superbly opportune. He recalled to the jury "a well-looking little girl" who had given some minor evidence on behalf of the defense. "Why, Martha Chagnon, that was here a day or two ago, stepped on the stand and began to talk about Mrs. Chagnon as her stepmother. Well, I advise the City Marshall to put a cordon around *her* house, so that there will not be another murder there. Right here, in your presence, she spoke of her stepmother, and Mrs. Chagnon herself came on the stand afterwards, and I believe the blood of neither of them has been spilled since."

It was the kind of illustration that a country jury loves: concrete, local, about people they had seen. They pouted again and shook their heads a little; didn't seem much in the stepmother business either. . . .

The lawyers and reporters listening to the speech, who were well acquainted with Geroge Robinson's quick wits, had never doubted his ability to score whenever circumstances offered the tiniest of openings. But they waited with deep interest to see how he would handle a matter in which they discerned no opening at all: the matter of the note "from someone who is sick."

The defender did not dodge the point; he could not if he would. And if it made the weakest part of a very powerful speech, no possible blame can be attributed to him.

"A person may say," he said: " 'where is the note?' Well, we should be very glad to see it. Very glad." Nobody could doubt that this sentiment was sincere. If the note had materialized, it might have proved decisive. "Very likely Mrs. Borden burned it up. But then they say nobody has come forward to say they sent it. That is true. You will find men living perhaps in this county who do not know that this trial is going on, don't know anything about it, don't pay much attention to it; they are about their own business; don't consider it of consequence. Sometimes people don't *want* to get into a courtroom even if a life is in danger."

Robinson's manner was as confident as ever, but the content of his argument now wore a little thin. The jury looked puzzled. His grip on them was loosening. Up to now they had gone all the way with Guv'nor Robinson, but they didn't feel happy with this talk about the note. Did it make sense? They tried to imagine what they would have done themselves—the test that he was always asking them to apply. Would *they* not have known that the trial was going on? Would *they* have hung back, if it meant somebody's life? But there wasn't really time to think the problem out; Robinson was moving on to another, better point. . . .

Robinson now ranged to and fro on ground that was congenial: the burning of the dress (where Miss Emma lent him strength), Miss Lizzie's supposed attempts to tempt Bridget to town ("If she had undertaken these deeds, think you not she would have sent Bridget out on an errand?"), the Commonwealth's uncertainty about the murderer's weapon. Nor did he forget to offer his own theory. "The side door, gentlemen, was unfastened from about nine to eleven. . . . Bridget was outside talking to the next-door girl; she couldn't see the side door when she was there. Lizzie was about the house as usual. What was she doing? The same as any decent woman does. Attending to her work, ironing handkerchiefs, going up and down stairs. You say these things are not all proved"—Knowlton had stirred restlessly—"but I am taking you into the house just as I would into your own. What are your wives doing now?"

The jury felt homesick. They were suddenly out of this oppressive, crowded court; they had ceased to be the center of the waiting world; they were back there on the farm, with a cool breeze blowing and the missus putting on a good New England meal.

"What are your wives doing now?" Robinson's voice wound its way into their thoughts. "Doing the ordinary work around the house, getting the dinner. Well, where do they go? Down cellar for potatoes, into the kitchen, here and there. You can see the whole thing. It was just the same there.

"Now suppose the assassin came there and passed through. Where could he go? He could go up into that bedchamber and secrete himself to stay there—until he finds himself confronting Mrs. Borden. Now what is going to be done? He is there for murder; not to murder her, but to murder Mr. Borden. And he knows that he will be recognized, and he must strike her down. A man that had in his mind the purpose to kill Mr. Borden would not stop at the intervention of another person, and Lizzie and Bridget and Mrs. Borden, all or any of them, would be slaughtered if they came in that fellow's way.

"And when he had done his work, and Mr. Borden come in, as he could hear him, he could come down. Bridget was upstairs, Lizzie outdoors. He could do his work quickly and securely, and pass out the same door as he came in."

Robinson had very nearly finished, but, like most master advocates, he had nursed and husbanded his most dramatic stroke.

Steadily he gazed upon the close-packed jury box. His tones were level and imperative.

"To find her guilty, you must believe she is a fiend. *Gentlemen, does she look it?"*

The speech had gone full circle. "Is it possible?" "Does she look it?"

They looked, and saw Miss Lizzie with her high, severe collar; her modestly groomed hair; her long, slender hands and her sharp, patrician features; her unmistakable air of being, above all else, a lady.

They looked at her, and her advocate had played his strongest card. . . .

As Robinson sat down, amid that buzz of tongues which bursts forth uncontrollably of the slackening of tension, Knowlton slowly rose, like a man oppressed with care, and resolutely started on his grim, ungrateful task.

He grappled at once with the greatest of his difficulties. "My distinguished friend says: 'Who could have done it?' The answer would have been: 'Nobody could have done it.' If you had read an account of these cold and heartless facts in any tale of fiction, you would have said: 'That will do for a story, but such things never happen. . . . It was an impossible crime.' But it was committed. Set any human being you can think of, put any degraded man or woman you ever heard of, at the bar, and say to them 'You did this thing,' and it would seem incredible. And yet—it was done; it was done."

He particularly deprecated Robinson's suggestion that the murders could not have been committed by a woman, and permitted himself a few general observations on the temperament and nature of the female sex. "They are no better than we; they are no worse than we. If they lack in strength and coarseness and vigor, they make up for it in cunning, in dispatch, in celerity, in ferocity. If their loves are stronger and more enduring than those of men, their hates are more undying, more unyielding, more persistent." In a disdainful phrase he struck at a main obstacle to cool-headed decision. "We must face this case," he said, "as men, not as gallants."

Through the twelfth afternoon and through the thirteenth morning, Knowlton continued his remarkable address; gravely exhorting, patiently explaining, impeccable in literary style and moral tone. His thesis was twofold: that Miss Lizzie's story was in itself incredible; that anybody else could have done it was impossible. . . .

No passage in his speech was more impressive in its thoughtfulness, and cunning in its horror, than that in which he sought to analyze Miss Lizzie's motives. The order of the crimes, he said, supplied their key. He reversed Robinson's theory that the woman met her death through coming upon and recognizing a murderous intruder who had got into the house to lie in wait for Mr. Borden. "No," said Knowlton," it was Mrs. Borden whose life that wicked person sought, and all the motive we have to consider bears on her." And whatever might be said about old Andrew, except for Miss Lizzie (and the absent Miss Emma) his harmless wife had not a single foe. "There may be that in this case," said Knowlton very solemnly, "that saves us from the idea that Lizzie planned to kill her father. I hope she did not. I should be slow to believe she did. But it was not Lizzie Borden who came down those stairs, but a murderess, transformed from the daughter, transformed from the ties of affection, to the most consummate criminal we have read of in our history. She came down to meet that stern old man. That man who loved his daughter, but who loved his wife too, as the Bible commanded him. And, above all, the one man in this universe who would know who killed his wife. She had not thought of that. She had gone on. There is cunning in crime, but there is blindness in crime too. She had gone on with stealth and cunning, but she had forgotten the hereafter. They always do. And when the deed was done, she was coming downstairs to face Nemesis. There wouldn't be any question but that he would know the reason that woman lay in death. He knew who disliked her. He knew who couldn't tolerate her presence under that roof."

As a work of abstract art, this speech of Knowlton's has surpassing merit. The language is choice, the mood exalted, the reasoning taut and deep. It is excellent to read. But the study is one place, the courtroom is another, and the best advocacy seldom makes the best literature. The jury, simple folk that they were, may well have found George Robinson more comprehensible. They may have felt more at home with his less august style.

Before he ended, Knowlton made a brave attempt to lift the issue of the trial onto a spiritual plane. "Rise, gentlemen," he cried, "to the altitude of your duty. Act as you would be reported to act when you stand before the Great White Throne at the last day. . . . Only he who hears the voice of his inner consciousness—it is the voice of God Himself—saying to him 'Well done, good and faithful servant,' can enter into the reward and lay hold of eternal life."

This peroration has real grandeur. It puts to shame George Robinson's humble "Gentlemen, does she look it?" But one wonders which stood uppermost in the minds of the jury as they sat in their little private room deciding Lizzie's fate.

By five o'clock that afternoon it was all over. Miss Lizzie had been acquitted in a tempest of applause. With her faithful sister Emma at her side, she was on her way home to celebrate her vindication. George D. Robinson, well pleased with himself, walked away from court amid the cheering of the crowds. Only in the office of the District Attorney, Knowlton and Moody sat apart from the rejoicings. They alone, perhaps, were at that moment capable of beholding the Borden trial through the eye of history.

Miss Lizzie lived thereafter for four and thirty years, with every indication of an easy conscience. She had inherited a comfortable fortune which she placidly and soberly and decently enjoyed. She never married. She occupied herself—as she had formerly done—with a variety of charitable works, and in her will she left thirty thousand dollars to a society for the prevention of cruelty to animals.

Her death let loose in public a flood of speculation that had gone on in private ever since the trial. Students of crime and detection endlessly debate: was the Borden verdict right?

Others remember Lizzie for a different reason. A catchy little jingle, probably written before she was acquitted, has linked itself imperishably with folk and nursery lore.

> Lizzie Borden took an ax
> And gave her mother forty whacks.
> When she saw what she had done
> She gave her father forty-one.

Students may argue about her as they please. In the wide world that is her epitaph.

APPENDIX

Robinson's aim is clear. He achieves it with the last question of this sequence, when he gets Bridget to agree that she never saw any "quarrelling, or anything of that kind." But he dares not ask this baldly, without careful preparation, because he cannot foresee the terms of her reply. Supposing she says, in response to a blunt query, "Miss Lizzie and Mrs. Borden quarrelled all day long." His cause will then be far worse off than if the matter had not been raised at all. So he needs to approach the question circumspectly, advancing only one step at a time, and at every stage leaving channels of escape which he can use without grave loss of face.

He starts with just one hard fact to work from. Bridget has been in the Bordens' service for close upon three years. That dictates the form of his first question.

"Did *you* have any trouble there?"

If Bridget says "Yes," Robinson can retort, without fear of

contradiction, "But you *did* stay there three years," and then, accepting the danger signal, ride off to some less inflammable topic with a specious air of having scored a point. If Bridget says "No"—as she does—he has strengthened his hand, improved his position, and gained a better sight of the ground ahead.

It does not take him very far. But it enables him to venture next on a question that appears superficially a mere rephrasing of his last. In fact, though, by an almost imperceptible change in stress, it is designed to bring him closer to his target.

"A pleasant *place* to live?" he askes.

This imports the idea that not only were things all right for Bridget personally, but the Borden household was all right in general. And yet he can be fairly certain that Bridget will say "Yes" to this after her affirmative reply to the previous question. The two sound so alike. If, surprisingly, she does say "No," Robinson's escape is open as before, but with additional virtue—"But you stayed there three years *and* you never had any trouble.'

This, however, does not arise. Robinson safely collects another "Yes."

Now he comes to the most delicate point in the sequence. He must ask, however broadly, about the family themselves. He has, it is true, buttressed himself by the two preliminary questions, but this is the danger spot, and he knows it.

"It was a pleasant *family* to be in?"

Bridget's answer raises a problem. A downright "Yes" would have brought the advocate almost home. A downright "No" would have driven him from the trail; it would have been far too dangerous to press her further. Robinson would have made off under cover of a volley of safe questions. ("Pleasant enough to make the place pleasant, eh?" etc.)

But Bridget's reply is enigmatic. "I don't know how the family was," she says. "I got along all right."

Is this to be taken at its face value? Or is she hinting that there were family dissensions and that she kept out of them? Robinson has gone a long way now; he does not want to withdraw without his prize. But the utmost care is called for.

The next question, so artless in appearance, packs into its small compass a life time's experience and skill.

"You never saw anything out of the way?"

"Out of the way" is exactly right. Respectable girls—and Bridget is a very respectable girl—do not describe places as "pleasant" where "out of the way" things occur—as Robinson will, if necessary, remind her. But Bridget gives no cause.

"No, sir," she says.

Now he is practically secure. If any quarrelling is mentioned, they are ordinary, everyday domestic quarrels, quarrels that could not be considered "out of the way." He can go straight forward.

"You never saw any conflict in the family?"

Even if, contrary to expectation, Bridget should say "Yes," Robinson is well protected. But Bridget says "No" and he reaches his goal.

"Never saw any quarrelling or anything of that kind?"

'No, sir. . . ."

And few of the spectators are aware that they have heard a little gem of the cross-examiner's art.

THE "TORSO MURDER" CASE

Frank Monarski
for the prosecution

vs.

F. Lee Bailey
for the defense

by F. Lee Bailey

This case has a multiple fascination, for it marks the first courtroom appearance of one of America's great trial lawyers, F. Lee Bailey. Fresh out of law school and hungering to test his untried talent in a court of law, Bailey virtually stumbled into a major murder case on the basis of his youthful expertise in the new field of polygraph ("lie detector") testing. What we have here, as a result, is a fine trial story, a commentary on techniques of trial preparation, cross-examination and summarization, an introduction to the mysteries of the polygraph, and—most important—a description of how it feels in the gut to go from law-school classes into a courtroom struggle for a client's life.

The woman's body had been scooped up in pieces from the Merrimack River, an otherwise innocent stream that winds through northeastern Massachusetts. The head was never found, which gave the newspapers a ready-made title: "The Torso Murder." The body was identified as that of Betty Edgerly, a Lowell, Massachusetts, housewife. Within a few weeks her husband, George, was indicted for her murder.

In the spring of 1960, I was finishing law school and preparing for my bar exam. All I knew about the Torso Murder was what I read in the papers. But less than a year later, I was to tell the members of a jury why they should not send George Edgerly to the electric chair. The most sensational murder case to hit Massachusetts in years would mark my first appearance as a trial lawyer. And I would enter the trial when it was already in progress—after half the evidence had been heard.

I was admitted to the bar on November 16, 1960, and for the first few months my investigative service paid the rent for my Boston office. By the following February, when the Torso Murder trial was making headlines, I had fewer than ten open files in my legal drawer.

One of them was that of Willard Page, a man accused of rape almost four years after the crime. The polygraph—or, as it is popularly and mistakenly called, the lie detector—was shaping up as an important part of Page's defense. A polygraph test had indicated that he was innocent. But in Massachusetts, like most states, polygraph results are not admissible as evidence unless both sides agree. In Page's case, the prosecution was understandably reluctant. So as I saw it, there was only one thing to do—set a precedent and establish new law by getting Page's test before a jury. After doing a great deal of research on the polygraph, I had arranged for a panel of experts to come to Boston and testify to its reliability. The trial was set for May.

Meanwhile, the Edgerly trial was titillating the public as the lurid sort of details that never fail to make news came out. Betty had once served time for rolling GIs; George was a philanderer of the first order. But the banner headline that struck me as sensational was straightforward enough: "Edgerly Flunks Lie Detector Test." A polygraph examiner had testified that Edgerly had taken a test whose results indicated his guilt. At first I thought my precedent had been set. Closer reading of the story showed that this was not the case. Under the mistaken impression that the test results favored Edgerly, his chief defense counsel, John H. Tobin, had asked that they be admitted.

The following day I got a phone call from Charlie Zimmerman, the highly experienced polygraph examiner who had tested Willard Page for me. He said the Edgerly defense wanted some quick advice on how to cross-examine the lie-detector "expert" who had done in Edgerly. This was during the weekend; the cross-examination was to start on Monday. At Charlie's suggestion I went on Sunday to see John Tobin, who had suffered a seizure of some sort late Friday afternoon and was resting at his home in Cambridge. John told me what had happened, and it was clear that he was not just being outmaneuvered by the prosecution. In poker terms, he had been sandbagged.

During their investigation, police had given Edgerly two polygraph tests. Edgerly told Tobin about them, and the lawyer called Captain Michael Cullinane, the state police polygraph examiner, to check the results. Cullinane, a police officer with a well-deserved reputation for honesty, said the tests were inconclusive.

At the trial, however, one of the investigating officers spiced his testimony with repeated references to some "tests" Edgerly had taken. He was careful not to say "lie-detector tests," as this would have been automatic grounds for mistrial. But the implication was clear—Edgerly had been tested on the polygraph, and the results were being withheld. Tobin then made what seemed to him to be a foolproof move; he demanded that the tests be produced. He was surprised when prosecutor Frank Monarski agreed.

Now Cullinane took the stand. He repeated what he had told Tobin: the tests had been too inconclusive to warrant any opinion. And, yes, Edgerly had been cooperative in taking them. Tobin at that point had every reason to believe that his strategy in calling for the test results had paid off.

Then the prosecution called Augustine Lawlor, a Lawrence, Massachusetts, pharmacist. A graduate of the Keeler Polygraph Institute in Chicago, Lawlor was acquiring testing experience by working free for local authorities. Lawlor testified that he, too, had tested Edgerly. He exhibited several charts and said that, in his opinion, Edgerly had "not told the truth" when he denied complicity in his wife's murder.

Tobin turned angrily to his client and asked him why he hadn't mentioned the Lawlor tests. He had forgotten about them, said Edgerly. Besides, he'd been told they just represented practice for the examiner and that they proved nothing.

Up to this point, the prosecution had been the underdog. Now, it looked like a winner—and George Edgerly looked like a candidate for the electric chair.

Unless, of course, the defense could shake Lawlor's testimony in cross-examination.

I told John Tobin everything I knew about the polygraph, a fairly simple device first used in crude form about 1920. The modern polygraph has three components that measure physiological changes in the person being questioned. The first component is a replica of the standard blood-pressure cuff used by doctors. But whereas the physician's device has a small dial that records the readings and is attached to the cuff itself, the polygraph's cuff is attached by a rubber tube to a stainless-steel pen. Every time the subject's heart pumps, the pen moves up. As the blood flow ebbs, the pen moves down. The pen records on a moving paper chart that, when the test is complete, will show any changes in the subject's blood pressure as well as any variance in the frequency of his pulse-beat. Both of these are significant in detecting deception.

The second component is an accordianlike expandable rubber hose that is fastened around the chest. A piece of rubber tubing connects the hose to a second steel pen on the machine. When the subject inhales and his chest expands, the pen moves up. When he exhales, it moves down. The regularity of his breathing can then be studied after the test is complete. Changes that coincide with psychologically stimulating questions can strongly indicate deception.

The third component, the galvo or GSR, measures what is known as the galvanic skin response. It consists of a highly sensitive galvonometer capable of measuring the flow of a minute electrical current. Two electrodes are placed on the skin, and the instrument measures the amount of resistance that the skin offers a current passing from one electrode to the other. This, too, is recorded by a steel pen, which swings from the top of the chart to the bottom, indicating the changes in conductivity. There are various theories about why the galvo is significant in reading truth, but I think it's fair to say that no one really knows. The most common view is that lying induces perspiration, which affects the skin's conductivity. Whatever the reason, the galvanometer is of proven value, especially with certain individuals. When a person is a good galvo reactor, many examiners will say that the other two components need not be used. Conversely, some people can tell blatant lies without significant galvo reactions.

This, then, is the machine itself. On the whole, it is dependable; the critical factor in any polygraph test is the examiner. In the United States, polygraph examiners range from experts who rarely err to rank amateurs who should be locked up for posing as experts. There are no formal educational requirements, and only fifteen or sixteen states license examiners. Consequently, in any state where examiners are not regulated, anybody can buy a machine and put up a shingle. That is why attorneys and police officers should choose polygraph examiners as carefully as most people choose doctors and accountants. A first-rate polygraph examiner must have intelligence, skill at interrogation, and considerable knowledge of both psychology and physiology.

To begin with, there are the questions. The examiner must be equipped with the known facts of a case. The right questions must be asked in the right way. The questions must all be answerable with "yes" or "no." And they should be written out before the machine is activated. The subject should at least know the areas the questions will cover. For one thing, an unexpected question may cause a reaction that has nothing to do with deception. For another, the very fact that a subject anticipated a question will cause him to build emotionally toward it and react all the more emphatically when it comes.

Because of the pressure on the upper arm's artery caused by the blood-pressure cuff, tests are limited to no more than seven minutes. The subject sits with his back to both the examiner and the polygraph, so that he won't be distracted by the fluctuation of the pens. As each question is posed, a mark is made on the moving graph indicating the place where it was asked. Then a second mark is made indicating whether the subject answered "yes" or "no."

Finally, it is up to the examiner to interpret the finished chart correctly. The term "lie detector" is a misnomer; "truth verifier" would be more accurate. Essentially, the polygraph has a single function—it separates those who have told the whole truth from those who have not. This is all it can do. Anyone can pass a polygraph test—all he has to do is to tell the *whole* truth. A person can tell the *literal* truth and still show deceptive responses.

By way of illustration, suppose John, suspected of killing Mary, is asked: "Did you kill Mary?" John didn't do it, but he knows who did. Or he had a secret desire to knock her off. Either way, he may react very much as if he were the killer. And he will not be able to clear himself until he tells the examiner everything.

Although civilian courts regard the polygraph as a threat to the jury system, it is widely used by law-enforcement agencies and by military and industrial authorities. In some places, a suspect who passes a police polygraph test is automatically eliminated as a potential defendant. This makes good sense because it eliminates the need for indictment and trial, an experience from which few people recover even if they are acquitted. They may have been found not guilty, but so far as much of the public is concerned it was just a case of some smart lawyer getting them off. This is a flaw in our system that could be remedied with proper use of the polygraph.

Maybe, I told John Tobin, the Edgerly case could help.

John Tobin was seventy-two years old; he was tired and ailing, and the trial had etched new lines of strain across his face. I was twenty-seven, a young fighter hot for combat. We talked for several hours about the polygraph. Then John stared at me.

"Lee," he said, "would you be willing to come into the case to cross-examine this guy Lawlor? I don't think there's another lawyer in Massachusetts who would recognize a lie detector if you dropped one on him. I think you could help us."

I had reason to hesitate. In the Page case, I was fighting to prove the polygraph's reliability—now Tobin was asking me to cast doubt on the results of a polygraph test. But offering me a chance to appear in the Torso Murder case was like offering the advocate inside me a slice of the moon. I said yes.

It was evening when I left Tobin and returned to the small apartment across the street from my Boston office. I knew more than most lawyers about the polygraph, but all my research had been done from a positive viewpoint: I had never concentrated on attacking a test or its examiner. I had to go back to the books, and I had one night to do it in.

My ability to cram, a hangover from student days, stood me in good stead. So did my friends. I called Dan Bloomfield, then my chief investigator, and Phil Halloran, a law-school classmate. We sat in the apartment drinking coffee and reading books on the polygraph then Dan and Phil briefed me on the material they had studied. When we finished, the third pot of coffee was empty and the sky was getting light. It was time to get ready for court.

I put on a black suit and vest, shined my shoes, and dumped an armful of polygraph texts and some magazines into a briefcase. On the way to my first appearance as a trial lawyer, I forgot the polygraph. Instead, I reviewed everything I knew about the most devastating weapon in the trial lawyer's arsenal —cross-examination.

We all cross-examine. Parents cross-examine children, executives cross-examine subordinates, politicians cross-examine aides and each other. But for the trial lawyer, cross-examination is a deadly speciality. Through his questions, he must destroy the evidence amassed against his client—he must diminish it, limit it, explain it away. As the prosecutor tries to build, the defense counsel tries to tear down. Attorneys who don't understand this should stay out of court.

Unfortunately, they're in court every day. Most law schools teach little or nothing about cross-examination. There should be courses in the methods and principles of cross-examination, and the courses should be followed up with practice sessions. Instead, the new lawyer must learn cross-examination in real trials at the expense of real clients. To me, this makes about as much sense as it would make to let medical interns practice surgery on living people instead of cadavers.

Good cross-examination also suffers at the hands of public misunderstanding. This achieves serious proportions because it is the public that fills our jury boxes. Too many jurors are waiting for Perry Mason; they expect the lawyer to bring the witness to a point where he cries out that the defendant is innocent, that *he's* the one who killed the go-go dancer. Well, it happens—on television.

In fact, the first rule of cross-examination is DON'T. Unless the witness has said something that can be used against him, unless there is a chance that the effect of his testimony can somehow be diminished, a lawyer should smile and say: "No questions."

Until a witness is firmly committed to a definite statement or position, he can parry a question or sidestep it with some kind of explanation. The cross-examiner's first task is to pin down all that the witness claims to know about the subject and all that he says he doesn't know. What he doesn't know is equally important because it is often from the lack of evidence that reasonable doubt must flow.

Obviously, the witness has made some commitment under direct examination. But this testimony usually is brief and lacks detail. So before going on the offensive, the cross-examiner must ask questions patiently and methodically until the witness has taken some position, either positive or negative, as to everything he knows about the matter in dispute. The most common error lawyers make in cross-examination is that of immediately attacking a witness who has not been sufficiently pinioned. The result is that the witness escapes.

The cross-examination of an expert witness, which is what

I was about to do, poses added problems. He's a professional who understands the trial process; he knows how much he can get away with; he knows how to answer questions. And usually, though not always, he is thoroughly versed in his field. Give an expert a broad enough question, and he may bury you. That's why a trial lawyer has to be a crammer; he has to know his stuff well enough to catch any weakness on the part of the witness.

Such was my task with Augustine Lawlor, the small-town druggist who in the space of two days had come to represent a pivotal point in my life. As I walked up the steps of the old East Cambridge courthouse that icy February morning, I thought about the drawbacks. I hadn't seen Lawlor's test charts, I had never met him, I knew little of his background or his capability as a witness. I had never cross-examined anyone before a jury. I had been in practice for less than three months.

The courtroom that was my very first arena might have been built in England in the 1800s. It was high ceilinged with dark mahogany furnishings, an antique defense table, an ornate judge's bench. The acoustics were ridiculous; many of the thrill-seekers in the spectator section could barely hear what was happening. But the room was jammed all the same. . . .

In the courtroom I met George Edgerly. He sat in a wire cage, a barbaric contraption used until a few years ago in all Massachusetts capital cases. Edgerly, I soon discovered, had a quick sense of humor, an excellent memory for details, and an almost clinical attitude toward the trial. He made $10,000 a year as an auto mechanic, and his boss described him as both skilled and dependable. He was also a man of the world, at least his world. Some of the trial's most colorful testimony had come from his wife's sisters, who described trips George had taken with them, going into such details as who had stayed with whom in various hotels.

Edgerly examined me from inside his cage. "You think you can tear this lie-detector guy apart?"

"I don't know," I said, "but I'll sure give it a try."

"Okay," he said. "I hope you know what you're doing. He sure doesn't or he would of never said I was lying. I didn't kill my wife."

For the moment, I had to take Edgerly at his word. I had to presume that Augustine Lawlor had made a mistake, or that he hadn't gone far enough in his testing. I might at least be able to establish that although Edgerly's reactions did not show innocence, neither did they prove guilt.

Now court was in session, and Augustine Lawlor and I faced each other. Lawlor was in his middle thirties, scholarly-looking, very erect. He didn't seem the least bit nervous. I introduced myself to the jury, explained that John Tobin was sick, and summarized the testimony Lawlor had given on Friday.

"Mr. Lawlor," I said, "it is correct to say that the so-called lie detector, or polygraph, does not detect lies. Is that right?"

Lawlor hesitated, glanced at Frank Monarski, and then answered, "Yes, that's correct."

I saw the jurors react. Monarski had laid very little foundation for the polygraph technique in his direct examination of Lawlor, and the jurors were startled by what seemed to them a surprising disclosure.

It was essential to establish what polygraph texts Lawlor, as an expert, might regard as authoritative. Unlike a lay witness, an expert is permitted to give an opinion or conclusion. If he endorses a text or professional publication in his field, he may be questioned closely on it, and may say something that contradicts the book. In many instances he will have a hard time explaining the contradiction.

Very few books have been written on the subject of polygraph testing. The one generally considered most authoritative was written by Fred E. Inbau, a Northwestern University law professor, and John E. Reid, one of the country's top examiners. I showed a copy of that book to Lawlor and asked whether he had read it.

"I've read most of it," he said.

"Do you regard it as authoritative?"

"No," said the prosecutor's expert. "I do not."

"Tell me, Mr. Lawlor, is there any book on the subject of polygraph testing that you regard as authoritative?"

I walked to the defense table and put my hand on a stack of about eight books. I'm sure Lawlor thought all of them were books on the polygraph, which is precisely what I wanted him to think. A few of them actually were.

"No . . . no, I can't think of any such books."

"Have you written a book on the subject, by chance?"

"No, I haven't."

"Have you written any articles for any of the police or crime-detection publications?"

"No." He was beginning to look irritated.

"You have of course read such articles, and know that a number have been published from time to time?"

"Yes, I have read some of them."

"Are there any articles you regard as authoritative?" I reached into my briefcase and began to draw out magazines.

"No. There are none that I remember that I regard as an authority in the field."

Gus Lawlor seemed immovable. But I had another lever.

"I understand, Mr. Lawlor, that you use a Keeler polygraph?"

"Yes."

"You regard the Keeler as a reliable instrument, do you not?"

"Yes, I would say so."

"And you consider the Keeler Company as expert in the teaching and manufacturing of polygraphs, is that correct?"

"Yes."

"What model do you use—would it be a 6303?"

"It is."

There was something else I wanted to establish here. "That, by the way, is a *three*-pen machine, isn't it?"

"Yes."

"Now then, when you bought your instrument, did you receive a handbook on its use and the administration of polygraph tests published by the manufacturer?"

"Yes, the handbook came with it."

"Good. Now, having in mind your opinion that the Keeler Company knows what it's doing in the field of polygraph testing, wouldn't you say that at least their handbook on how to run the instrument is an authoritative publication?"

Lawlor sighed. He had to commit himself. "Yes," he said, "the handbook is authoritative."

"You have read the handbook, of course?"

"Yes."

I moved closer to the witness stand and showed him a standard handbook for a Keeler 6303 polygraph. "Your copy is just like the one I am holding here?"

"It is."

"And it is your practice, no doubt, to conduct your polygraph examinations in the manner that this handbook recommends?"

"Well, yes," he replied. "I go by it pretty much."

I had him pinned down on one item. And then I used another basic tactic of cross-examination: I dropped the subject. There was something in the Keeler handbook I intended to use, but not while Gus Lawlor was thinking about it.

"With respect to your practice as a polygraph expert, Mr. Lawlor, I take it this is not a full-time occupation?"

"No," he said, "it's not full-time."

"You are a *druggist* by profession?"

"I am a pharmacist."

"You make most of your income from the business of druggery—er, excuse me, pharmacy?"

"Yes."

"And when I say most of your income, I mean ninety-nine percent. Would that be correct?"

Lawlor nodded.

"That is because, is it not, you are not *paid* for the testing you do?"

"I run my tests free, yes. I have an interest in law enforcement."

"Many other examiners run tests for law-enforcement officials, do they not?"

"Yes."

"And many of them charge for their testing, true?"

Again, Lawlor nodded.

Now I was ready to get back to the handbook. Prior testimony had suggested that due to an excess of boozing—and, by innuendo, wenching—Edgerly had not been in the best shape during some of the interrogation sessions. "Mr. Lawlor," I asked, "it is true, is it not, that on the morning you tested George he appeared to have, shall we say, a bit of a hangover?"

"He may have."

"Well, he told you that he hadn't slept much that night before, isn't that right?"

"I believe he mentioned it."

"You wanted the tests to be as accurate as possible?"

"Of course."

"And you wanted the tests to be fair to Edgerly, didn't you?"

"I always try very hard to be fair to the subject."

I turned to the counsel table, and scooped up the Keeler handbook. "In this book," I said, waving it at him, "in this very book it says that in any proper polygraph test the subject must be well rested and in good physical condition. You know that, don't you?"

Lawlor glanced at Monarski. "I believe it says that."

"And you agree that this is so, don't you?"

"Yes, I suppose so."

"But you nonetheless ran a test on George Edgerly, knowing that he had neither complete rest nor good physical condition?"

No answer.

"In a *murder* case, Mr. Lawlor, did you run this polygraph test knowing that the subject was not fit physically? Did you do that in a *murder* case?"

"I was not told that it was a murder case," he answered frostily. "I thought it was a missing-persons case."

"Do you mean, Mr. Lawlor—do you mean that when you tested this defendant you did not know that he was supposed to have killed his wife? Is that what you mean?"

"Well, yes—in a sense. I mean, I could only go on what I was told."

"Of course," I said sympathetically. "Had you known that this was a murder case, and that you might be called upon to testify, you would have insisted on more stringent conditions for the test, wouldn't you?"

"Yes," said Lawlor, he would have decided to stop. . . .

When the recess was over, I took Lawlor through a description of the principles of polygraph testing and we discussed the three components of the machine. Lawlor had used the blood-pressure cuffs and the pneumograph, but not the galvanometer. Actually, earlier machines had no galvo and some examiners questioned its usefulness. But I was not about to point that out.

"You told us your machine had three pens, Mr. Lawlor?"

Lawlor looked uneasy. "Yes," he said. "It has."

"And when you attended the Keeler School you were taught to use all three?"

"Yes."

"I notice that in testing the defendant you elected to omit the galvanometer that you earlier explained. Is that so?"

"No, I didn't use it."

"Tell the jury why."

I was taking a chance. Generally, cross-examiners avoid "what," "when," "where," "why," and "how" questions, all of which give the witness, especially the expert, far too much latitude. But I felt that there was no way for Lawlor to talk himself out of the corner into which I had pushed him.

"I believe," he said, "that the galvanometer adds very little to the test and may in fact confuse it. It is nowhere near as dependable as the other two components, and I don't like to rely on it."

"You were taught how to use it?"

"Yes."

"Would it be fair to say, Mr. Lawler, that your reason for omitting the use of the GSR is your concern that you might not be able to competently determine the results of its tracing? That you really don't understand it?"

"This is not the reason at all. I can read it perfectly well."

I turned to his charts, which I had pinned to the blackboard next to the witness stand so that the jurors could see them. There is nothing more frustrating for a juror than to have a lawyer go into a long discussion of some photograph or document the jury cannot see.

With the charts in view, I asked Lawlor to point out the responses where he felt Edgerly had not told the truth about his wife's disappearance. He indicated several.

"Do you believe, Mr. Lawlor, that the defendant's name is George?"

"Why yes . . . I have no reason to believe otherwise. . . ."

"Would you point to that portion of the chart where you put the question to him: 'Is your name George?' "

Lawlor took the pointer and complied. "I see that when you asked this question there was a rise in the defendant's blood pressure," I said. "Do you say that the defendant's answer was untruthful?"

"No," said Lawlor, "I do not consider that to indicate deception."

"But his blood pressure did rise, as your chart indicates?"

"Well, yes, it did rise some—but not necessarily deception."

"Might his, er, poor physical condition account for the change we see here?"

"Yes, it very well could."

"To be fair, then, might we not say that the same poor physical condition could account for all of the similar responses we see on both of these charts?"

Lawlor was boxed in. The word "fair" challenges the heart of an expert's integrity.

"It could," he conceded, "but in my opinion there is a difference between the responses to the various questions. . . ."

I'm sure that he was more than willing to explain, but I wasn't about to give him the chance. If Monarski had been fully briefed on the polygraph, he might encourage Lawlor to elaborate on redirect. For instance, Lawlor could discuss the pneumograph pattern, which showed somewhat more damaging reactions than the blood-pressure lines. As it was, Monarski decided to let well enough alone. I stopped, and there was no redirect examination.

If I had done nothing else, I'd pleased my client. "That was pretty good," George Edgerly said. "How about sticking around until the case is over?"

I thanked him, but told him I had just come in to handle the polygraph evidence, and that I was sure John Tobin would be back with him soon. The judge called a recess for lunch, and I was through with the Edgerly case. At least I thought I was.

I lunched with two friends, feeling both glad and sorry that the encounter with Lawlor was over. In any case, I thought, I hadn't made a fool of myself. And I had established some ground for doubt.

I couldn't resist returning in the afternoon as a spectator. I wanted to hear McCarthy's opening statement. He told the jury the defense case would be built around the testimony of George Edgerly himself. Using the testimony of other witnesses as to when and where they had last seen Betty, he would show that Betty had been alive after the time of death claimed by the state.

I was about to return to my office when John Tobin called to say he'd had favorable reports about the Lawlor cross-examination. Would I like to stay with the case and handle some of the witnesses?

The trial had been going on for two weeks, and a lot of ground had already been covered. But it was like asking a kid singer who's been playing roadhouses if he'd like a shot on the *Ed Sullivan Show.*

I didn't need any urging to say yes.

My first assignment from John Tobin was to handle a witness I'll call Louis DuBois. Although his real name appears in the trial transcript, I'm changing it to spare him any more misery than he's already suffered. Louis DuBois put himself on the line in coming into the case, and what happened to him was a damned shame.

DuBois was a figure out of Betty Edgerly's checkered past. She and DuBois were ex-business associates; he had been sentenced to jail, along with Betty, for rolling GIs some years before. After his release, DuBois went straight. He married, got a steady job, and won the respect of his neighbors, most of whom were unaware of his criminal record.

When the Edgerly trial opened, DuBois had a difficult decision to make. He had seen Betty Edgerly on the street in Lowell six weeks after she was supposed to have been murdered. He had gone to the police at the time, but his involvement was not made public, and the defense knew nothing about him. Appearing as a witness would mean his exposure as an ex-convict, notoriety and perhaps shame for his family. But if George Edgerly got the electric chair, Louis DuBois would always wonder whether his testimony would have made a difference. When the trial was in progress, DuBois contacted the defense and told his story.

He repeated it on the stand, and he was a beautiful witness. His manner was quiet but forthright, and his answers were convincing. He testified that when he was agonizing over the consequences of getting involved in the case, he had first gone to a priest for advice. The priest had gone with him to the Lowell station house.

Monarski stepped forward to cross-examine, a piece of paper in his hand. He looked confident.

"You claim, Mr. DuBois," he said, "that you talked with Lieutenant Wilson in the presence of this priest, is that so?"

"Yes, I did."

Now Monarski waved the piece of paper at DuBois. "Have you at some time signed a statement for the Lowell police?"

DuBois looked down. "Yes, I did."

"Is this your signature at the bottom of the statement?"

DuBois nodded.

"And in this statement do you not say that you did not get a good look at the woman you thought was Betty Edgerly on the day in question, and could never be sure that it was she?"

DuBois nodded again, and Monarski sat down. It was my

turn. DuBois had never told me about the statement, and I had to try to repair the damage in redirect examination. Almost sobbing, DuBois testified that police had told him to sign a statement or else. They said that exposure of his past could only bring him trouble, that the best way to stay uninvolved was to become a "nonwitness." He signed the statement.

But now he had chosen to get involved. He was willing to say under oath that the statement to the police was a conscious falsification, and that his testimony was fact. It took courage, which I felt had to impress the jury.

John Tobin agreed with me, but he began an intensive search for the priest who had accompanied DuBois to the precinct house, and who had since been transferred to a parish outside the state.

Tobin also asked me to handle the direct examination of George Edgerly. Edgerly's testimony was crucial. If the defendant sits on the stand, invariably he is his own star witness—if the jury believes him when he says he didn't do it, his acquittal is certain.

Obviously, the questioning of George Edgerly was a rare opportunity as well as a challenge for a young lawyer just starting to practice. And it was a chance to do something for John Tobin. There was a real fear on the part of everyone involved in the trial that the strain of taking Edgerly through his story could be too much for John.

There were also manifest drawbacks in my taking on the assignment. I had not seen half the trial. I was not aware of what evidence had had the greatest impact on the jury. I could read the transcript, but if I spent the time studying all seventeen hundred pages, I would have little if any time to go over the case with Edgerly. And that was vital for both of us—for me, because the facts as the defendant knows them are often quite different from the facts supplied by the other witnesses; for Edgerly, because if I put him on the stand cold, he would have trouble knowing what I was driving at with each question.

Except for occasional references, I decided to forget about the transcript. I would stick with Edgerly himself; he had both an excellent memory and, for a layman, an almost uncanny sense of what was significant as evidence. I would let George do it—I would rely on him to tell me what testimony had been given that required explanation or rebuttal.

All through that night, and the next two nights, my secretary (and wife-to-be) and I worked with Edgerly. The jailkeeper and his wife, who lived on the prison grounds, let us use their home and even helped keep us going with coffee and sandwiches. I questioned Edgerly, and Wicki took down everything in shorthand. Bit by bit, we assimilated the facts of the Torso Murder case.

The background was relevant. George and Betty Edgerly had had more a truce than a marriage. If it was correct to say that George strayed, you would have to say Betty traveled. She was likely to disappear for days and then return home without any explanation of where she'd been. George's motto on these occasions was live and let live; he didn't ask questions.

The night she disappeared, they had gone to dinner at a restaurant not far from the coast. This was in December, 1959, and it was snowing as they drove home. Although they had not argued, Betty was sullen on the ride back and seemed upset. George suspected that she might be having an affair at the time, and that this could have caused her moodiness. But if he was right, he had no clue to the identity of the other man.

As they were driving through Lowell, their car got stuck on the slippery road. George left Betty in the car and went to get help. At the top of the rise, he spotted an orange truck plowing the street but was unable to flag it down. When he returned to the car he found it empty. He looked around for Betty and called her name. What the hell, he thought, Betty had disappeared on him before. This time, he never saw her again.

Edgerly insisted that he had no reason to kill his wife and added that the prosecution had failed to show any strong motive. He told us Betty had some friends who might have been involved in the sale of narcotics. There was a possibility that she had come to know too much about their operations and was killed as a potential risk. But he didn't have enough solid information for us to put this theory before the jury.

Edgerly also discussed the testimony that had already been given by other witnesses. His perception and grasp of nuance were amazing as he went into details of who said what, how they said it, and how the jury reacted. For long stretches I simply listened, occasionally nodding to Wicki to indicate that something should be underlined.

When we left the jail the first night, we had more than enough material for the first day's testimony. Since there wasn't time to have the shorthand notes transcribed before court opened, I got permission from Judge Dewing to allow Wicki to sit at the counsel table with me. The press immediately named her "Della Street."

Edgerly was on the stand for two days. He told the story the way he had told it to me at the jail; not a fact was changed.

When Monarski's turn to cross-examine came, the tension in the courtroom reached a high point. All the curious were waiting to see whether George Edgerly would crumble. Monarski, experienced and capable, carried a thick pad of notes. He probed for inconsistencies, he searched meticulously for shadows of doubt. When the cross-examination began, Edgerly was up against the wall. When it ended, he had stood up well.

The next morning, I got a phone call from an attorney for

whom I had conducted investigations. He made a few remarks about young lawyers who start at the top with murder cases, and then came to the point. He was calling for a woman client who was afraid her name was about to come out in the Edgerly case. Around the time of Betty Edgerly's disappearance, his client had gotten somewhat stoned in a bar and had left with a drinking companion. They stopped on the way home and found themselves together in the back seat of the car he was driving, but their attempted coupling was halted by his discovery that she was having her period. Later she learned that her new acquaintance had borrowed the car from an old buddy—George Edgerly.

At this point in his narrative, the attorney, a man I both liked and respected, paused and asked whether the story rang a bell.

"Sure," I said. "The prosecution put in evidence that blood was found in the back seat of George's car, and hinted strongly that it was Betty's. I've got to prove it wasn't. The boyfriend's going to testify."

"Look, Lee," he said, "the girl is in the middle of a messy divorce, and this could ruin her. Leave her name out of it, can't you? The way it looked in the papers, you've got it beat anyway."

"For chrissake, Ed," I said, "I can't leave out any evidence that might explain the blood. Suppose I don't put it in and they convict him? What do I do then? Go to the judge and ask for a new trial because I deliberately withheld some evidence?"

"Oh, come off it," he said. "It's not going to be that important. They haven't identified the type of blood or anything, have they? This is a decent girl who never even met Edgerly. Why do you have to drag her through the mud?"

"I'm sorry, Ed. This guy has to testify. He won't mention the girl's name, but Monarski can demand it on cross. There's nothing I can do."

"Oh bullshit!" he yelled, and hung up.

Actually, the favor he asked was not unreasonable. Many times, a lawyer will try to avoid hurting an innocent third party. But not when the defendant's life is at stake. I put the evidence in, and I presume the woman suffered some embarrassment. Defending a murder case is one of the best ways I know to lose friends.

At Edgerly's urging I had turned up another witness who saw Betty after she was supposed to have been killed. The witness was sure of his identification; he testified he had been dancing with her. We also brought in the weather reports for the night Betty disappeared and the records of a snow-removal contractor—an orange plow had been exactly where Edgerly said it was that night. After tying up as many loose ends as possible, we rested our case.

Monarski announced that he had a rebuttal witness, and the Torso Murder case took another twist. The witness was Lieutenant Wilson of the Lowell police—the officer to whom Louis DuBois had gone with a priest to report spotting Betty Edgerly on the street.

"The whole story is false," Wilson told the jury. "DuBois did not come to me and report seeing Betty. There was never such a meeting with the priest."

It was hard to imagine that a police officer would lie about such a matter. But I found it even harder to believe that Louis DuBois was lying.

I turned to Leonard Mullen, an associate defense counsel who was a longtime colleague of Tobin's. "We'd better find that priest fast," I said. "If the jury believes this copy, they'll have to believe we dreamed up DuBois. They might convict on that alone."

I stood up to cross-examine Wilson.

"You did meet Mr. DuBois at some point, Lieutenant?"

"Sure," said Wilson. "I took his statement where he said he didn't see Betty Edgerly. But that was after we found her body, long after."

"And you do know the priest he claims was with him when he met you, do you not?"

Wilson nodded. "I know him. He was a good friend. But I never met him with DuBois."

Challenging Wilson on the statement that DuBois said he had been pressured into signing, I failed to rattle him. Wilson, it seemed, had put the prosecution back in the lead.

There was other rebuttal, but nothing comparable to Wilson's testimony. All of us were depressed, except Edgerly. He was furious. "Where the hell is that priest?" he raged.

By that evening the priest had been located in upstate New York. He wouldn't discuss the case by phone, but he would come to East Cambridge the next morning. All we could do was wait. We had no sure way of knowing whose credibility he would destroy—Lieutenant Wilson's, the cop's, or Louis DuBois's. We did know that if he destroyed Louis DuBois, he would also probably destroy George Edgerly.

The next morning we waited at court for half an hour, but there was no word about what action the priest had taken. Then a court officer summoned us to Judge Dewing's chambers. John Droney and Frank Monarski sat against one wall; Tobin, McCarthy, Mullen, and I sat against the other.

"Gentlemen," said the judge, "I have conferred with this priest at his specific request, and because, as I understand it, both sides wished me to do so. Is that correct?" We nodded.

"He has told me that he does know Lieutenant Wilson, and that he does know DuBois. I have explained the conflicting testimony, and he says that Wilson is not telling the truth, but that what DuBois has said is completely true."

It was impossible for the defense to keep quiet in the face of such good news, but Judge Dewing stopped us short.

"Just a minute," he said, "It's not quite that simple. It appears that Lieutenant Wilson called the Father last night, and asked him not to come to this court because he would be destroyed by the Father's testimony. The Father feels that this was in the nature of a priest-penitent disclosure and is unwilling to testify to this fact. Indeed, he is not anxious to testify at all, and since he did not come here under subpoena, he may not be compelled to testify. Any suggestions?"

I knew what I wanted. I wanted the priest put on the stand. I wanted Wilson's hide. The penalty for perjury in a capital case was life imprisonment, and that was what the lying bastard deserved. On the other hand, I felt that a clergyman ought to have protection against having to testify to something told him in confidence.

Tobin, however, had been around a great deal longer than I had, and he knew juries better. He agreed to compromise with a stipulation—a statement, agreed to by opposing counsel, which could be used to replace testimony. Ordinarily, it is not an agreement as to the truth of what it states, but only means that if the witness is called, such will be his testimony. Either side may then argue that the testimony stipulated to is not the truth.

"That seems like a sensible solution," said Judge Dewing.

Tobin was sure that a simple statement to the effect that the priest did recall the station house meeting and corroborated DuBois in every detail would be enough.

I realized Tobin was probably right, but I didn't want to give in completely. "John," I whispered, "you can bet they want a stipulation more than we do. Only it will close the evidence. If we present final argument this afternoon, Monarski will have all night to pick through it and give up the business in the morning. Let's agree to stipulate if they'll agree to suspend until tomorrow."

He grinned at me. "Very good," he said. "You'll be a

lawyer yet." He explained our terms, and the prosecution agreed. The jury was informed in open court that if the priest had appeared, he would have corroborated DuBois. As dramatic endings go, it wasn't bad. Now only the final shouting remained, and we had to decide who would shout for George Edgerly. In some states, each lawyer involved in the case is allowed to make his own summation; in Massachusetts, each side gets just one summation and one man.

I wanted to be our man. Maybe it gets me back to that question interviewers invariably ask me: what makes me run? I burn, dammit, that's why. I like to run. But this was John Tobin's case, and I knew the decision wasn't mine to make.

When we asked Edgerly how he felt, he left it up to John. "If you feel up to it," he told Tobin, "you're my lawyer. But if you want the kid to do it, it's okay with me. I don't want you to kill yourself with this case."

Tobin was silent for long minutes. Finally, he turned to me. "You think you know the evidence well enough to sum it up —even the part you didn't hear?"

"I think I do." I had read the transcript and had gone over all the testimony with George.

"All right," he said. He seemed tired and a little relieved. "We'll come to your office tonight and go over it with you. You make an outline of what you think should be covered. You'll do the talking."

By the time we met, I knew my way. I'd learned long before the Edgerly trial that the best defense is a good offense. So far as I was concerned, Edgerly had been arrested and indicted simply because no other suspect could be found, and because it was politically expedient to come up with *some* solution to a frightening crime. It was not entirely irrelevant that a number of officials, including the district attorney, had been up for election between the time Edgerly was arrested and tried. To the public, mere arrest implies solution—the general feeling being that the trial is just a game. And the American people do not equate jury acquittal with innocence. That's one of the reasons a criminal lawyer doesn't win popularity contests.

And so the Torso Murder case came down to a bitter cold March morning when I stood before a packed courtroom and looked from one juror to another—hoping I was finding something receptive in each face. "Ladies and gentlemen," I began, "this is the beginning of the end of the Edgerly Case. . . ."

I spoke for two hours; it was the longest summation I have ever given, and probably the longest I will ever give. I covered all the aspects of a criminal trial that I knew; I went into the responsibilities of the jury, of counsel, of the judge. I turned over every piece of evidence. I castigated Wilson and his prosecution allies for everything they had done, especially for the rebuttal perjury. I denounced political influence. At one point, I walked over to the D.A. and shouted: "Here's a man so callous as to try to put a man in the electric chair for something he didn't do just in order to get reelected." I denounced everything but the American flag.

When I sat down, Tobin patted me on the shoulder. "That was good," he whispered.

I was physically whipped; I was almost glad to let Monarski have the floor. He argued skillfully, picking at weaknesses in our case. At times I felt like jumping up and reminding the jury that the prosecution, not the defense, shouldered the burden of proof. When he finished there was a brief recess, and then Judge Dewing gave his charge.

Our system calls for the jury to determine what the facts are, and then to apply to those facts whatever law the trial judge describes as appropriate. Unfortunately, we operate ass backward. Before the jurors have been able to discuss the testimony or vote on it, they're flooded with more rules of law than a bright law student might be expected to learn in a month.

Looking at the transcript, I would have a difficult time picking out a solid error in Judge Dewing's instructions. But at the time, they seemed slanted toward the prosecution. The judge was a former prosecutor, and perhaps it was his inflections that bothered me. Perhaps it was my own fervor as a defense lawyer. Whatever the reason, I took exception to the charge on the ground that it was slanted in favor of the state. The judge nodded without comment. He knew such an exception was meaningless under Massachusetts law.

The jury went out shortly before 4:00 P.M. Observing what was considered local tradition in East Cambridge, I walked across the street to wait in the Esquire Bar.

The press was there in force, its members in the relaxed frame of mind that is their style when juries are out. They took pity on a young advocate who was breaking his back to look casual and not having much success. They even bought the drinks, perhaps recognizing that whereas their pay was miniscule, mine was nothing at all.

The court officers in East Cambridge all know enough to call the Esquire when a jury comes in. Whenever the phone rang, I jumped in my seat. At about 7:00 P.M., Eddie Corsetti of the *Boston Record-American* nudged me and said: "Quit worrying. The jury will be in at two in the morning with an acquittal."

Other reporters varied in their estimates of time and verdict. Most of those who bet on conviction figured it would be in the second degree. I kept fidgeting and drinking Scotch. I had done little boozing in the service, and I couldn't afford liquor while I was in law school. But I drank like fourteen fishes while the Edgerly jury deliberated. Interestingly enough, the liquor had little effect on me. Perhaps it had something to do with tension. Or with adrenalin. All I know is that most trial lawyers drink. And the good ones can hold their booze.

Hours later, the phone rang for what seemed the thousandth time. The jury was ready. In the courtroom, we waited for the judge to come back from his hotel. When he finally ascended the bench and the jurors filed into their box, it was two o'clock in the morning.

The clerk took the written verdict from the foreman of the jury. He read it, turned toward the jury, and asked: "Mr. Foreman, how say you? Is the defendant guilty or not guilty?"

The next second bordered on forever. And then: "We find the defendant, George Edgerly, not guilty."

The exhilaration mounted slowly. Shouting, back-pounding, and then it all broke loose and I was soaring. I was all alone in a velvet sky, and the weather was wonderful. How about that Eddie Corsetti? I would buy him a drink, and one for Wicki, and one for myself, and . . .

The night had been a mélange of television cameras and microphones and gin in paper cups and George Edgerly wearing the only grin in the room bigger than mine. But now it was the morning after the verdict, and my phone was ringing. "Lee," said a voice, "the power company just cut off our electricity. You haven't paid the bill for three months."

The following Sunday, my mother was in church. One of the front-row spinsters approached her and said she had read about me in the papers.

"Yes," said my mother, full of pride. "Lee just tried a murder case."

"Well, it's nice that he has some cases," said the spinster. "I suppose when he's starting out, he has to take whatever kind of cases he can get."

THE CUTTER LABS "POISON VACCINE" CASE

Melvin M. Belli
for the plaintiff

vs.

Wallace Sedgwick
for the defense

by Albert Averbach
and Charles Price

This is a civil case—a lawsuit brought against a manufacturer of Salk polio vaccine on behalf of children who contracted infantile paralysis after being vaccinated with defective vaccine. An open-and-shut case, you say? Far from it! In this description, told largely in Melvin Belli's own words, we see that a great trial lawyer may have to help make new law in order to win his case. Here the "King of Torts" gives us a blow-by-blow account not just of the trial but of its preparation, which is nine-tenths of any courtroom victory, and the appeal, which can turn victory into bitter defeat. After reading this, you will understand why "Belli for the plaintiff" strikes terror into the heart of many an able defense attorney.

Shortly after five o'clock on the evening of April 25, 1955, Dr. Walter E. Ward, medical director of Cutter Laboratories, in Berkeley, California, received in his office a chilling telephone call from Chicago. On the other end of the line was an officer of the Public Health Service reporting that a local child had contracted a case of what was suspected to be poliomyelitis. The child had recently been given an innoculation of the vaccine developed not too long before by Dr. Jonas Salk, and the shot he had been given had been traced to a batch of vaccine processed by one of the five pharmaceutical houses licensed to market it: Parke Davis; Eli Lilly; Wyeth; Pitman-Moore; Sharp and Dohme; and Cutter. There was no doubt about it—this batch had been processed by Cutter.

At home, that same evening, Dr. Ward heard by telephone of another case, this one in California. By six o'clock the next evening, six cases had been reported. By the end of the week, seventeen had been reported. At the end of two weeks, forty-four cases had been reported, of which thirty-eight had been directly traced to Cutter-produced vaccine. The remainder had received the vaccine of other firms. But, as a spokesman for Cutter was to put it later, "the association of paralysis with site of injection appeared to be significant only with respect to Cutter vaccine."

The site of injection of a shot of vaccine was the discriminating factor between Salk vaccine in general and that produced by any of the five pharmaceutical houses in particular. Field trials of Salk vaccine had not guaranteed it to be one hundred percent effective in making a person immune to polio. It was still possible to contract the disease after having been vaccinated without the vaccine itself giving it to you. If, however, the paralysis most quickly and most severely affected that part of the body into which the needle had been inserted, then the cause of the disease could be laid directly to the disease itself, in which case it had certainly been improperly processed. Not as formulated, but as tested. Or produced. Or manufactured. By whichever house had been responsible.

By the sixth of May—twelve days after the first case had been reported to Dr. Ward—nobody was receiving Cutter vaccine any longer. On the morning of April twenty-seventh the National Institute of Health had directly requested Cutter to withdraw all the vaccine it had distributed throughout the country, which it did by promptly notifying all local health departments and wholesale druggists and by notifying newspapers, the wire services, and radio and television stations. But, by this time, an estimated seventy-nine cases of polio would eventually be contracted from shots that had already been given of Cutter vaccine, and an incalculable number of other people had to wait in dread to see what would happen. Nobody wanted to guess how many others would get polio while the doctors were trying to replace good vaccine for the Cutter brand they could not use.

On the twenty-sixth of April, Mrs. Josephine Gottsdanker was traveling through Calexico, California, with her husband and three children when, having stopped at a roadside stand for ice cream, her five-and-a-half-year-old daughter, Anne, suddenly complained that her head hurt. To Mrs. Gottsdanker it seemed like a "casual" complaint at the time, and she thought only that perhaps the child's ponytail had been pulled back too tightly. Nevertheless, she decided to take her daughter's temperature. It was 101 degrees. That night Anne was up several times, vomiting. Her mother realized then that she had a sick child on her hands. The following day, the upper part of

Anne's right leg began to ache. Then the ache began to move down the leg. As her mother was to recall later in a hospital where it was determined that Anne had polio, Anne had been inoculated eight days before in the right buttock with Salk vaccine—*Cutter*-Salk vaccine.

On the twenty-seventh of April, Mrs. Elizabeth Phipps, of San Francisco, noticed that her thirteen-month-old son, Randy, had started to run a slight fever. This was on a Wednesday. Between then and Saturday he had been irritable off and on, but by Saturday his irritability had become marked whenever he was moved. While changing his diaper, Mrs. Phipps put Randy's weight on the back of his shoulders. He objected violently. When she gave him his bottle the next morning, he couldn't hold it. She put him on the floor to see if he could crawl. His left arm and shoulder gave way. He couldn't support his weight on it. When Randy's condition had been diagnosed as polio, Mrs. Phipps was able to recall that he had been inoculated on April nineteenth in the upper left arm with Salk vaccine—*Cutter*-Salk vaccine.

Both the Gottsdanker child and the Phipps baby had clearly received poliomyelitis at the site of injection. In other words, they had received shots from a batch of vaccine that had been prepared in a way other than Dr. Salk had said it should be prepared. The formula was right. It was the product that was at fault.

Cruel as polio is to a child and heartbreaking as it is to a parent, it is also crushingly expensive to treat. Since there had been no precedent for either case, the question of who was to pay for such treatment would be a matter for the courts to decide. In one of the most logical moves anybody who lives in California could make under the circumstances, both the Gottsdankers and the Phippses appealed to attorney Melvin Mouron Belli, of the San Francisco and Los Angeles firm of Belli, Ashe and Gerry, the most spectacularly effective battery of personal-injury lawyers in the history of American jurisprudence.

As in everything else, in law, there are trial lawyers and then there are trial lawyers. At one extreme is the inarticulate, ill-read, soft-spoken neighborhood attorney, dressed in a bow tie and a suit right off a pipe-rack, who gets an otherwise solid citizen off a drunk-driving charge by showing the judge a letter from his client's minister. He learns his law out of a textbook. Then there is Melvin Belli, who might very well have written the book.

There are those, many of them lawyers themselves, who say that Melvin Belli has to be seen to be believed. Belli had a full head of flawlessly barbered hair composed equally of strands of silver and white. Underneath it he displayes an engagingly handsome smile that is especially resistless to small children and old ladies. His suits, which cost in the neighborhood of a good motorcycle, have an Eastern cut to them with certain distinctly Western embellishments, such as red silk linings, and trouser pockets that are cut parallel to the waist, like riding pants. For footwear, he uses Congress gaiters, black leather boots that rise halfway up his calves and cost $75 a pair. With his thumbs in his vest, he looks a little like Hopalong Cassidy without a horse.

There are also people—again, many of them lawyers—who say Mel Belli has to be *heard* to be believed. Of certain leaders of the American Bar Association, with which Belli has been feuding for years and his contempt for which he displays by hanging his membership plaque upside-down in his bathroom, Belli has said, "They want the American lawyer to be a conforming, second-rate professional—a sort of athletic supporter to insurance companies and big business." . . .

In court as well as out, Belli may well be the most aggressive, ingenious, histrionically endowed trial lawyer since Darrow. At seventeen, he successfully sued the principal of his high school for withholding his diploma when Belli failed to put in an appearance to give the valedictory address because he, Belli, was hung over. He has won cases for, among others, a woman who had been sold a dress that had been returned from a mortician after it had once dressed a corpse; the smell of embalming fluid had come out at an overcrowded cocktail party and made her ill. He got the sentence of a rapist reduced from four hundred years to two hundred years, comically but significantly enough, by proving that some of the women had actually cooperated with his client. He won a case against a theater because his client had sat on a seat which someone else had just used as a toilet. Another client Belli successfully defended was a young man who had to be castrated because his doctor had carelessly diagnosed cancer of the penis as a wart. Using Dr. Kinsey as a reference, Belli estimated that his client had been deprived of 5,929 orgasms before his life expectancy would have run out. "Ladies and gentlemen of the jury," he said in his summation, "what value can we place on this? Can we place an arbitrary value upon a loss so devastating? Can we say that he should be awarded one dollar per occasion, or five dollars, or. . . !" The jury awarded Belli's client $100,000. . . .

However bizarre other lawyers may regard Belli's courtroom posture to be, none but the most obviously envious would deny that he is an extraordinary lawyer out of the courtroom and a truly great one in it. He is the universally regarded "King of Torts," the master at righting civil wrongs. He is a "people's lawyer," in the sense that Darrow, Michael Fallon, and Samuel Leibowitz once were, a courtroom Robin Hood who lives quixotically by getting rich insurance companies to pay for the misfortunes of the oppressed and the destitute. ("Bankers," he points out, "seldom get hit by trucks.") No other lawyer has ever tried, or won, as many malpractice suits against doctors and hospitals. In fact, it is a toss-up as to which group dislikes Belli more—the American Bar Association or the American Medical Association. Probably it is neither but, instead, the American Society of Insurance Adjusters, from whose clients Belli annually extracts more than a million dollars. "The trouble with insurance-company executives," he has said, "is that they forget that the money their companies are worth is money they are holding in trust, given to them by you and me in order to protect anyone you or I happen to injure. Now, God knows you and I don't want to shortchange cripples. But the insurance companies do, and will, if you give them half a chance. They stupidly think that money's *theirs.*"

Like a lot of famous lawyers, Belli has had his share of celebrated clients. But he has handled the infamous with equal alacrity. He has represented everyone from Errol Flynn to Caryl Chessman, from Maureen Connolly to Mae West, from William Kapell to Mickey Cohen. In addition to Jack Ruby, he has also represented more than a hundred other murderers. While rightwing lawyers may deplore his techniques, law-school deans and professors, on the other hand, have publicly applauded him. "He is the best trial lawyer I have ever seen," says Judge Theresa Meikle, of the San Francisco Superior Court. "This," says another judge, "is the most brilliant lawyer that ever came into my courtroom." That remark might be expected to have been made by one of Belli's drinking buddies. Actually, it is credited to Judge Joe Brantley Brown of Dallas, the man Belli openly fought with in court during the Ruby trial, has since publicly insulted, and whose tactics Belli still abhors. . . .

From the outset, Belli regarded the case as "the Cutter case." Anne Gottsdanker and Randy Phipps were "just a couple of pathetic kids who never would be normal again." It was the

Cutter people Belli was after, not for personal reasons, but for a principle that had been in the back of his mind for some time. "I would be depicted as a man who would say Cutter didn't care," Belli has since said. "I disavow that. I think—and thought then—that the Cutter people cared very much. The only point of difference there, perhaps, might lie in my estimate of just what it was they cared very much about.

"The preparation of a lawsuit, an old professor of mine was fond of saying, turns a lawyer into a general preparing to fight a battle. The better prepared he is, the better his chances of winning the fight. This is by way of reciting the obvious, and I can hardly question its wisdom. But there are times when you do not prepare for just a battle. You prepare instead for a *war,* of which the immediate battle is only a part. 'One more victory like this,' cried King Pyrrhus, 'and we are lost!' And so it is, I believe, in the practice of law. . . ."

Belli's council of war turned out to be a brilliant example of what happens when a twelve-cylinder collection of attorneys get together with a sure hand like Belli's at the wheel. The group met at an oaken table in a nondescript seafood restaurant on Kearney Street, in downtown San Francisco, one evening over dinner. Among them were Lou Ashe, one of Belli's partners, various other members of the firm, and assorted lawyer friends, one of whom was Bernard Witkin, a widely recognized authority on California law.

"There were two counts we could go in on here," Belli recalls. "The first was negligence. Cutter vaccine, and Cutter's alone, was causing these polio cases. Obviously, Cutter seemed negligent in their preparation of the serum.

"The other count was warranty. Here there was no law at all, by way of precedent. Foodstuffs, yes—any number of cases had shown that the original dispenser of a food was responsible for its edible condition once it reached the consumer, regardless of 'privity,' which is to say, the number of stages of hands it had gone through in being distributed from manufacturer to vendor to buyer to consumer.

"But drugs—that was something different. Here there was no law. An article of food was sold. An article of medicine was prescribed, dispensed, administered. The essential point here was one of *service* as opposed to *sale,* even though the medicine was paid for. An outstanding test case had shown the original supplier of blood plasma not to be guilty when the blood, upon eventual injection into the patient, caused an untoward result.

"Warranty—all warranty says is, 'We stand behind our pledge.' And, as I say, that little matter of privity, compounded by the factor of intervening service (as opposed to sale), made this a concept totally apart.

"True, where drugs were concerned, we had on our side an interesting concept of legal precedent—the ancient code of Hammurabi, sixth king of the Amoritic dynasty of Babylonia, whose reign extended from 2067 till 2025 B.C. Said Hammurabi: the doctor is responsible for his treatment. Should the patient lose an arm, let the doctor lose *his* arm by way of recompense.

"But this was not a medical malpractice case. We were not after the doctors who had given the shots to Randy and Anne. All our old friend Hammurabi could do for us was to set down the ancient principle of *absolute liability* from which, century after century, the world had begun to swing away. But now —I felt—it was beginning to swing back.

"And here, I thought, was where we should make our stand, in this battle in this immense war. On warranty, and warranty alone. Let the vendor stand behind his goods: let generations of *caveat emptor*—'let the buyer beware'—become *caveat vendor*—'let the seller beware.'

"My colleagues, in that meeting that night in that little fish restaurant, looked at me as though I was crazy. They talked persuasively and well. There was no law to fall back on in warranty, they agreed, and no Hammurabi to testify. Furthermore, if we tried the case on warranty and lost, and some other lawyer, representing some other Cutter victim, tried his case on negligence and won, we ourselves could be sued by our own clients for malpractice! And, doubtless, rightly so.

"Now it was my turn to talk again. At times I can be persuasive too. How, I asked them, could we prove negligence?

"*Res ipsa loquitur*—that was their answer. 'The thing speaks for itself.' As we'd said before, Cutter vaccine, and Cutter's alone, was causing these polio cases.

"No," Belli said. "When I said how do we *prove* it, I meant *prove* in the lawyer's sense." By that, Belli meant, to convince the jury. "The thing speaks for itself," he continued, a little sadly, "except in Oakland."

Oakland was where the trial would be held. It was next door to Berkeley, where Cutter Laboratories was an old and highly influential institution. The entire weight of the community, the press, the powerful drug industry, the even more powerful American Medical Association would slam down upon them. They would be savagely accused as people who were trying to impede the progress of medicine and the safety of millions, for no drug company would continue to experiment in its laboratories if a single untoward result could bankrupt it in the courts.

What *was* the thing that spoke for itself in this case? Was it negligence? Negligence in what respect? Were the laboratories' testing rooms unclean? Cutter would say they were clean. Who would testify otherwise for Belli? Was the vaccine prepared according to formula? Cutter would say yes. And before Belli could say no, such a preponderance of scientific gobbledygook would assail the jury that they would be convinced the side with the most impressive witnesses had to be right.

"The thing that speaks for itself here," Belli argued, "is not negligence—it's *warranty!* The public was told this stuff was safe. It wasn't safe. That's it. Period."

"Yes," Bernard Witkin said, "but the law of warranty applies to a sale, not a service. You have it in foods. But not in drugs."

Each camp in that council of war was arguing that the other side could lose. None of them was talking about how they could win. "Essentially," says Belli, "we were telling the other fellow what was wrong with his idea, not what was right with our own. Which is all right. The time to be pessimistic about a case is before it starts. And God knows we had enough to be pessimistic about."

The ultimate decision they reached was simplicity itself. They would go in on both counts: negligence *and* warranty. . . .

The making of Salk vaccine depended not only on the ingredients but, as one might test a baked cake by sticking a straw into it, on a timetable of production. Live virus, grown in the kidneys of monkeys, was what went into Salk vaccine. This virus had to be inactivated by the addition of formaldehyde, for active virus in the serum would be dangerous. It could, in fact, cause polio.

As the inventor of the process, Dr. Salk had specified that manufacturers' lots of the vaccine should be tested while the formaldehyde was being added; that each time you tested, a "good" lot of vaccine would show fewer remaining "live" particles until finally no available measuring device could show any "live" virus elements remaining.

This did not mean no "live" virus was left. You could not tell, because the amounts were so small they could not be measured. It did mean that a finding of "zero" on available testing devices showed the serum to be safe. Dr. Salk had found that if you put a dot on a graph for the number of active particles still alive each time you tested, then connected those dots with a line, the result would be a *straight* line.

Cutter admittedly did not find a straight line in its tests. They were finding a curve instead. Since the entire process was a new one, they claimed, and because Salk found safety in a straight line, it did not necessarily follow that getting to zero on a curve, instead of on the straight line, proved the vaccine was bad. In other words, they stated that while Salk's product was good, his theory behind it was neither good nor bad. Certainly, it was not binding.

The government itself wanted to be extra-safe in licensing this vaccine to the general public. They insisted that no one lot be judged by itself alone. A zero reading for one lot in an overall batch could be misleading—maybe just an accident. So for protection's sake, all the lots in any greater overall batch of vaccine were to be checked one against the other.

For instance, suppose you had twenty-eight lots in a batch, and ten proved "bad." If you got fewer and fewer bad lots as you went along, it meant you were on the right track. So your final readings of "zero" on the last lots would have some real meaning.

But here, in the sequence produced, is the reading Belli and his staff found in one batch of twenty-eight lots of Cutter vaccine:

Lot No.	*Good*	*Bad*	*Lot No.*	*Good*	*Bad*
1	x		9	x	
2		x	10	x	
3	x		11		x
4		x	12		x
5	x		13	x	
6		x	14	x	
7	x		15	x	
8	x		16	x	

Lot No.	*Good*	*Bad*	*Lot No.*	*Good*	*Bad*
17	x		23		x
18	x		24	x	
19	x		25		x
20	x		26		x
21	x		27	x	
22		x	28		x

From this, it can be seen that of the ten bad batches, five were concentrated among the final seven—the precise opposite of the Salk finding, recognized by the government as instrumental.

It was recognized early by the government in this work that a single negative test itself was inadequate to establish safety with sufficient significance, but that a sequence of negative production lots is of increasing significance.

But having licensed the production of Salk vaccine according to Salk formula, the government in effect paid only lip service to what it had assumed the manufacturers would obviously obey in any event—Salk *theory.* And since only Cutter was producing bad vaccine, and only Cutter was named in the lawsuit, and the other drug companies rallied round their stricken comrade, it can be imagined the problem faced when the other companies started saying that they, too, were getting curves, not straight lines, in their testing.

As preparation for the trial dragged on, each day seeming to make the outcome of the case appear more and more unfavorable, Belli felt sure he and his staff "were going to get the socks beat off" them at negligence. And so, while preparing for negligence, his thoughts went back more and more to the concept of warranty, the all-consuming idea that "let the buyer beware" should be altered to "let the seller beware."

But in warranty there was nothing to prepare. There was no law, no precedent. There was only an idea, and a shaky one at that, for there was always that seemingly insurmountable legal fact that what was held true for foods was not held true for drugs. It just could not be argued that, as articles "fit for human consumption," drugs were the same as food. So be it, Belli thought to himself. Then, an entirely new tack would have to be taken. He would have to demonstrate an astonishing new concept of just how things are humanly consumed. No, he thought, drugs are not the same as food; they are even more so! There was the inescapable fact that with the bad Cutter vaccine, infection had set in at the site of injection, where it was consumed.

Many foods, ranging from lemon juice to bicarbonate of soda, have medicinal uses, Belli told himself. And many foods, ranging from sugar to coffee, are now administered other than by mouth. Down through the years, "food" and "mouth" had had the same connotation. But why, when there are so many other inlets to the body?

If, for instance, you were to put into your mouth some lemon juice contaminated by something, you could smell, touch, see, or even taste that contamination before you swallowed it. Under certain circumstances, you might do all four. But even though you did none of the four, your stomach could easily reject the contamination for you by throwing it back up.

But if you were to receive that same contaminated lemon juice rectally, a quite standard medical procedure, none of your senses, nor even the stomach itself, would then be able to warn you or reject the contamination. The law then, for many years, had protected you against bad food taken by mouth. But neither the law nor anything else could protect you if you were to ingest the food any other way. The law protected you where you needed it least, Belli told himself, and failed you where you needed it most.

Suddenly, Belli knew, they were not talking about drugs at all, but about food. From this line of reasoning came two paragraphs in his brief to the appellate court, two paragraphs that represented the breakthrough in the field of tort law in general and warranty law in particular:

> Nothing can be more immediately "consumed" by an individual than an injection directly into the human tissue or bloodstream. In the case of food, the eyes, nose, or the sense of taste may warn. The natural vomiting defense of the alimentary canal may reject the noxious food foreign object invader. The other defenses of the body have opportunity to mobilize against the not-too-unexpected invasion of contaminated food.
>
> There is no defense against the unwholesome enemy hidden in the barrel of an inoculation needle. (Even the good doctor who gives the shot tells the child to "look away.") The minor plaintiff never sees the vaccine. What would it tell his senses if he did? He does not smell it; he cannot taste it. The regurgitating defenses of the digestive tract are bypassed; the devasting *live* enemy is at work in the entire human body within minutes; there is no time for defenses to mobilize.

From this point on, Belli was not again to think in terms of drugs but in terms of food. If trichinosis from pork could excite a court in justified defense of the public health, how much more wrathful would it become over an unwholesome live virus injected into the bloodstream? Belli would argue drugs in front of the jury, but he would talk *food* to the judge. As for legal precedent, he could call upon any one of a number of food cases, asking if these same foods could not have been taken into the body by means other than the mouth, even under medical orders.

Still, there was another, even closer precedent. Belli recalled the case of *Boyd* vs. *Coca-Cola,* in Tennessee in 1915. Mrs. Boyd was the lady in delicate health who would drink an occasional Coke for its tonic effect. Hence, Coke had been regarded as a food and a tonic at one and the same time. A food and a *tonic!*

"Hey, fellas," Belli said to his partners when this thought crossed his mind. "We've got 'em!"

As it is to all trial lawyers, who know that any successful case is nine-tenths preparation, the trial itself came only as an anticlimax to Belli. "We knew how it was going to come out," he has said, "and we knew what would happen along the way. Let me clarify that at once: you never know what will happen in a lawsuit. You can lose an uncontested divorce case, if you don't look out. What I mean to say is that in this instance we realized the preponderance of probability. Much more so than the defense. They didn't know what to expect, for the uproarious reason that, having blocked our access to information in every way they could, they now could not tell how much we knew!

"If a man is charged with murder and the state has to prove it, it is, beyond doubt, the accused murderer who loses sleep. Not only is he the one who has to pay the penalty if convicted, but he and he foremost of all *knows* the degree of guilt! He has to sit there and wonder how much the other side knows.

"It would have startled them, how little we actually knew! We had prepared this case over months and had expended literally scores of thousands of dollars in time and money. But nothing we could do could overcome the one thing that made this case, and for this reason alone, one of the most stunning in the history of tort law.

"If I hit you with my car and you sue me for damages, then you are alleging that a tort has been committed. And you and I can wind up in court, with our various witnesses, to testify about what happened.

"In the Cutter case, however, we were on that weird middle

ground where people doing the complaining were there to testify to the crime—and yet nobody except the defendant saw it happen! Randy Phipps, Anne Gottsdanker—and, to be sure, Mel Belli—weren't in Cutter's laboratory when that vaccine was readied, tested, packaged, shipped. Who was? *Only Cutter!*

"And so, under the rituals, the checks, the balances of our magnificent system of law, does it sometimes come full circle: the more your crime went undetected, the less the other side will know about it. But the less they know, the less you can know what it is they *do* know! Does that sound like a game? It ought not to. Under the 'rules of discovery' now available, both sides can know much more of what should be known. And that is good. But no 'rules of discovery'—no rules of anything—can remove from a guilty party the stain of his guilt. He knows. He *knows!* And he sits there, wondering how much you know.

"In my judgment, it is seldom that the good lawyer has to bring out this part of it in a courtroom. Perry Mason may do it one way on television, but all he does—outside of giving the public a fairly distorted view of courtroom activity—is to express the fiction writer's ridiculous conceit that since all lawyers are smart, the hero has to be smarter than the villain.

"Next time you are in your lawyer's office, look at his diploma. It does not say how smart he is. Sometimes, it pays not to be smart. Be un-smart. But let your opponent be un-smarter than you! It happens.

"And so it happened here. When it was the turn of the eminent Wallace Sedgwick, star attorney for the defense, to cross-examine Mrs. Phipps, here is what took place.

SEDGWICK: Now, I believe that you said that you took the boy Randy to get his shot on April ninteenth. Do you recall whether it was Monday or Tuesday? Was it Tuesday?

MRS. PHIPPS: Yes.

At the counsel table, Lou Ashe, Dick Gerry, and Belli exchanged glances. What was this for? Belli shrugged.

SEDGWICK: The only reason, there seemed to be some question about it. I really don't know. How do you happen to remember the date particularly as to the nineteenth or Tuesday? Could it have been Monday?

MRS. PHIPPS: No, I believe it was a Tuesday.

Belli shot a look at the jury. Some of them were frowning —wondering the same thing, no doubt.

SEDGWICK: We all have a little problem on this date?

MRS. PHIPPS: I don't know. I would say it was Tuesday, and I believe it was the nineteenth. I remember the days rather than the dates.

Now Belli was beginning to smile. He had mentally "hired" Mr. Sedgwick, remember, but he hardly dreamed he would be working for him this early in the case. He could not let go of that Tuesday.

SEDGWICK: You think it was a Tuesday?

MRS. PHIPPS: Yes.

SEDGWICK: Is that your recollection?

MRS. PHIPPS: I believe so.

"That was five questions about Tuesday," Belli recalls. "There were five more questions, and the witness was dismissed. Given the opportunity to impress the jury with evidence of a nature beyond their normal comprehension, Mr. Sedgwick had chosen to concentrate his fire on something that had no bearing on the case: was the shot given on a Monday or a Tuesday?

"And, now abandoning that ridiculous course, he displayed on his own the fact that the Monday-Tuesday nonsense bore no relationship to the issue at hand. He had simply chosen to throw himself on the defensive. He could not have done so more obviously had he defended a gunslayer on the basis that the gun was purchased on a Thurday instead of a Friday. Even worse than that, in this case the lady was right—it *was* a Tuesday.

"Knowing what we knew, it was things like that we had to depend upon. We hardly believed they would exhibit themselves in this stark a fashion, but here it was. You have ten world-renowned scientists at your beck and call to testify that there was nothing wrong with the vaccine that infected a child, and you take five questions in a row to find out if the mother of a child can remember a day of the week more than two years ago when that infection took place. There is only one thing more stupid than asking her if she remembers that date. That is finding out that she does!

"What was behind that line of questioning, of course, was Sedgwick's uncertainty. He did not know how much we knew, as I have explained, and he showed it every time he appeared in court. We counted on him to do so. He did not fail us. . . .

"The chief antagonist, when all was said and done, was Dr. Ward—Cutter's medical director. At the outset of the trial, we could see what it was we could expect from him.

BELLI: May we call the first witness, Your Honor? I don't believe it will take long.

THE COURT: All right.

BELLI: Dr. Ward, will you step up, please? May the record show, if Your Honor please, we are calling Dr. Ward as an adverse witness.

THE COURTS: All right.

BELLI: Dr. Ward, I have just one or two questions. I would like to have you tell the ladies and gentlemen of the jury if the vaccine that Cutter sold and from which the Phipps child and the Gottsdanker child were vaccinated was subsequently tested by you in your laboratory and contained live virus?

SEDGWICK: There is no showing he knows which one it was.

BELLI: Certainly by now you must know which of your vaccines was injected into plaintiffs, right?

DR. WARD: No, I can't positively state, because, as I think is well known, there are a number of suits, there are a number of lot numbers, and I would have to refer to the records.

BELLI: And in the number of suits, you checked all of those lots of vaccine and found that the vaccine contained live virus, did you not?

DR. WARD: I don't think that is true. I would have to review records to answer.

BELLI: Come now, Doctor, can't you tell the ladies and gentlemen whether the vaccine that was injected into the Phipps plaintiff and the Gottsdanker girl contained live virus?

DR. WARD: As I sit here, having been in court all day, I

do not know the answer because I have to review the records.

BELLI: Can you tell the ladies and gentlemen of the jury how many lots of the vaccine that you sold and you later recalled contained live virus?

DR. WARD: No, I can't. I haven't reviewed the records recently. I just don't know.

BELLI: You haven't reviewed the records recently?

DR. WARD: That is correct, sir.

BELLI: When did you last review them, Doctor?

DR. WARD: I can't recall.

BELLI: Could you give me just a hint or suggestion?

DR. WARD: No, I am sorry. I couldn't.

The Honorable Thomas J. Ledwitch, presiding at the trial, was the first to show irritation. "Have the records here at nine-thirty in the morning," he snapped at the defendants.

Thus finally, while the trial was actually in progress, was Dick Gerry enabled to unravel the code and come up with the table reprinted earlier.

BELLI: Will you tell the ladies and gentlemen of the jury whether there was or was not live virus in the polio vaccine of which Anne and the boy were inoculated?

DR. WARD: I reviewed the record over the weekend, and based on the tests that we did after April twenty-seventh, we had negative findings on those two lots.

BELLI: You had negative findings on those two lots?

DR. WARD: That is correct.

BELLI: Do you mean to tell the jury that you put out the vaccine not knowing what the word "consistent" meant?

DR. WARD: Yes. And as far as I know, everyone else did too.

BELLI: Didn't that prove to you one of two things—one, that your tests were not accurate, or two, the way you were manufacturing it was wrong?

DR. WARD: Well, I can't answer your question. Something odd, or something was going on which scientifically you couldn't explain.

BELLI: You knew, then, in some of the tests—one-third of them, in fact—you were getting live virus, and that something odd was going on, to use your words. Either these tests were not good or your manufacturing was not following the Salk process?

DR. WARD: I just can't answer that question.

To most questions, though, Dr. Ward could answer. Several he answered more than once—and differently each time.

BELLI: Did you sell any to the public when scientifically there was something odd going on you couldn't explain?

DR. WARD: We never sold that material, no.

Later:

BELLI: You told us that some of your Cutter vaccine had live virus in it that you had returned, is that right?

DR. WARD: Right.

BELLI: But you told us on your test that the lots that were

used on the Phipps boy and the Gottsdanker girl, according to your tests, did not have live virus?

DR. WARD: That is correct.

BELLI: Is that still your answer today?

DR. WARD: That is still my answer today.

Later the same day:

BELLI: It is your opinion presently that there was live virus in the lot in which Anne Gottsdanker was inoculated and in which James Phipps was inoculated?

DR. WARD: That would be my best opinion, yes.

So, it would seem, there was live virus in the vaccine Cutter sold to the public, although they never had any doubts about the vaccine they sold to the public. And there was no live virus in the Gottsdanker or Phipps lots, except that there was. Belli now appealed to the physician's common sense:

BELLI: There is a label on the poliomyelitis vaccine box that you sold, is there not?

DR. WARD: Yes.

BELLI: "Inactivated"—is that right?

DR. WARD: That is correct.

BELLI: And that was to be the same inactivation as came from the minimum standards?

DR. WARD: That is correct.

BELLI: And that meant what it says on there to a person of ordinary intelligence and prudence, is that right?

DR. WARD: Yes.

While Dr. Ward's testimony may have made sense to the technicians at Cutter Laboratories, it wasn't making much sense to Belli in that court. He looked at the judge beseechingly.

The question now arose as to what Cutter did with a lot of vaccine that *did* test bad. Did they throw it out completely? Did they mix it with other vaccine? Did they continue to treat it until it tested negative? Or what? A man from Cutter's laboratories testified that operating procedures were drawn up to follow Dr. Salk's written method. But having found a way to treat vaccine so that it turned out good, Dr. Salk had never thought that anybody would continue to treat vaccine that had turned out bad. So the possibility of "reinactivation" of serum that had not tested inactive the first time was never even in the minimum requirements.

> BELLI: So if you were going to reuse that, like a stew, or making a cake, or something that was baked and didn't turn out right, and you were going to do something about it, then you would have to follow your own procedures about how long to reinactivate it or how long to bake it, right?
>
> DR. WARD: Yes.
>
> BELLI: You were on your own?
>
> DR. WARD: That is correct.
>
> BELLI: That is, Cutter's own?
>
> DR. WARD: Yes.

Round and round the questions and answers went; eventually to come back to what Belli subsequently nicknamed "innocence by association." A veritable welter of scientific stars, virologists, immunologists, and serologists testified that Salk was not necessarily right, and if he was, then Cutter in any event was not violating any of the minimum standards. Dr. Wendell Stanley, a Nobel Prize winner, testified that Dr. Salk could hardly be considered the final word on his own process. Yet, earlier, he had told a congressional committee that Salk was "the last word" on polio research.

Belli even brought out the fact that the United States Public Health Service was unaware that Cutter had been getting one-third bad results in their own lots of vaccine. Belli asked Dr. Howard J. Shaughnessy, an adviser to the government, "And if you had information at that time that one of the manufacturers was getting one-third bad lots . . . certainly you wouldn't have recommended licensing, would you?"

Dr. Shaughnessy replied, "I would not have."

"Of course," says Belli, "he *didn't* know that. And there was nothing to say Cutter had to inform him. And the government team that went in to examine Cutter's premises and processes found no negligence!"

What about that question of consistency? The "straight line" theory? Dr. Ward had the answer to that one: "It was my feeling . . . that the inactivation did not follow and had never followed, even in Salk's hands, a straight line. . . . The straight line was a theoretical concept which, if checked very carefully, probably was an erroneous theory."

Thus rested the Cutter defense, to Belli's way of thinking, in an atmosphere of irony, for they who had done the damage had argued the benefits of doing something "very carefully." As everybody waited anxiously for the verdict, Belli thought he and his team had only one thing going for them: the deceptively simple fact that something had gone wrong with that Cutter vaccine.

The Cutter lawyers had argued the bad batch was an unforeseeable accident that is often the price of medical research. To Belli's mind, it was not a bad argument, except for one line of thought. They had set out to deal with the facts, not the people. But, as Belli is fond of pointing out, a lawsuit *is* people. And time and again the defense had missed that point. There was, for one thing, the curious tenacity of the star defense lawyer to wrest from Mrs. Gottsdanker the jokingly inconsequential fact of whether the inoculation had been made on a Monday or a Tuesday. That blunder had done its work, as could be seen when the jury at last came in with its verdict.

As the verdict was read, Belli experienced one of the strangest few minutes in his long courtroom career. He had won the case, and damages were awarded in the amount of $131,500 for the Gottsdanker girl and $15,800 for the Phipps boy. But appended to the verdict, in an unprecendented action on the part of a jury, was a two-page memorandum, handwritten by the foreman, a bank clerk who looked every inch the role. When the jury was being chosen, Belli had noticed that he dotted his i's with circles and that he kept his loose change in the same pocket as his handkerchief, to muffle the clinking of coins. But Belli had also made note that he was a prospective father, and he had hoped that this prospect might overcome any ultraconservatism. As Belli was about to learn, he had been wrong. The document read as follows:

> Your Honor:
>
> On the assumption that the attached forms of verdict were prepared for us merely as a convenience, we submit that it is our right and duty to expand upon it briefly. We feel that the court would wish to know the full extent of the verdict agreed upon.
>
> The jury took as first consideration the matter of negligence, and from a preponderance of the evidence concluded that the defendant, Cutter Laboratories, was not negligent either directly or by inference in producing and selling poliomyelitis vaccine under conditions prevailing at the time of the Cutter incident.
>
> With regard to the law of warranty, however, we feel that we have no alternative but to conclude that Cutter

> Laboratories came to market a lot of vaccine which when given to plaintiffs caused them to come down with poliomyelitis, this resulting in a breach of warranty. For this cause alone we find in favor of plaintiffs.

Judge Ledwitch stared at the document and blinked. He shook his head, as if to clear it. "Frank," he said to the court clerk, "have your ever run into anything attached to a verdict?"

"Way back," the clerk said. "I just can't recall all the details. . . ."

Belli had the frightening thought that he had accomplished what he had proposed *not* to do! Won the battle but lost the war!

The wording of the extraordinary piece of jury theory made it look as though they had followed the normal instructions of the court, as to warranty, against their own free will. They had found Cutter not guilty on the count of negligence. The best, therefore, that Belli could now hope for here was an award less than what it should have been, for the acquittal of negligence, as a statement in Cutter's favor, of course softened the warranty blow to come.

Had he gone in on warranty alone, as he had wanted to do that night so many months before in that little fish restaurant . . . Well, he hadn't done so. And now he had to fight in the appellate court, just to stay even.

Yet, bad as things seemed, they had their good side. If the verdict could be upheld, then a fantastic step forward had been taken in the field of warranty law. Belli could try ensuing Cutter cases on warranty alone.

It was left to Belli to write the firms' appellate brief. Once again, he would be confronted by the weight of organized business, pharmaceutical houses, and the medical profession. And once again, he trusted that the lawyers on the other side would help him do his work for him. They did not fail. And little Randy Phipps, the boy who had won too small a verdict, played his part. . . .

"This is not just going to be a brief," Belli told Ashe and Gerry. "This is going to be an outline of new law in the field of warranty. It is going to change the face of our legal map. We'll have thousands of them printed, ship them to law libraries and offices and jurisdictions all over the world."

They agreed. There was no doubt about it. The firm had made law. For both in the judge's instructions and the jury's verdict, they had jumped—almost without anyone's noticing it—the barrier of drugs vs. foods.

This had been accomplished in three ways. First, by demonstrating the obvious: that Cutter in selling the product, not a doctor in administering it from a sealed ampul, was the source most responsible for causing illness in the victims. And down fell the structure of "service, not sales."

Secondly, there was Mrs. Boyd and her Coca-Cola "tonic," and Belli's argument that drugs should be classified as foods —even, to be sure, more so, in that no ordinary defenses of the body against bad food could be marshaled here. "The regurgitating defenses of the digestive tract are bypassed," Belli had said. "the devastating *live* enemy is at work in the entire human body within minutes; there is no time for defenses to mobilize."

There was one more sentence to that paragraph. It told the whole story in one sentence. It was the reason the Cutter case *made law.* Though no one case ever should be said to rise or fall on a lawyer's words rather than its own merit, this came as close as you can come to it. It is the most often quoted single sentence from that widely circulated Cutter brief, and it not only cannot be answered, but stands by itself. "The enemy in the Cutter case," Belli had written, "came in the guise of a defense against that very enemy."

And now Cutter tried to answer. Most of all, Belli suspected, they hated that one sentence, and therefore tried to answer it.

Belli had showed time and again in his brief how the public had been assured, even urged, that getting these polio shots was of vital importance to them and their children. Now Cutter's attorneys, in answer to the brief, said, "These are advertisements, *not by Cutter,* but by the National Foundation for Infantile Paralysis . . . the posters, radio, TV, magazine and news stories *were not Cutter's* . . . this was a representation, *not of Cutter,* but of the National Foundation . . . this was an appeal, *not of Cutter,* but jointly of the National Foundation, the AMA, the American Academy of Pediatrics, and the American Academy of General Practice . . . *not urging or warranty by Cutter* are advertisements by Parke Davis, *not Cutter.*"

"Using the technique I discussed," says Belli, "we had provided the paper bag, and Cutter's lawyers had obediently pulled it over their heads and now were trying to fight their way out of it. The harder they fought, the funnier it became. They wound up saying, 'It wasn't our fault Parke Davis made better stuff than we did. We never said our stuff was any good!' The laughter increased when it turned out that Parke Davis, through the American Pharmaceutical Association of which it was, on size alone, a stronger member than Cutter, paid its share to hire a lawyer to defend Cutter in an associated defense brief. This brief was really brief—only eighteen pages —its major point being that the pharmaceutical industry had been subjected to 'the danger of becoming the victim of its own excellence.'

"The almost unbelievable insouciance of that statement was typical of the extremes to which the defense had been driven. They had won on negligence, had lost in a field where there was no precedent in law, and the form of jury verdict could easily suggest to the nimble legal mind some way in which the judge's instructions to the jury might be thrown out by a higher court.

"Yet they played down these strong points, and time and again, instead, underlined the point that a certain number of bad results are inevitable in the dispensing of a mass pharmaceutical. What they were saying, in so many words, was that if you are the one person in a million who gets a bad result from our drug, it means there's something wrong with you, not us . . . *and therefore we owe you nothing!*

"Had Cutter defended itself alone, with silent help from the sidelines, we would have had a far tougher job. But now the very element that cost us a negligence verdict—the very weight of the 'big boys' on Cutter's side—was proving out in our favor. The big boys didn't know when to quit. Why should Parke Davis, which had no bad Cutter vaccine, be screaming now on Cutter's behalf? You don't have to guess the answer. The briefs spelled it out: 'Because not only the polio stuff can go wrong, but anything else we make, too!' If I'd been a judge reading those defense briefs, I would have stuck with the headache they gave me rather than go down to the store and take the chance of buying an aspirin.

"They were right about one thing, the big boys. In claiming the license to put out products that might have bad effects on people, they did indeed have the precedent of the law on their side. But they overlooked what in our judgment was the critical point in this case—that the law does not stand still. It is said that only plaintiffs 'make' new law. That in itself is one of the most exciting things about the tort field in which firms like Belli, Ashe and Gerry operate so prominently. But I have always had the private suspicion that it is the defendant's attorneys whose option it is to exploit opportunity. If a wrong is done, and there is no law to cover it, we must always wonder *why* there is no law. The skillful defense lawyer will not only point out why there is no law, but will *refrain* from bringing in extraneous material. Such extraneous material can only help the other side, simply because it has no reason for existing, and thus, however unintended, gives rise to the suspicion that you think the guts of your plea cannot stand by themselves.

"Thus, *it did not matter* whether Randy Phipps got his polio shot on a Monday or a Tuesday. For the defense to have asked a single question about that was to do themselves harm. For them to have asked five in a row about it was just incredibly stupid. A small thing? Perhaps. But it is emblematic of the way they conducted their defense throughout. They had more artillery than they needed. Instead of harboring it, they used it all.

"What would happen now was obvious. The appeals court would probably not overturn the negligence verdict, and they certainly would not overturn the warranty verdict. Because of the negligence verdict, the actual award in the case of Phipps and Gottsdanker was, as I have said, less than it should have been. And so we lost the battle. And so, simultaneously, we won the war."

The appellate court said simply that the jury verdict must stand.

"By now we knew where we were," Belli recalls. "Our answer brief was not a major document, by any means. It had one interesting element to it, though. It was warranty, warranty, warranty! We thundered about it, roared about it. We were out to win the war now, and the battlefield of negligence, as I had tried to say in that little fish restaurant now so long in the past, was a losing one."

The Supreme Court of the State of California refused to review the case, and so the verdicts stood. . . .

FANNY HILL IN HACKENSACK

Ronald Picinich
for the prosecution

vs.

Charles Rembar
for the defense

by Charles Rembar

In the long series of court cases that established the American public's right to read sexually stimulating books, the case of John Cleland's *Memoirs of a Woman of Pleasure (Fanny Hill)* is a landmark. Before the U.S. Supreme Court decided the *Fanny Hill* case, it had established that certain erotic works which were also deemed great works of art—like *Ulysses, Lady Chatterley's Lover* and *Tropic of Cancer*—could not be banned from publication in that they had "redeeming social value." But *Fanny Hill,* although possessing some undoubted literary value, was obviously in the main a delightful piece of pornography. This meant that the courts would now have to grapple with the question of whether government suppression of pornography could be justified on the ground that reading erotic books is harmful to the normal reader. When *Fanny Hill* made it through the courts, the barriers to free publication of porn were definitively breached.

The following, often hilarious, selection shows us a master at work—Charles Rembar, who represented Grove Press in the *Lady Chatterley* and *Tropic of Cancer* cases, as well as in that of *Fanny Hill.* Rembar is perhaps the finest obscenity case lawyer in the country, an urbane, elegant practitioner with a razor wit. The selection is in the form of direct quotations from the trial transcript, with comments by Rembar in the footnotes. (I have abridged the transcript slightly in order to eliminate legalistic squabbles which might distract the reader from the main points at issue.) The Hackensack case was one of a series of *Fanny Hill* trials which also took place in Boston and New York. In this case, the judge decided against Rembar and the publisher, but his decision was later effectively reversed by the Supreme Court's opinion in the Massachusetts case.

The account of the trial begins here with the prosecutor, Mr. Picinich, attempting to prove through expert witnesses that reading *Fanny Hill* is bad for you, while Rembar's cross-examinations plant a series of delayed-action bombs under the witness chair. The first witness will be William Reilly, an official of the Citizens for Decent Literature, who swears to tell the truth, the whole truth, and nothing but the truth.

William P. Reilly, sworn[1]
Direct Examination by Mr. Picinich[2]

Q. With respect to the book, John Cleland's *Memoirs of a Woman of Pleasure,* introduced in evidence, have you read that book?

A. Yes, sir.

Q. Can you state for the court what the dominant subject matter of that book is? . . .

A. The overall theme, the dominant theme of this book, is a portrayal of abnormality and perversion as being normal.

Q. What does the book deal with?

A. The book deals with abnormal sex.

Q. Now are there instances of abnormal sex portrayed in this book?

A. Definitely.

Q. Can you point to some of those instances which you consider to be abnormal?

A. Sure. I don't know if you want the exact page or not but there are certain articles in here in which voyeurism

---

[1]Dr. Reilly's face was highly mobile, rather fleshy and generally beneficent. Except under stress, he had a jolly look, a sort of secular Friar Tuck.

[2]The testimony on the witness's qualifications is omitted; its substance appears below.

is indicated, which is abnormal; homosexuality, which is abnormal; flagellation, which is abnormal; fetishism, which is abnormal; if you want the specific mentioning of these I will be glad to do that. . . .

Q. My next question is, what effect would reading this book have upon the average person?

A. The effect on the average person of this kind of material is definitely detrimental to their mental health, and I say definitely. To the average person a constant perusal—a constant perusal of this kind of material—would definitely stimulate them to acts of sexual activity. . . .

BY THE COURT:

Q. You consider this objectionable—from your standpoint, just stimulation in itself?

A. Stimulation as such?

Q. Yes.

A. Of course not. I am referring, of course, when this is being geared to the average person and it isn't under the proper circumstances. For example, if a husband and wife were to be reading this book, say, when they retire to their bedchamber at night, I don't see where it would be so bad, I grant you that, but we are speaking to the average person under ordinary circumstances.

Q. You condone the book under the setting you just described?

A. I wouldn't condone anything. Your Honor, I am simply saying taken in that broad context that it would not be too bad.

THE COURT: Go ahead.

BY MR. PICINICH:

Q. This stimulation to sex, would you say that the normal person would react to this, the stimulation would be normal, or a healthy or a wholesome stimulation?

A. It would be an abnormal, an unhealthy stimulation.

Q. In what way, and how does that differ from the normal and healthy stimulation?

A. If you make sex as the end-all and be-all of existence, as the pleasures of sex and nothing else, without assuming the responsibilities that go along with sex. Sex as we know it is a God-given act. It is able to evoke the most intensive human pleasures with a definite reason behind it, as most average people will see it, as procreation of the races, to perform your functions of civic-minded citizens, to take your place as citizens. But when you make the sexual pleasure an end in itself you are going to end up with anarchy, you have nothing else left. Hedonism, which is what this is, is pure pleasure for pleasure's sake. It offers nothing. It offers nothing to a society.

Q. And would the manner in which the author treats the variety of sex weigh in that analysis that you have just made?

A. Of course it does; certainly.

Q. In what way?

A. For example, we would have many kinds of books in the field of medicine where we do have certain types of books that we use for young people getting married to explain sex in its entire effect. That is a beautiful thing.

There are certain parts of the human body which were intended to be stimulated for pleasure as a direct result of the married act, with the end result in most cases the idea of procreation, quieting the passion, and things of that type. But in this particular situation it is made sex for sex's sake, just a pleasure in itself. This type of book, certainly we would not take it into our home, read it aloud. I would never be allowed to read this over the TV. I would never be allowed to read this over the radio.[3] . . .

Q. Now do you find in this book any reference to people receiving pleasure out of pain or rather a painful experience?

A. No question about it.

Q. Where did you find that, in what instances?

A. There are a couple of instances here, in one of which this young idiot boy who was seduced by this—I can't think of the girl's name, I think Louisa—and his penis was described, with all due apologies to the ladies in the audience if there are any, described as practically as big as her arm, and she couldn't hold this boy back, but she enjoyed it tremendously even though she was practically, not exactly, screaming in pain, but she was willing to bear this pain because of the exquisite nature of this that accentuated her sexual pleasure. This belongs in the field of abnormality. This is not normal sex by any means. That is one item.

Q. Are there others?

---

[3]This testimony is obviously objectionable, on the ground, among others, that it is not responsive to the question that was asked. I made no objection, for reasons that follow.

A. Oh yes.

Q. Do you find in this book anything of a philosophy expressed?

A. Yes, there is a philosophy of pleasure for pleasure's sake, hedonism.

Q. Do you find anything redemptive in this book?

A. No.[4]

Cross-examination by Mr. Rembar. . . .

Q. You mentioned that all the states of the union make the publishing or selling of obscene literature a crime?

A. Yes.

Q. Except, I believe you said, New Mexico.

A. That's right. It is part of the education law in New Mexico.

Q. Do you know whether—so far as behavior is concerned as distinguished from reading—whether the general moral level in New Mexico is any lower than that of the other states?

A. I don't know. . . .

Q. You don't know whether there is a higher incidence of sexual offenses in New Mexico than there are in the other states?

---

[4]It may be noted that during Dr. Reilly's direct examination there were many more interruptions from the court than from counsel—an inversion of the usual situation. After the doctor had been on the stand for a while, it appeared to me that the revelation of his habits of thought and underlying attitudes was weakening the prosecutor's case and strengthening ours. I decided that giving his biases full display was worth whatever loss might come from allowing him to make all the points he wanted to, whether or not they constituted admissible testimony.

A. No, I don't know.

Q. You mentioned, I believe, just the theme of the book before the courts is the portrayal of abnormal sex.

A. Yes.

Q. Does it deal with the portrayal of normal sex?

A. No.

Q. How do you define normal sex?

A. Normal sex? Normal sex, I would say, would be the actual act of sexual intercourse between male and woman with the avowed purpose of married people; I would say it is an act between married people for the avowed purpose of fulfilling the marriage contract, primarily with most people to procreate the race and with quite a few people as a second motive the quieting of passion. . . .

Q. Now I want to give you a specific hypothetical situation so that you may give me a very precise answer. You have a married couple. They definitely do not want any children. They do not want to procreate the race, for whatever reason, and they engage in sexual intercourse, taking every care possible to see to it that there is no precreation of the race. Do you regard that as normal sex or abnormal sex?

A. In the context of the statement that is normal sex. I mentioned that to you before.

Q. That is normal sex?

A. I would say that is normal sex, yes. . . .

Q. Now let me add one more item to the situation. They are not married. In your view, is what they are doing normal or abnormal?

A. Abnormal.

Q. Abnormal?

A. Yes.

Q. You, in one of your answers on direct examination, postulated a situation in which a married couple in bed read the book.

A. Yes.

Q. I think you said under those circumstances the stimulation it gave was one that you did not disapprove of.

A. I would go along with that.

Q. Well now, I would like you to explain that to me. Are you saying that you feel that this book is obscene in some circumstances and not in others, depending on what the situation in which it is read may be?

A. In one situation, Mr. Rembar, one situation, which I felt it may not be abnormal.

Q. What may not be abnormal, the book?

A. To read the book itself, I will have to rephrase that in the one situation a married couple in bed, where almost anything goes in marriage as long as the sex act ends up where it is supposed to go, stimulation of almost any type may well be accepted. Under those circumstances, I will say the stimulation engendered by the reading of this book would not be considered abnormal.

Q. Then you are not talking about the book, you are talking about the reaction of the people?

A. The reaction of the people to reading of this book. What could I say about the book? The book is an abstraction here. . . .

Q. On direct examination you stated that this book had a detrimental effect because it advocated hedonism, because it advocated sex as a pleasure in itself, right?

A. Yes.

Q. And because it advocated sex outside of marriage?

A. Yes.

Q. Let me give you another hypothetical. You have a book, not fiction, in the form of a treatise, in which a writer of the highest argumentative skill—say, a man whose skill rivals that of Cardinal Newman—takes the view that hedonism is a good thing, that sex outside marriage is a good thing, and that sex as a pleasure in itself ought to be pursued, and in this book with all that skill he urges very strongly upon the reader that the reader should follow his ideas. What is your feeling about such a book?

A. I have to determine myself what is the dominant theme of that book. Is it an appeal to pruriency or isn't it?

Q. I'm telling you the dominant theme of this book very simply is that the reader go out and pursue sex as a pleasure in itself. . . .

A. If the dominant theme of that book was one of an appeal to pruriency, it is up to the court to make the decision, and not to me.

Q. I am asking you for *your* opinion about that book. You gave your opinion about *this* book.

A. Yes.

MR. PICINICH: Your Honor, may I state for the record I object to the question. I am certainly confused, and I think the witness is confused as to what conclusion he is being asked to draw.

THE COURT: The witness has not said he is confused. If he is, I would like to know it from him.

MR. PICINICH: I would object on the ground it is ambiguous.

THE COURT: I will overrule your objection. I think it is a proper question. If you understand the question, please answer. . . .

> A. If it portrays hedonism, the philosophy of hedonism as such, just as an abstract philosophy without going into all these gross details as this book does, I would have to say no—as a philosophy, an abstraction, without going into all the details on it, of course I couldn't. You have asked me the question. I said this book is hedonism as philosophy, but I am not disputing hedonism as such.
>
> Q. Even though the average reader may very well get the idea from this that it is a good idea to go out and pursue sex as a pleasure in itself.
>
> A. If the average person in this country and the great majority of people, national standards and so forth—the great majority of people felt this was so, I have nothing to stand on, I grant you that. But I doubt very much they would feel that way.[5] . . .

[5]Although the syntax of this answer is a bit difficult, its purport and effect are clear. In the several preceding answers Reilly has agreed that there should be no suppression of a book which, perhaps even more than *Fanny Hill,* would induce people to commit acts Reilly regards as "detrimental." His reserving decision where the book is "prurient" is irrelevant. He was not called as an expert on prurience; he was called to testify on the harmful consequences of reading, and he and Picinich have been

Q. You mentioned homosexuality, flagellation, fetishism, voyeurism. Is there any sex in this book that you regard as normal? . . .

A. In the broad context of the book, no; individually, yes.

Q. What individual examples do you regard—

A. As it describes the plain ordinary intercourse where she was with this fellow Charles at one point after she realized how much she loved this man, that the ordinary description of the sexual act to me with the describing of the intensity of the pleasure, I would go along with that particular part as such, but in the context of this book I see nothing normal of any sexual activity whatsoever.

Q. Then the only normal sexual activity you find in this book is the intercourse between Fanny and Charles. Is that your answer?

A. After the first or second time they had relations, I would say that particular part in describing normal activity, describing normal activity with the pleasure that was induced in her and shown that there was a certain amount of actual love here, but only in that particular thing.[6] . . .

Q. Dr. Reilly, I won't keep you much longer, but I want to read something else to you and ask you whether you

making the point that *Fanny Hill* should be suppressed because reading it will lead to sexual activity that Reilly regards as abnormal—for example, sex out of wedlock. But he is now saying that even though the hypothetical book would cause the same bad conduct, he would not have such a book suppressed.

[6]It would be pointed out in the post-trial brief that the instance of normal sex the witness cited did not fit the rule of normality he had proclaimed earlier. Fanny and Charles were not concentrating on the procreation of the race; "fulfilling the marriage contract" was hardly their "avowed purpose"; and they would have recoiled from the suggestion that they should "quiet their passion."

find yourself in agreement or disagreement with it. . . . This that I am reading you is from an opinion in a federal case: "Although the whole subject of obscenity censorship hinges upon the unproved assumption that obscene literature is a significant factor is causing sexual deviation from the community standard, no report can be found of a single effort of genuine research to test this assumption by singling out as a factor for study the effect of sex literature upon sexual behavior. What little competent research has been done points definitely in a direction precisely opposite to that assumption." . . .

A. I disagree very strongly with the content of that statement, and I am prepared to elaborate on it.

Q. I will be happy to give you that opportunity, Doctor. What is the factual basis for your disagreement?

A. The basis of my disagreement is this: Frankly, I am not too sure when that particular statement was made. But we at the present time have a hard-core group of evidence proving within a certain reasonable degree that there is no question in the minds of eminent psychiatrists, psychologists, social workers and so forth—there is a definite cause-and-effect relationship between the reading of this type of literature and the increase in vandalism, juvenile delinquency, promiscuity, et cetera, et cetera.

Q. You mentioned you have a—what was it, a hard core of evidence?

A. Yes.

Q. Do you have it with you?

A. I have it downstairs, yes. I can quote you if you wish

the quotation. I spoke before the New York Academy of Medicine.

THE COURT: We are not getting into that, Mr. Rembar, so don't invite him to go downstairs and get it. . . .

Q. I gathered from your testimony on direct examination, Dr. Reilly, that your chief concern about the class of books that you disapprove of is that they contribute to juvenile delinquency. . . .

A. As a witness, I am not concerned primarily with juvenile delinquency; as a pediatrician, of course. But as president of the Citizens for Decent Literature, I am concerned with the effect on the average person.

Q. Did you tell me in answer to my previous question that you have evidence—

A. Yes .

Q. —that the literature you are referring to—

A. Yes.

Q. —has damaging effects—

A. Yes, definitely.

Q. —on the average person?

A. And I am prepared to name them.

Q. Name whom?

A. The different psychiatrists who have done the work so far.

Q. You are not talking about evidence then in the sense of empirical results? You are talking about evidence in the sense of statements of other individuals?

A. Empirical results at the present time are being worked upon by Dr. Frederick Wertham in New York.

Q. Do you have any of those results?

A. Not with me.

Q. Do they exist?

A. They exist. They have not been published as yet.

MR. REMBAR: That is all. . . .

Joseph F. Zigarelli, sworn[7]
Direct Examination by Mr. Picinich

Q. Dr. Zigarelli, are you a licensed physician?

MR. REMBAR: I will concede that Dr. Zigarelli is a medical expert.[8]

MR. PICINICH: Let's go into some of the background. I think it's valuable for the court if we go into some of the background.[9]

Q. Are you a licensed physician, Doctor?

A. I am.

Q. Have you specialized in any particular field?

---

[7]There was a marked difference between the prosecutor's first witness and his second. Dr. Zigarelli was urbane, highly articulate, calm and confident. He looked and sounded important. He had neat gray hair, and a set of neat features gave off an air of knowing tolerance. Quite evidently his testimony was the product of careful thought; he did not waste words. That is, he avoided gratuitous statements that would not be helpful to a position he was advancing; he spoke at length when he felt it accomplished something.

[8]Where you know, or can anticipate, that the items of experience by which your opponent's expert will be qualified are likely to be impressive, it is better to concede the qualification and avoid the recital.

[9]Picinich was aware of this too.

A. Yes, neurology and psychiatry.

Q. Do you belong to any organizations within the medical profession within these fields?

A. Yes, I do.

Q. What organizations or societies would they be?

A. I am a diplomate of the American Board of Neurology and Psychiatry. I am a fellow of the American Psychiatric Association, a member of the New Jersey Neuropsychiatric Association, a member of various organizations in New Jersey referable to neuropsychiatric electroencephalography. That's my qualifications. . . .

Q. Doctor, have you read the book that is introduced into evidence, John Cleland's *Memoirs of a Woman of Pleasure?*

A. Yes, I have. . . .

Q. These sexual acts and these sexual experiences that are portrayed in this book by this author, can you tell me whether this in toto is healthy or a normal or wholesome treatment of sex?

A. In my psychiatic opinion, it is not.

Q. In what manner is it not healthy, normal and wholesome?

A. One, it portrays perverted acts of sex.

Q. Such as, Doctor?

A. Such as voyeurism, various phases of homosexuality, masochism, sadism. Two, the description by the author of these various acts, in my opinion, could stimulate abnormal sexual desires in the average individual as we see them, the average individual in all age levels. Three, it portrays in my opinion, again psychiatrically, sex in a debased way. It portrays the life and experience of a prostitute. Sex in itself need not be described that way in my opinion. These are just the major factors.

Q. Apart from this sex which you have described, Doctor, is there any expression of a philosophy, any other type of philosophy in the book?

A. Here again, if the author was attempting to portray a philosophical note I was unable to grasp it. If he were attempting to be another Voltaire, I don't know. I did not get any philosophical note from this book. . . .

Q. Now you have described masochism. This book deals with physical harm or pain, doctor.

A. In certain areas the particular experience of the female in her experiencing of pain and discomfort is masochistic; that is in this book.

Q. Is this a healthy or a normal view of a person? Is this a normal person who enjoys this pain?

A. Masochism is definitely an abnormal perverted act sexually. . . .

CROSS-EXAMINATION BY MR. REMBAR.

Q. Did I understand you to say on direct examination that the reading of this book would stimulate an abnormal sexual response in a normal individual?

A. I did not use that particular terminology. I said that it could, it could stimulate.

Q. It could?

A. It could. It is possible that this could, yes.

Q. Could other types of books—say, *Mother Goose* or Andersen's fairy tales—stimulate an abnormal sexual response in a normal reader?

MR. PICINICH: I object to the question, Your Honor, on the basis that the position of the State is that we should not be going into any other comparisons. What is on trial here is *Memoirs of a Woman of Pleasure.*

THE COURT: I don't think *Mother Goose* is being used here by way of comparison to *Fanny Hill.*

MR. PICINICH: Do you know where we are going?

THE COURT: I think I understand the avenue counsel is seeking to travel by way of cross-examination. I am going to allow it, if the doctor can answer it.

A. I will answer it with a question by saying, your Honor, that the normal reader is a vast domain. What do you mean by normal reader?

Q. I am using your answer, Doctor; I did not suggest the term. You answered a question put to you by Mr. Picinich. You said as I copied it down—I may be wrong—that this book could stimulate an abnormal sexual response in a normal individual. So it is your phrase.

A. A normal individual need not be a normal reader.

Q. All right, then; normal individual.

A. All right. Yes, I do feel that any literature in certain circumstances can stimulate sexual activity, but not abnormal sexual activity.

Q. Does the book have to deal with abnormal sexual activity in order to produce the effect we are talking about?

A. Not necessarily, no.

Q. So that a book that had no description of abnormal sexual activity could produce this abnormal response.

A. Not abnormal response—sexual reponse. Sexual response and abnormal sexual response are two different things.

Q. You are saying this book could produce the abnormal sexual response.

A. In my opinion, it can.

Q. In a normal individual?

A. In a normal individual.

Q. In a normal individual who is—take the instance of homosexuality—an individual who is fully matured sexually, has no homosexual contacts in his make-up, he can be stirred by this book to commit an act of homosexuality? Is that what you're saying?

A. No. In my opinion he can. He can be stimulated. Now I disagree with your statement that an individual who is normal has no homosexual components.[10] We all do normally. All normal individuals have an unconscious homosexual component in their make-up. This book can stimulate homosexual activity in my opinion in a normal individual. It can excite the homosexual factors. For example, if this book were read by a sailor in a destroyer and there were no women around I think he could masturbate.

Q. He *could* masturbate?

---

[10]A statement I had not made.

A. Yes.

Q. Do you think he would be provoked to commit an act of overt homosexuality?

A. This is the field of probabilities.

Q. What is your opinion? You have been asked for your opinion.

A. My opinion would be that if the confinement in that ship were long enough, yes.

THE COURT: What is your next question?[11]

Q. My next question is, taking what you consider to be the great mass of readers, not sailors confined in a ship for an extraordinary period, would you give the same answer to my question? . . .

A. There again the answer would have to be in some way qualified, your Honor. I can't answer directly.

Q. You would say there would have to be some special circumstance such as confinement in a ship for an undue period?

A. The particular situation in each individual question would have to be specific, specific in the sense that there are so many variable factors, that each factor would have to be ascertained before giving an answer specifically to your question.

Q. Let me ask you whether you can answer this question, and if you cannot, simply say so. Taking a normal individual defined as you have, and I take it in your view the normal individual includes a latent homosexual compo-

[11]I had paused to make sure the judge had heard that answer.

nent or some homosexual component—is that what you are saying?

A. Here again, don't misquote me. When I say homosexual factor, we individuals go through what we call a homosexual phase in life. We grow through homosexuality. This latent homosexuality exists in all of us. Taken in the proper concept of the individual then—latent homosexuality going back to the age of four, five, six, seven, or eight years is what I am talking about; I am not talking about the latent homosexuality which borders on being abnormal—taking it that was then, I still feel that this could excite homosexual activity.

Q. Let me finish that question then. Taking such an *individual* who lives here in Hackensack, who is an adult, who leads what we would all regard as a normal life—are you saying that the reading of this book is likely to stimulate him to an act of overt homosexuality?

A. Again in my opinion if you are speaking of the male, yes. If you are speaking of the female, yes. Both.[12] . . .

[12]This is a turning point. What has happened since the time he said "it could" has induced Zigarelli to take a more extreme position. Perhaps he sensed from the questioning that the "could" kind of statement was not going to get him very far. Any book may be said to hold the possibility of producing a given response in some one of its many readers. If *Memoirs* was to be suppressed on the basis of the behavior it caused, something more than that would have to be said. So Zigarelli went farther. But now his statements, while they were more meaningful, were much more vulnerable.

Cross-examination could not directly negate the testimony the prosecution was presenting. It was not like, say, the opinion of an orthopedic surgeon on a physical injury, or even that of a psychiatrist describing a psychosis; such testimony may be countered by questions relating to accepted medical knowledge, to the history of the particular patient, or other factual material. On the subject of reactions to erotic writing, however, there is almost no factual material; there is nothing with which the

William Scott Morton, sworn[13]
Cross-examination by Mr. Rembar

Q. Dr. Morton, I guess the most convenient thing is to pick up where we left off. When you gave your answer to the question put to you by Mr. Picinich, what limits of candor were you referring to —in what area? Of conversation, among people in social groups, motion pictures, television —what?

A. I was referring, I believe, to the tenor of conversation among sophisticated people and among average peo-

---

witness can be confronted that will compel him to contradict himself. It seemed to me, therefore, that the best way to deal with the prosecutor's witness was to lead him into excess.

It may occur to the reader that a strong point might have been made by demanding that Zigarelli back up his general proposition with specific facts—by asking him whether in his practice he had ever encountered a situation where a book had in fact caused abnormal sexual behavior. It also occurred to the writer; it would have been great to have had him admit that well, no, he had never actually seen a case. But suppose he had said why, yes, of course, and ticked off a few. I would not have believed him, but there would have been no way of disproving what he said, and the lawyer's opinion of the testimony is not what decides cases. It was better, I thought, to let his cross-examination end with the witness making unsupported statements that are inherently improbable.

[13]The Reverend Morton provided a further contrast. Dr. Zigarelli's amiable urbanity was replaced by the reverend's rather truculent earnestness. He had a high arching forehead, steel-rimmed glasses and a downturned mouth. There were now no smiles from the witness chair.

During direct examination he stated that he was a doctor of divinity and had lectured at universities; his subjects were "Mainly the Far East cultural civilization of China and Japan, comparative ethical matters and comparative religious fields and in the cultural, of course, a good deal of literary comparisons too." He then said that the sexual experiences described in the book were "unhealthy," that the plot was "very weak," that there was a philosophy expressed in the book but one he disapproved of, that there were other historical sources for "the customs, manners and so on, ideas of the eighteenth century," and finally, that the "content and subject matter of the book greatly exceed the average of candor in discussion of the matter." I had made an objection to his testifying on the last item, on the ground that it was a legal conclusion.

ple, taken overall, on topics of life and literature combined . . .

Q. You are talking about two things: conversation, social intercourse?

A. Right.

Q. And literature?

A. Right.

Q. I am now taking examples of current literature. Are you familiar with the novels of James Baldwin?

A. Yes.

Q. We referred previously specifically to *Giovanni's Room* and *Another Country.* Are you familiar with John Updike's *Rabbit, Run?*

A. I have dipped into all these works.

Q. You have not read them as a whole?

A. Not as a whole, no; not these ones that you have mentioned so far.

Q. How about James Joyce's *Ulysses?*

A. Yes, I read a good deal of that.

Q. Including the famous soliloquy?

A. I can't recall it. . . .

Q. To refer to a work in which I am sure you have done more than dipped in, are there instances of abnormal sexual behavior in the Bible?

A. Certainly.

Q. In your opinion, does reading a description of abnormal sexual behavior make it likely that a normal reader will commit an overt act of the same type?

MR. PICINICH: I object to the question, your Honor.

THE COURT: I will overrule the objection. You may answer it if you can, Doctor.

A. Yes. I think very often description of such behavior does incite people to it.

Q. Do you think it is likely?

A. I think it is likely. I think it is likely.[14] I think in the case of the Bible it has done so if the person has not read the rest of the Bible and tried to get the whole spirit of the book, the purpose of the author or authors of the book. Then I think this can happen.[15] . . .

MR. REMBAR: That is all, Doctor. Thank you.

My main defense against this psychiatric-clerical attack were, first, to argue (in my briefs, and by objection during trial) that whatever such witnesses might say was irrelevant, and then to try to show by cross-examination that what they did say was incredible. For safety, though, I thought we had better have a witness on our side; we brought to court Wardell B. Pomeroy, one of the three co-authors of the Kinsey Report.

Pomeroy had a pleasant, earnest, youthful, all-American look—a sort of cultured Ozzie Nelson. In contrast (perhaps)

[14]Zigarelli's Syndrome was, I was pleased to see, contagious.

[15]A cross-examiner can begin to enjoy himself too much. Shortly after this, in the middle of a question, it struck me that Dr. Morton's testimony was at this point as good for our side, and as bad for the other side, as it would possibly get. Keeping him longer on the stand could only make it less good for us and less bad for them. I ended the cross-examination.

to the subject matter of his research, his manner was studious and reflective rather than worldly. He withstood cross-examination very well. At one point, Picinich was going over, one by one, the various aberrations in the book; he referred to the character Norbert:

> Q. Would you say that it is a practice which is accepted by the people of today, deflowering of virgins?
>
> MR. REMBAR: May I ask under what circumstances?

My interruption, which was a valid objection to the form of the question put by Picinich, was intended to direct Pomeroy's attention to the interesting problem of how the human race would survive if people were to reject the practice of deflowering virgins. Picinich finally got his answer:

> A. Yes. Every woman is deflowered at one time or another. This would be nearly one hundred percent.

Pomeroy's direct examination (which came on the second day of the trial) was devoted partly to showing the spread of the sexual stimuli through the environment, in support of my argument that appeal to prurient interest could not mean appeal to sexual interest. In other trials I had simply asked the court to take judicial notice of the state of our culture; here I said that this testimony gave "the support of factual data to matters of which the court may take judicial notice." But the main reason for Pomeroy's presence was to contradict the prosecution's witnesses on what would happen to people who read *Fanny Hill.* He testified that sex books did not rank especially high among sexual stimuli. Where the prosecution's doctors based their statements on their individual practices, Pomeroy's were based on the interviewing of over eighteen thousand people, eight thousand of whom he interviewed personally. (Among the products of this research was the finding that criminals convicted of sex offenses were less often aroused by reading erotic literature than the rest of the male population. . . .

In addition to Pomeroy, we had our witnesses on literary value and on the treatment of sex in contemporary literature. They were particularly good in this case, partly because of the experience of the earlier trials and partly because of their own abilities, which Picinich's prodding cross-examination gave them ample opportunity to demonstrate. J. Donald Adams was present again—large, good-looking, white-haired and of an age to command respect. His manner was one of relaxed dignity, and as in the New York trial two years earlier, his failure to remember details seemed only to put the judge on his side and draw greater attention to his general statements. "Do you recall the character William, the young male messenger?" asked Picinich. "Not by name," answered Adams. Whereupon the judge told Picinich to refer to the incident rather than to "say Willie or John; that did not make much of an impression upon Mr. Adams." Later, when Picinich asked about "the introduction to the characters Harriet, Louise and Emily," the judge admonished: "The principle still applies. Tell him about the incident. Never mind Harriet. . . ."

Another veteran—of the battle of Boston rather than New York—was Fred Holley Stocking. His testimony in Boston had been so good that I asked him to come down to New Jersey. He was a strong witness, his delivery deliberate, his statements clear and emphatic. Frequently in making his points, especially on cross-examination, he smiled, perhaps out of courtesy, perhaps in amusement at the thought that the answer was not going to be what his cross-examiner wanted. He began by countering, almost shocking, Zigarelli:

> Like a previous witness I think I should explain the ground on which I base a professional opinion. . . . I am a professional teacher of literature and my subject is an art, and my greatest expertise, if I have any, is in teaching young men how to interpret and understand literature as an art. And I firmly believe as a critic and teacher of literature that there is a difference between a sound or intelligent interpretation of a work of art.

He gave reasons why a reading of *Memoirs* that finds value in the book is sound and intelligent. On cross-examination, Picinich brought up something that he might reasonably have thought would embarrass a professor, particularly the head of a department:

> Q. Mr. Stocking, do you require your students to read this book?
>
> A. I do not require my students to read this book.
>
> Q. Is this the type of book you would want a young college student to read?
>
> A. Definitely.
>
> Q. Do you think that the sexual experiences described in this book would have any deleterious effect on the young college student? . . .
>
> A. One sentence. If he were to read this book in a course of mine and his chief response were the arousal of sexual passion and that dominated every other response, he would flunk my course.
>
> Q. You mean that?

THE COURT: Publish that answer up at school so the boys can find out.

Q. You mean that if a college student were stimulated as a result of reading this book he would be reading with the wrong purpose in mind. Is that what you mean?

A. That's not what I said.

MR. REMBAR: I think the question has been answered.

A. I said if his chief response were the arousal of sexual passion, he would flunk my course.

Q. Well, if he were sexually stimulated, would he flunk your course?

A. Not unless that were his chief response. My students get sexually stimulated from reading *Anthony and Cleopatra,* but that isn't their chief response.

The next witness was John Owen McCormick, another department chairman—of comparative literature at Rutgers. McCormick was the most elegant of the witnesses. He had his own accent, and a musical voice, heavy on the woofer and light on the tweeter. Some of his words were hard to catch, but what he had to say was worth hearing, and the judge was willing to lean forward. Picinich taxed him with the "exaggeration" in *Memoirs;* the witness said he could think of very few novels that "do not exaggerate aspects of human experience. That is part of what novel writing is." Picinich then asked:

Q. How about the incident where all the inmate prostitutes tell about their defloration? Is that an exaggeration?

A. Again I couldn't say. One of the things about this novel, you see, that is fantastic is the attempt on the part of Cleland to place himself in a woman's mind. This is a very interesting attempt. And it is a very difficult thing to do in any literary work. As I said earlier, for a male writer to place himself in a female writer's mind, or vice versa, very rarely comes off. I think this comes off, that it succeeds. For the male reader this becomes more so of course; obviously this is a man's view, so how can one say?

MR. PICINICH: Yes.

This was a smartly executed exchange of roles, followed by a ruminative pause on the part of counsel.

THE COURT: What did you say the next question was, Mr. Picinich?

In his questioning, Picinich suggested—as prosecuting attorneys had, from the time of *Chatterley*—that there was no legitimate reason for Cleland to write the way he did. I dealt with the suggestion on my redirect examination of McCormick:

Q. [by Mr. Rembar]: You were also asked whether a book designed to stimulate sexual response would necessarily contain certain scenes which my brother described on cross-examination. It is possible that a book could create sexual response in the reader without having any of those items that he mentions?

MR. PICINICH: I object, your Honor.

THE COURT: I am going to allow him to answer.

A. Yes.

Q. In other words, you might have a book without defloration, without homosexuality, without flagellation, that might arouse a sexual response in a reader.

A. We have them.

Q. You might, would you not say, even have a book without any sexual intercourse at all that could arouse a sexual response in a reader?

A. Definitely, yes. . . .

The trial closed with the testimony of two young professors of English—Paul Fussell, Jr., from Rutgers, and David Burrows, from Douglass (the Rutgers women's college). Each managed to make some literary comments that sounded fresh despite anything that had gone before. Picinich devoted a great deal of cross-examination to Fussell, who was cool and resourceful and, with the possible exception of Stocking, knew *Memoirs* better than any other witness in any of the trials. He should have; he had read the book twelve times. "Did it," I asked, "improve or diminish in your eyes as you reread it?" "It improved as a literary work," he answered, "it diminished as an erotic work. . . ."

The prosecution's witnesses, I thought, had failed to demonstrate that *Fanny Hill* would cause harm, or that any reading might cause harm. This does not mean that such a case could not be made.

I do not agree with those who say books can work no evil. The assertion is an affront to intellect. Books have great influence, much of it bad. But the risk that inheres in reading books is precisely the risk that the First Amendment contemplates. All the conflict is in the mind itself, and this is the conflict we cherish. . . .

THE AL CAPONE TAX CASE

George E. Q. Johnson and
Dwight H. Green
for the prosecution

vs.

Michael J. Ahern
and Albert Fink
for the defense

by Francis X. Busch

Alphonse Capone—"Scarface Al"—"Public Enemy No. 1"—is the classic American folk villain. Almost everyone knows the story of Capone's bloody rise to power in the Chicago underworld during Prohibition days, of the feud with "Bugs" Moran's gang which culminated in the St. Valentine's Day Massacre, and the ways in which Chicago politicians, policemen and judges were "persuaded" to grant Big Al and other gangsters virtual immunity from prosecution. The fact that Capone was finally tried, convicted and sentenced, not for murder or racketeering but for evasion of federal income taxes, is also familiar history. What most people do not know, however, is that lawyers and criminologists still debate the merits of the Al Capone tax case. In one sense, it seems clear that justice was done. The herculean efforts of federal investigators and prosecutors, very well described below by veteran trial reporter Francis X. Busch, resulted in the imprisonment of one who was certainly a menance to society. Like the Jimmy Hoffa case of a later era, however, the Capone trial raises some disturbing questions for believers in due process of law. Did the prosecution really prove its tax-evasion case? Should the judge have admitted certain disputed evidence? Was a ten-year sentence justified? Some, even now, would be inclined to agree with defense attorney Fink that ". . . if the defendant's name were not Al Capone, there would be no case. . . ." The reader will have to make up his own mind about this.

We pick up the story in the year 1931. Following the gangland-style murder of Jack Lingle, a newspaperman reportedly associated with Capone, a group of prominent Chicagoans known as the "Secret Six" began working with federal investigators seeking evidence of tax evasion by racketeers. Their efforts, as we will see, soon bore fruit. . . .

Capone soon became concerned by reports that agents were investigating his affairs. They had already caught up with beer-runners Frankie Lake and Terry Druggan, with Jack McGurn, with Frank (The Enforcer) Nitti, with Capone's brother Ralph and with Capone's friends, Joe Fusco and Jake (Greasy Thumb) and Sam Guzik. Capone hastened to employ an income-tax "specialist" and to attempt a compromise.

The Federal investigators, on their side, were not finding it easy to prove something on Capone. To any but the experienced, resourceful and persistent men from the Federal investigating offices, unearthing evidence to sustain a conviction would have been an impossible task. Capone had kept no personal books, had no bank accounts in his own name, had never made a financial statement and had never filed an income-tax return. It was common talk that he ran a string of fancy brothels, that he was the owner or partner in a half-dozen gambling houses and was interested in over a thousand bookie joints, that he operated several dog tracks, that he controlled a number of breweries and sponsored twelve hundred speakeasies and that he got a cut on every case of whisky that found its way into Cook County. But no one who knew of these ownerships and interests would come forward to testify to them. There was also abundant evidence of Capone's regal style of living; his well-appointed home on Prairie Avenue in Chicago, his estate at Palm Island, Florida, his huge food bills, his lavish banquets and entertainments, his largess, his high-powered armored automobiles, his retinue of henchmen and his fantastic expenditures for personal wearing apparel.

To the man on the street this might be proof enough that there was an income and a big one, but the government's investigators had to prove by *direct* corroborative evidence, calculated to satisfy a jury of twelve beyond a reasonable doubt, that in one or more specified years Capone had derived from defined sources a net income subject to Federal tax.

For nearly two years the agents worked. Avenue after avenue closed at a dead end, but finally the break came. Special agent Frank J. Wilson told of it much later in one of the national weekly magazines. Wilson was rummaging through a mass of old books and papers which had been seized in a raid on a Cicero gambling house, The Ship, just after the murder of Assistant State's Attorney McSwiggin. The Ship was one of Capone's reputed holdings, and Wilson thought there might be a clue among the papers. His diligence was rewarded. He found a dusty cashbook containing a record of the joint's income.

Painstakingly Wilson and his assistants collected handwriting samples from every hoodlum known or suspected to have had associations with Capone. These samples came from voting registers, police-court bonds and bank-deposit slips. After a long process of comparison and elimination the agents discovered in a Cicero bank a deposit slip which matched the handwritten entries in The Ship's cashbook. The handwriting was that of one Lou Schumway. It was easy to establish that Schumway was a trusted henchman of Capone's who had once been a bookkeeper at The Ship.

Wilson traced Schumway to Florida and found him at a dog track at the Biscayne Bay Kennel Club. Schumway was frightened into talking. He identified numerous entries in the cashbook as his and, in Wilson's words, generally "played ball" with the government. The government stored him in California for "safekeeping" until he should be needed.

Continued examinations of transactions in Cicero banks led to an investigation of a mysterious "J. C. Dunbar" who had brought upward of $300,000 in cash to one of the banks to purchase cashier's checks. Dunbar turned out to be Fred Ries, a former employee of one of Capone's gambling houses. Ries was traced to St. Louis and questioned. When he refused to talk about his past affiliations, Wilson and an assistant agent arrested him and had him committed to what Wilson describe as a "special jail" in Danville, Illinois. The only "special" thing about it seems to have been its extraordinary infestation with vermin which so harassed Ries that after five days he was prompted to change his mind and talk. He was "sneaked in to the grand jury room in Chicago" where he gave his testimony. Then he was packed off to South America with government agents to guard him until he was needed in court. The Chicago Secret Six supplied the money for the expedition.

There was other evidence—a good deal of it—submitted to the Federal grand jury, and on June 5, 1931, that body returned indictments charging Alphonse Capone—alias Alphonse Brown, alias Al Brown, alias Scarface Brown, alias Scarface Capone, alias A. Costa—with twenty-three separate violations of the internal-revenue laws. He was charged specifically with failing to file an income-tax return for the years 1928 and 1929 and with attempting to evade the payment of income taxes due for the years 1925, 1926, 1927, 1928 and 1929. Capone's bond was fixed at $50,000. It was provided for him and he was released pending the outcome of the trial. . . .

From the day the indictments against Capone were returned there were persistent rumors that he intended to plead guilty. When he appeared with his lawyers before District Judge Wilkerson on June 15 he confirmed the rumors by entering formal pleas of guilty to the indictments charging him with violations of the income-tax and the prohibition laws. Judge Wilkerson entered the pleas and set the disposition of them for June 30.

On June 29 Capone's attorney, Michael J. Ahern, appeared

in court and requested a continuance. Capone, he claimed, had become involved in some civil litigation in Florida which required his presence there. The Government agreed to a postponement until July 30 and the Court entered an order to that effect.

Had that been all, there would have been no occasion for the concern which permeated the Capone camp after the hearing. But apprehension arose because of an exchange between Ahern and the Court. Attorney Ahern suggested to the Court that on pleas of guilty similar to Capone's eighteen months was the longest sentence that had ever been imposed. Judge Wilkerson, with what one of the newspapers characterized as a "mysterious seriousness," replied, "There are conspiracies and conspiracies and tax violations and tax violations, but I'll hear you fully on July 30." The perturbation of Capone and his counsel was measurably increased when the judge, on July 16, directed United States Attorney Johnson to "have all of the income-tax witnesses in court on July 30," and announced that he expected to have a full hearing.

All parties were present in court on July 30. At the outset the judge said that in addition to hearing the Government's witnesses he would expect also to hear from the defendant if he was pleading for a mitigation of punishment. All of this, while perhaps out of the ordinary, was strictly in accordance with law. The trial judge has the responsibility for sentence on a plea of guilty and has the right, if not the obligation, to advise himself fully of all the facts and circumstances before passing sentence.

Mr. Ahern did a quick shift and told the Court he had never intended to enter an unqualified plea of guilty. He said that he, the District Attorney, the Attorney General and the Assistant Secretary of the Treasury had agreed on a recommendation which District Attorney Johnson would make to the Court, and he expected the Court, under the usual practice, to follow it. The "compromise," he added, took in both Capone's civil and criminal liability. He concluded that if he had had any idea the Court would not follow the District Attorney's recommendation he would never have pleaded his client guilty.

Judge Wilkerson answered that he would give due consideration to recommendations made by the United States Attorney, but would not obligate himself to follow them. He reminded the attorney that the responsibility for the sentence was his and his alone after he had fully informed himself of the facts. "And," said the Court, "if the defendant asks leniency he should be ready to answer all proper questions put to him by the Court touching the matter he has confessed in his plea."

Mr. Ahern then moved to withdraw the pleas of guilty in all the pending cases, and the Court set the hearing of that motion for September 8. On that date Judge Wilkerson filed a memorandum restating his position. "The Court," the paper read, "has ruled that all pleas of guilty must be unconditional, and that in a hearing thereon there can be no understanding which precludes the Court from ascertaining the facts and entering at the conclusion of the hearing the judgment which is proper under the facts. "But," he added, "there being no objection by the United States, the motion to withdraw the pleas of guilty will be granted."

On September 10 the pleas of guilty were formally withdrawn and, by leave of Court, demurrers to the income-tax indictments were heard and overruled. The two income-tax cases were consolidated for trial and set for hearing on October 6.

At 10:00 A.M. on the day appointed, counsel for the government and defendant Capone, accompanied by his counsel and bodyguard, worked their way through the crowded corridors to District Judge Wilkerson's courtroom and the trial began.

This trial brought together a judge and lawyers of exceptional competence. A contemporary newspaper account of the trial referred to the presiding jurist and the attorneys, for both the Government and the defense, as "the cream of the bar." Appearing for the Government were United States Attorney George E. Q. Johnson, Special Assistant Attorney General William J. Froelich and Assistant United States Attorneys Dwight H. Green, Jacob I. Grossman and Samuel G. Clawson. Michael J. Ahern, who had represented Capone in the preliminary actions, was now associated with a second defense attorney, Albert Fink.

Judge James H. Wilkerson was one of the best-qualified lawyers ever appointed to Federal District judgeship. As a practicing attorney he had been actively engaged in the trial of important civil and criminal cases. He had made a distinguished public record as United States Attorney and as chairman of the Illinois Commerce Commission. In the eleven years he had been on the Federal bench, he had established an enviable reputation for integrity, ability, judicial poise and impartiality. . . .

Mr. Johnson had served for five years as United States Attorney and in that service had gained a reputation as an honest, able and forceful advocate. Mr. Johnson's principal assistant, Mr. Dwight H. Green, was an experienced and able trial lawyer. Mr. Grossman, Mr. Clawson and Mr. Froelich were all lawyers of recognized ability.

The array for the defense was equally impressive. Michael J. Ahern was one of Chicago's most erudite and successful trial lawyers. Albert Fink was a distinguished criminal lawyer with a record of many notable successes.

But it was the defendant himself, rather than the distinguished presiding jurist or the lawyers, who drew the attention of the curious onlookers. "Scarface Al" was easily identified. His hulking frame, his broad, scarred and heavy-jowled face, closely shaved and powdered to a chalklike whiteness, and his faultlessly tailored clothes, colored silk shirt, polished tan shoes and pearl-gray spats set him apart from the more modestly attired lawyers. And he was attended by an equally dapper personal bodyguard, a nattily dressed, well-groomed, swarthy young athlete named Phil D'Andrea. D'Andrea followed closely on Capone's heels, both inside and outside the courtroom, and during the trial he occupied a chair immediately behind the defendant.

Under the questioning of the Court, the impaneling of the jury proceeded with dispatch. By midafternoon three retail grocers, two journeyman painters, a patternmaker, a real-estate broker, a stationary engineer, a hardware merchant, an insurance agent, a farmer and a clerk had been sworn to give the defendant a fair and impartial trial.

Assistant District Attorney Green outlined the Government's case in an opening statement. There were, he said, two indictments being tried together. One contained a single count and related to the year 1924; the other contained twenty-two counts and related to the years 1925, 1926, 1927, 1928 and 1929. The prosecutor emphasized that Capone had filed no income-tax returns and had paid no income taxes whatsoever for the years 1924, 1925, 1926, 1927, 1928 and 1929, whereas his income and taxes due had been:

For 1924, net income $123,101.89;evaded tax, $32,489.24;
For 1925, net income $257,285.95;evaded tax, $55,365.25;
For 1926, net income $195,677.00;evaded tax, $39,962.75;
For 1927, net income $218,057.04;evaded tax, $45,527.76;
For 1928, net income $140,536.93;evaded tax, $25,887.72;
For 1929, net income $103,999.00;evaded tax, $15,817.76.

. . .

The first Government witness called was the director of the Income Tax Division of the Bureau of Internal Revenue of the First Illinois District, Charles W. Arndt. Under Mr. Green's direct examination he testified that he had carefully examined the Bureau's records for the years 1924 to 1929 and that neither Alphonse Capone, Alphonse Brown, Al Capone, Al Brown, Scarface Capone, Scarface Brown, A. Costa or Snorky Capone had filed an income-tax return for any of those years.

Two men who lived in the suburban area west of Chicago testified to their participation in May 1925 in a citizens' raid on a gambling house known as the Hawthorne Smoke Shop in Cicero. The raid was initiated by a complaint for a search warrant sworn out by representatives of a voluntary law-enforcement agency called the Southwest Suburban Ministers and Citizens Association. The object of the organization, testified Chester Bragg, one of the witnesses, was "to make the western suburbs of Chicago fit places in which to live and raise children." Bragg was one of the raiding party and stood just inside the street door to prevent unauthorized persons from entering. He said he had just taken up his position when he "noticed a powerful man outside trying to force his way in." The witness, whose language did not seem to have been particularly improved by his association with the suburban churchmen, resented the intrusion and demanded of the would-be door crasher, "What the hell do you think this is—a party?" And the big man, according to Bragg, replied, "Well, if it is I ought to be in there. I am the owner of the place." Bragg said he then recognized the man as Al Capone and let him in. He said he followed him upstairs and heard him scold and threaten another of the raiders, the "Reverend Mr. Hoover," pastor of the Berwyn Congregational Church. Capone was quoted by the witness as saying, "Why can't you lay off me? Why are you always picking at me?" When Hoover replied, "We're not picking at you at all," Capone threatened, "You've pulled the last raid on me you're ever going to pull."

Bragg described the "upstairs place." "There were pool and billiard tables and a lot of other equipment that I was not familiar with—a roulette wheel, a chuck-a-luck table and racing forms." Bragg added additional testimony to illustrate Capone's elusiveness and the local law's shortcomings. He stated that a chief of police, a police magistrate, two patrolmen from a near-by suburb and a sergeant of police from the Cook County State Attorney's office arrived on the scene with a warrant for Capone's arrest "some hours afterwards." Capone had, of course, disappeared. "The follow-up," said Bragg, "was a rotten job."

Although Mr. Ahern's skillful cross-examination developed numerous uncertainties and inconsistencies in Bragg's recollection of some of the details of his direct testimony, the advantage, if there was any, was mitigated by the witness's dramatic statement of what had happened to him after the raid. "When I came out of the place," said Bragg, "I was set upon by about a thousand hoodlums. I was slugged over one ear. My nose was broken with a blackjack. One of my eyes was blackened—maybe two eyes—and I had to be taken to a doctor in Berwyn." . . .

The first of the Government's "star" witnesses was L. H. (Lou) Schumway. He was examined by Assistant District Attorney Grossman. Schumway testified that he "kept the sheets" and did the bookkeeping in five or six gambling houses in Cicero during 1924, 1925 and 1926. One of these was the Hawthorne Smoke Shop. The managers of the place, when he worked there, were Pete Penovich and West Side Frankie Pope. Jake (Greasy Thumb) Guzik came in frequently and the defendant Capone was there practically every day. The witness explained the layout; the gambling wheels, bird cages and horse-racing sheets were kept in the front rooms, while the money, books and accounting were handled in the rear room. "I often saw Mr. Capone in this rear room when we were going over the books and the money," Schumway said.

The prosecutor then produced a well-worn account book and had the witness identify the handwriting of various entries in 1924, 1925 and 1926. Some were in the handwriting of the witness; some were in the handwriting of Benny Pope, a brother of West Side Frankie Pope; others were in the handwriting of Jake (Greasy Thumb) Guzik. Capone's name appeared frequently as the recipient of cash.

Schumway testified that the money taken in at the Hawthorne Smoke Shop was transferred daily to a cafe in The Subway, another gambling parlor four doors up the street from the Smoke Shop. Capone, said the witness, showed great interest in this daily transfer of funds and personally superintended the removals. "Capone," explained Schumway, "was always worried about a 'stickup.' "

The witness remembered the ministers' raid on the Smoke Shop in 1925. "What happened after that?" queried the Government attorney. "Oh, we just packed up and moved across the street and opened another gambling place" was the blithe reply. "Charles Fischetti," he added, "sneaked out with the money."

Schumway's most solid contribution to the accumulating evidence against Capone was his statement, based on his recollection and the book entries, of the actual income of the Hawthorne Smoke Shop and the other Cicero gambling parlors where he worked. He testified they had a net profit of $350,250 in 1924, $117,460 in 1925 and $170,011 in 1926.

The cross-examination of Schumway accomplished but little. The witness did admit that his testimony concerning Capone was based only on hearsay and the circumstances he had related. He had no proof that Capone received any of the profits from the Cicero gambling places. He admitted also that Capone himself frequently placed cash bets, the same as any other patron, on the horses running at the various tracks which were listed on his sheets. . . .

The Government next called four employees of the Bureau of Internal Revenue to testify to the activities of one Lawrence B. Mattingly, the income-tax expert engaged by Capone in March of 1930 to work out a "compromise" of the government's income-tax claims. It was disclosed that Mr. Mattingly had had several interviews with a group of subordinate bureau officials, had allowed them once to interrogate Capone and had submitted a written statement to them.

This letter was produced, identified by the witnesses and offered as evidence of Capone's efforts to evade taxation. Mr. Ahern and Mr. Fink objected violently. They protested that the letter and Capone's and Mattingly's oral statements had been made in a bona fide attempt at a compromise of a pending, disputed claim, and that as such both the written and the oral statements should be privileged and not used as evidence.

The two bureau agents stated that both Mattingly and Capone had been warned before they made their statements that nothing they said would be considered privileged, that anything they might offer could be used against Capone in a later criminal proceeding.

There were long disputes on the admissibility of the evidence out of the presence of the jury. When counsel had been fully heard, Judge Wilkerson ruled the statements were admissible on the ground that a compromise, in the legal sense, meant a meeting of opposing interests, where both sides, properly authorized, come together to settle a genuinely disputed claim. Those elements, he said, were lacking in the case before him. Capone and his agent, both uninvited, had approached minor government officials and made the statements, although they had been warned that any declarations might be used against Capone.

It was a severe blow to Capone's defense when Mr. Clawson, who presented this part of the Government case, read Mattingly's letter to the jury. The letter stated that Capone had no taxable income in 1924 and 1925, for at that time he was working for Johnny Torrio at a salary of $75 a week. Then, and this was the crucial part, it admitted unqualifiedly that Capone had had a net income of not more than $26,000 in 1926, of not more than $40,000 in 1927 and of not more than $100,000 in both 1928 and 1929. There was indisputable confirmation of the Government's earlier testimony that Capone had never filed an income-tax return and had earned a taxable income. . . .

The stenographic record of Capone's own replies to the inquiring government officials was interesting more for what the gangster dodged than for what he told. He was asked whether he furnished the money to buy the home at Palm Island. "I'd rather let my lawyer answer," said Capone. Mattingly then stated that Capone had supplied $10,000, the title had been taken in Mrs. Capone's name and she had signed a mortgage and mortgage notes for $30,000. "What was the source of that money [the $10,000 cash paid on the house]?" pursued the Government examiner. "I'd rather not answer," Capone replied. The examiner tried to find out whether Capone held securities or brokerage accounts or other personal property in his wife's name and whether his wife or any other of his relatives had safe-deposit boxes. He asked whether Capone had any interest in dog tracks. But the same refusals to answer followed all the queries.

One prize understatement in the record drew smiles from the usually poker-faced jurors. When Capone was asked, "How long have you had a big income?" he replied, "I never did have much of an income."

The accumulation of evidence dragged on day after day. But on the fifth day of the trial there occurred an incident extraordinary enough to dispel monotony and to jolt even crime-accustomed Chicago. Throughout all the proceedings Capone had been watched vigilantly by his bodyguard. D'Andrea, in turn, had been watched vigilantly by the alert intelligence men of the Revenue Bureau, who had become suspicious of a bulging breast pocket in the bodyguard's flashy sportcoat. On this paticular day D'Andrea, as he trailed behind Capone from the courtroom to the elevator, fell into a position which pulled his coat tight. The agents were convinced. They seized him and hurried him to Judge Wilkerson's chambers. There he was searched and relieved of a fully loaded .38-caliber revolver, a supply of loose shells and, oddly enough, an official star of a deputy bailiff of the Chicago Municipal Court. Despite the protests of Capone's attorneys that D'Andrea had a permit to carry a gun and "in his ignorance of the law probably supposed that his permit extended to the Federal building," Judge Wilkerson committed him to the custody of the marshall, without bail, to answer a charge of contempt of court.

This flurry of excitement over, the Government next produced a long parade of witnesses to prove Capone's lavish disbursements during 1925, 1926, 1927, 1928 and 1929. Ten of them were from Florida. The admission of this testimony was bitterly resisted by Capone's attorneys, who contended that expenditures, however large, did not necessarily mean income during the years in which the expenditures were made. But the Court held otherwise. It ruled that a huge outlay of cash might be indicative of a corresponding income and was a proper circumstance to be considered by the jury in connection with all the other evidence in the case. . . .

According to the Government's proof, Capone's lavish expenditures were not restricted to Florida. Eighteeen witnesses were called to testify to some of his fantastic extravagances in Chicago.

One of the desk clerks and an auditor of the Metropole Hotel claimed that during 1925, 1926 and 1927 Capone maintained, under the registry of "Ross Brown," a five-room suite there. For six months in 1927 the room charges and incidentals ran up to $4,899. One of the incidentals was a single "party" which cost $1,633. Capone, said the witness, always paid in cash—usually in $100 and $500 bills. Sam Avery, the manager of the Metropole Hotel, testified that on the occasion of the Dempsey-Tunney fight Capone "threw a party which lasted two days and two nights." The total cost was $3,000 which Capone paid in cash. . . .

A salesman for B. Weinstein, a jeweler, identified a gold-and-diamond belt buckle which Parker Henderson testified had been given to him by Capone. The salesman said it was of thirty such buckles which had been purchased by Capone at $275 apiece shortly before Christmas, 1928.

Another jeweler, Abraham Quint, and one of his sales staff testified that in the same Christmas season Capone purchased twenty-eight combination cigarette-lighter watches at $13.50 each, and made wholesale purchases of sterling-silver tableware, glassware, candlestick holders, rings, bracelets, necklaces, beaded bags, perfume sets and "other knickknacks." Altogether Capone paid this dealer between $6,000 and $7,000 from 1928 to 1931.

Capone was a good customer of Marshall Field & Company and apparently patronized most of the departments of that well-appointed store. Seven witnesses, supported by the company's records, testified to his purchases. One spoke of the "truckloads of furniture" delivered to the Prairie Avenue house. Two from the custom-tailoring department testified that during 1927 and 1928 Capone had ordered twenty-three suits, three topcoats and one overcoat and paid $3,715 in cash for them. A fitter in the tailoring department added a neat touch to this testimony; it was Capone's order that "the right-hand pocket in all overcoats be made larger and stronger."

Another Marshall Field witness from the custom-shirt department testified that in 1927 Capone placed two orders for a total of twenty-nine specially fitted and monogrammed shirts. They ranged in price from $18 to $27 apiece. One bill came to $827, the other to $406. In 1928 six more custom-made shirts were added to Capone's wardrobe; the cost was $165.

Capone, it seems, also was partial to Field neckwear and handkerchiefs. His purchases of these items in 1927, according to a salesman from that department, amounted to $401.-50.

Capone was embarrassed only once during this protracted line of testimony—when one of Field's salesmen betrayed the gangster's penchant for numerous items of "glove silk" underwear. . . .

The last Government witness was Fred Ries, just returned from South America where he had been kept under wraps since his disclosures to Special Agent Wilson. Mr. Grossman conducted the direct examination of this "star" witness.

Ries identified himself as the former cashier of a number of Cicero gambling houses. During 1927 he had charge of all the finances of The Subway, the Smoke Shop and The Radio, all operated for Capone by Pete Penovich. In February of 1927 Ries began to handle also the receipts of The Ship, another Cicero gambling house. Since 1924 "Jimmy" Nundi had operated The Ship, but, as he told Ries, "Capone and his bunch had horned in and were going to take charge." Shortly after that Ralph Capone told Ries that Penovich would manage The Ship. At that time Ries became cashier at this latest establishment in the Capone chain.

Ries testified that he had never seen the defendant Capone in The Subway, but had frequently seen him at the Smoke Shop, The Radio, and The Ship in the company of Bobby Barton, Ralph Capone and Jake Guzik. Barton handled some of the profits of the Smoke Shop. Guzik took charge of the profits from the other three places. The witness and Penovich took their orders from him.

Ries was shown a cashier's check drawn on the Pinkert State Bank for $2,590, payable to "J.C. Dunbar."

"Who is J.C. Dunbar?" asked the prosecutor.

"Myself," Ries answered.

The witness testified that the $2,500 check was one of forty-three similar checks—totaling between $150,000 and $160,-000—which represented the 1927 profits of the gambling houses. He stated that he always turned them over to either Pete Penovich or Bobby Barton and they, in turn, delivered the checks to Jake Guzik. Guzik, said Ries, told him in February of 1927 to turn over money to no one—"not even to Al or Pete"—unless Guzik himself sent them down.

The checks were offered in evidence despite the defense's strenuous objection that they proved nothing against Capone. The Court ruled that in view of the previous testimony linking Capone and Guzik "they fitted into the chain of circumstances" and were proper evidence.

On cross-examination Ries testified that while he had frequently seen the defendant at The Ship, The Smoke Shop and The Radio in the company of Ralph Capone and Jake Guzik, he had never seen Capone handle any of the money of the enterprises, had never seen him take any bets, or in fact, do anything to indicate that he was in charge of or financially interested in the places.

The examination of Ries was completed on October 13 shortly after the opening of the afternoon session of court. There were still a number of unheard witnesses under Government subpeona, including Johnny Torrio, imported from Brooklyn, and Louis da Cava, alleged partner in Capone's safe-deposit box at the Pinkert Bank. The Government did not call these witnesses. Instead, United States Attorney Johnson announced that the Government rested. The prosecutors evidently were confident that they had proved their case against Capone.

The defense counsels were taken by surprise and acted with some uncertainty. They made a motion for a directed verdict of acquittal on the ground of insufficient evidence, but offered no argument in support of the motion. It was promptly overruled.

Unable to decide whether they should present any evidence in Capone's defense, the attorneys pleaded for a two days' continuance. The Court denied the request but gave them until ten o'clock the following morning either to go ahead with their evidence or to begin the summations to the jury.

When court reconvened on the morning of October 14, Capone's attorneys announced they desired to offer some testimony in his defense.

The first witness called was a Chicago cigar dealer who doubled as a handbook operator. He declared proudly that he was a good friend of the defendant. During 1924 and 1925 Capone had been a customer so highly valued that the witness personally called on Capone whenever the latter wanted to place a bet on a horse. These bets ranged in amount from $1,000 to $5,000. According to the witness, Capone was a chronic loser; in 1924 his total losses were between $8,000 and $10,000 and in 1925 they were between $1,000 and $12,000.

Several other witnesses of the same sort followed—"betting commissioners" and "bookies" operating out of prominent Chicago Loop hotels, well-known restaurants and so-called clubs. The aggregate of their testimony was that the defendant's bad judgment in picking winners had lost him $24,000 in 1924; $47,000 in 1925, $56,008 in 1926 and $90,000 in 1927.

All of these witnesses were sharply cross-examined. While admitting with apparent reluctance that Capone sometimes bought a winning ticket, none of them could remember a specific occasion when he won or the amount of his winnings. In fact, none was able to remember the name of a single horse that Capone had ever bet on. None required Capone to put up cash when he made his best. His credit, they all agreed, was excellent. As one of them expressed it: "Al Capone had a very honest reputation." . . .

After these various witnesses had indicated Capone's net income was much less than the prosecution had implied, the defense brought two governmental officials to the stand. The first, Elmer Irey, was head of the Intelligence Unit of the Revenue Bureau and was in charge of the preparation of evidence against Capone. Irey was asked when the present investigation of the defendant's financial affairs began, and he replied, October 18, 1928. The defense also asked the Government to confirm the date of Capone's sentence in the Holmesburg Prison for carrying concealed weapons. It was agreed that Capone was in prison from April 1929 to March 17, 1930.

The second government official asked to testify was Assistant United States Attorney Green. Mr. Fink asked Green whether Mattingly, Capone's income-tax specialist, had testified before the grand jury. Mr. Green's associates objected to this question because of the law that all proceedings before a grand jury are privileged. But Green volunteered to reply to the query and admitted Mattingly had so testified. Mr. Fink then demanded that the Government allow defense counsel to examine the transcript of Mattingly's earlier testimony and stated that this transcript would contradict the evidence revealed in his damaging letter to the revenue officials. This time the Government's objection that the testimony was privileged was sustained.

The defense rested. There was no rebuttal. Once again the defense asked for a directed verdict of acquittal and, failing to receive it, asked that the Mattingly letter and some items

Lizzie Borden listens as ex-Governor George D. Robinson pleads for her life in the famous "axe murder" trial of 1893. This sketch was drawn by B. West Clinedinst at the trial in New Bedford, Massachusetts.

Chicago Tribune

"Torso Murder Case" defender F. Lee Bailey makes one of his frequent appearances on television.

United Press International

Flamboyant Melvin M. Belli, the "King of Torts."

Ben Ng

Charles Rembar's defense of *Fanny Hill* wrote a new chapter in the law governing publication of sexually stimulating material.

International News

Al Capone, pictured in one of the few photographs showing why he earned the nickname "Scarface Al."

Alger Hiss arrives at the United States Courthouse in New York to surrender to federal authorities and begin serving a five-year jail sentence for perjury.

United Press International

Reies Lopez Tijerina and his wife, Patsy, leave the Bernalillo County Courthouse in Albuquerque, New Mexico, following his dramatic self-defense in the case of the "courthouse raid."

Brigadier General Billy Mitchell, seen here on his return from Germany in 1919. Mitchell had been Chief of the Air Service of the American Army of Occupation in Germany following World War I.

On the opening day of his trial in Jerusalem, Adolf Eichmann listens in his "glass cage" as his attorney, Dr. Servatius, makes an opening argument.

Associated Press

Lt. William Calley, Jr. waits in his quarters at Fort Benning, Georgia, for t
verdict of the six-officer panel which was deliberating his court-martial case. H
antiwar poster notwithstanding, Calley was accused of killing 102 Vietnamese me
women and children at Mylai.

of evidence linking Capone with Guzik, other gangsters and gambling be stricken out. The motions were overruled without argument and counsel was directed to begin the summations. The time for the arguments was limited by the Court to four hours on a side.

Mr. Grossman opened for the prosecution. The Government, he said, had proved that Capone spent $40,000 in 1927, $50,000 in 1928 and $26,000 in 1929—a total in three years of $116,000. And Capone, himself, said Grossman, had shown by his own witnesses that on horse races alone he lost $24,000 in 1924, $47,000 in 1925, $55,000 in 1926 and $90,000 in 1927—an additional total of over $200,000.

"Who is this man and where did he get his money?" Grossman demanded. The witnesses from Florida, he continued, had answered that question. Capone told them he was a gambler from Cicero and Chicago, that he was in the pressing-and-cleaning business and that he had an interest in a dog track. Even the defenses's witnesses, Grossman charged, revealed the nature of Capone's business and the extent of his power. Those who testified to Capone's betting losses were part of his organization. "You saw some of them on the witness stand," said the prosecutor. "They showed you themselves what a control he has over them. He pulls the strings and here they come."

Mr. Grossman was followed by his associate, Assistant United States Attorney Clawson. Mr. Clawson concentrated on the Mattingly letter, which unambiguously stated that for the years 1926, 1927, 1928 and 1929 Capone had an income of at least $266,000. And the letter admitted, said Clawson, that Capone had never filed an income-tax return and never paid a cent of tax on this money.

Clawson ridiculed Capone's contentions, made in Mattingly's letter, that he had no income in 1924 and 1925; that during that time he was just a handyman for Johnny Torrio making $75 a week. "Remember," adjured Clawson, "that in those same years, if you are to believe his witnesses, he was losing five times that much at the racetracks." . . .

After Mr. Clawson had finished, Mr. Fink took up the cudgels for the defense. First he lamented that the Government advocates had not analyzed the evidence logically in their summations. Then he launched into a two-hour argument, an argument as dexterous as any lawyer could have made under such an overwhelming weight of adverse evidence and circumstances:

> There are two principal questions involved in this case—one in which the defendant alone is interested, another which interests you and me, the present generation and future generations. The first question is whether there is any evidence at all which rises to dignity of hearsay indicating guilt on the part of the defendant. The second and most important question is whether, if there be no evidence of guilt, a jury can be persuaded and conned by the prosecution to bring in a verdict of guilty merely to appease public clamor.

Mr. Fink reminded the jurors of the "time-honored principle of the law" that Capone, the same as any other American citizen, was to be considered innocent until proven guilty beyond a reasonable doubt. Boldly he challenged the Government with the question uppermost in the public mind:

> Is the Government merely prosecuting this defendant for evasion of income tax, or is not this prosecution being used as a means by which to stow Al Capone away? . . . If this defendant's name were not Al Capone, there would be no case. You would be laughing at this so-called evidence.

Every count in the indictment, declared the lawyer, charged Capone with a "willful intent" to evade the payment of the tax and "willful intent" meant an intent with malice. "If I were sick on the day my income tax was due," he argued, "and failed to make a return, that would be no crime. And there are other circumstances in which one may fail to make a return and still not be guilty of an attempt to evade the tax." Mr. Fink then referred to the previously established fact that Capone had been released from the Philadelphia penitentiary on March 17, 1930—two cays after his 1929 income-tax return was due. He reminded the jury that six days after his release Capone was in the government tax office with Mattingly trying to determine a just amount and willing to pay whatever tax he rightfully owed.

Mr. Fink spoke bitterly of the lack of evidence:

> Surely, under this evidence, nobody could find that he had willful intent to evade his tax for 1929. There is no possible verdict on those counts [the ones dealing with the year 1929] save not guilty—unless, of course, you intend to return a verdict on no evidence at all.
>
> Capone is charged with evading taxes in 1924, and it is charged that he had an income in that year of $123,000. Where is the proof of it? Is there a scintilla of evidence that he made a dollar in 1924? Isn't it terrible, I ask you, that the Government should request you to violate your oaths and bring in a verdict on that count?

Mr. Fink followed the same line in dealing with the counts which related to the years 1925, 1926, 1927 and 1928. There was no proof, he declared, of net taxable income in any of those years. He attacked the prosecution's theory that the amount of income could be deducted from the amount of spendings. "We don't know what his losses were. How do you know that the money spent wasn't borrowed?"

The defense pictured Capone as a generous, openhanded "good fellow," a man of charity, a man respected and loved by all with whom he came in contact, "a man whose word bookmakers took for thousands." Then, with all solemnity, the defense inquired whether the jury could believe that such a man would defraud the government. . . .

United States Attorney Johnson, a mild-mannered, soft-spoken gentleman, made the closing argument for the Government. His quiet, conversational tone contrasted strikingly with the vigorous and often strident utterances of the defense counsel who had preceded him. Mr. Johnson explained to the jurors that it was peculiarly their province to judge of the credibility of the witnesses from their appearance and the likelihood of the truth of their testimony. The jurors must, he said, use the common sense derived from their own everyday experience in deciding where the truth in the case lay. The prosecutor commented sardonically:

> What a picture has been presented in this case. Here is a man who has never been engaged in an honest business and save for the purchase of a house in Florida has never engaged in a reputable business transaction. No income, and yet this defendant spent over $8,000 on diamond belt buckles! Counsel has pictured this defendant as a generous man who wouldn't beat the government, yet with all of his lavish spending he could not pay taxes to the government under whose protection he lived.
>
> During four hours of argument defense counsel here was strangely silent about the $77,550 in money transfers sent to Capone in Florida. Examine them. They came from the Lexington Hotel, and you remember the Lexington Hotel. Most of them were sent by Bobby Barton.

> You remember him as the man to whom, according to the testimony of the witness Ries, the surplus profits of the Smoke Shop were turned over. Others were sent by Charlie Fischetti. Fischetti was the man who Schumway testified sneaked out with the money when a Cicero gambling house was being raided. Others were sent by Sam Guzik, who is no stranger to the Federal courts. Did this money represent rights, inheritances or the proceeds of life insurance? From the pictures shown of Barton and Fischetti you can draw your own conclusions.
>
> The evidence in this case shows that this defendant was worried about not paying his income taxes, and that he finally commissioned Mattingly to try to settle the omission. Through Mattingly Capone admitted an income tax large enough to be taxable for the years 1925, 1926, 1927 and 1928.

Mr. Johnson also replied to Fink's charges that the trial was really an attempt to rid society of a gangster:

> They say we prosecute because of the name Alphonse Capone, but we can imagine a Federal case the result of public clamor? Consider the thousands of little men and women who earn only a little more than $1,500 a year and pay their taxes. It is public clamor to demand taxes due in a time of national financial stress and treasury deficit from a man who buys two-hundred-and-fifty dollar diamond belt buckles and twenty-seven-dollar shirts?

Mr. Johnson also countered the defense criticism that the Government had not called Mattingly to the witness stand. He declared that the written statement to the Revenue Bureau was in itself ample evidence of Capone's income—evidence so complete, declared the prosecutor, that "the Government will collect taxes on every cent of the money confessed in that letter."

The United States Attorney concluded with a simple but impressive appeal for a guilty verdict:

> The district attorney was never more sincere in the five years of holding office here than in this case. Never was there a case in my career where there was a more flagrant violation of the laws of the United States. This is a case which future generations will remember. There is no denying the public interest, but I am not asking you to think of this man as Alphonse Capone. Future generations will not remember this case because of the name Alphonse Capone, but because it will establish whether or not a man can go so far beyond the law as to be able to escape the law. . . .

It was in the early afternoon of Saturday October 17 that the Capone case was given to the jurors. After eight hours' deliberation they returned into court with a verdict which found the defendant not guilty on the indictment which charged evasion of 1924 taxes, and guilty on five, but not guilty on seventeen, of the counts in the second indictment. Translated into plainer terms this meant Capone was found guilty of a misdemeanor—willful failure to file an income-tax return for the years 1928 and 1929—and of a felony—willful attempt to evade payment of income taxes due on his income for the years 1925, 1926 and 1927.

Capone's lawyers moved that judgment on the verdict of guilty should be arrested on the ground that the second indictment was insufficient as a charge of crime and that numerous prejudicial errors had occurred during the trial. On October 24 their motion was argued and overruled, and the Court pronounced sentence: five years' imprisonment in a Federal penitentiary and a fine of $10,000 and costs on each of the three felony counts; one year's imprisonment in the county jail and a fine of $10,000 and costs on each of the two misdemeanor counts. The sentences on two of the felony counts were to run concurrently, but the sentence on the third felony count was to be consecutive and cumulative to the first two. The jail sentences on the misdemeanor counts were to run concurrently, and be served after the penitentiary sentence had been satisfied.

All these sentences were in addition to the six months' jail sentence imposed on Capone the previous April for contempt of court, but it was ordered that service of the penitentiary sentence on the felony counts would satisfy the contempt sentence. Altogether Capone, in satisfaction of his numerous convictions, would first serve ten years in a Federal penitentiary, then serve an additional year in the county jail and pay aggregated fines of $50,000 and costs.

The motion of the defense that Capone be admitted to bail pending appeal was denied. The same motion was made in the Court of Appeals and it too was refused. The once glamorous gambler took up a temporary residence in the Cook County jail.

The public's reaction to Capone's conviction was one of satisfaction, not unmixed with a sense of frustration—satisfaction that he "had been caught up with and put away;" frustration that with all of the heinous crimes imputed to him he was prosecuted and convicted for having failed to pay income taxes to the government on his ill-gotten gains.

None of the defense's efforts to alter the verdict was effective. The appeal proceeded with unusual dispatch. Ably written briefs were filed by both sides and oral arguments heard in the Court of Appeals within three months. The contentions of Capone's attorneys were limited to two points: (1) that the five counts of the indictment upon which the defendant had been found guilty were vague and uncertain and insufficient to charge him with a violation of the revenue laws, and (2) that the admission in evidence of the Mattingly letter and the verbal statements of Capone and Mattingly to the Treasury Department officials constituted grievous and prejudicial error. On February 27, 1932, the Court of Appeals handed down its unanimous opinion rejecting both of the defense contentions and denying the appeal. A petition to the Court of Appeals for a rehearing was overruled. On May 2 the Supreme Court of the United States denied an application to review the case.

The defense had exhausted the legal processes. Capone was promptly removed from the Cook County jail to the Federal penitentiary at Atlanta. After two years in Atlanta he was transferred to Alcatraz—the "rock" in San Francisco Bay. There he remained until January of 1939, when he was removed to Terminal Prison off the coast of San Pedro to serve out his jail sentence.

As soon as Capone entered Terminal Prison he was hospitalized. He was an extremely sick man. Shortly after his incarceration at Alcatraz he had suffered progressive deterioration of mind and body—the wages of untreated syphilis.

In November of 1939 relatives and friends (so it was said) paid the $57,692.29 in fines and costs assessed against Capone. The ailing gangster was was then released from prison. He had served seven years and six months.

News of his release stimulated rumors that Capone would resume the management of his underworld Empire. Jack Guzik, the former business associate of Capone, scotched the rumor: "Bunk," said Greasy Thumb. "Al's nuttier than a fruitcake."

And he was right. A harmless Capone retired to his Palm Island estate and the seclusion he now could find there. No more revels. Just the humdrum routine of doctors' visits, injections and medicines, with such innocent diversion as battling a tennis ball against a brick wall or playing gin rummy with his ministering relatives.

As time passed he grew progressively worse, and on January 25, 1947, he succumbed to an apoplectic stroke, complicated with pneumonia. He was forty-eight years old. Unlike Colosimo, O'Banion, Weiss, Lombardo, the Gennas, Scalisi, Anselmi and scores of his other friends and foes, he died as he had wished—in bed with his boots off.

Incredibly lavish displays had marked the last rites of some of Scarface Al's high-ranking gangster associates. In contrast, Capone's funeral was extremely modest. His body was shipped by rail to Chicago. In a casket that an appraising reporter said "could not have cost a dime over $2,000," covered with "only a sprinkling of gardenias and orchids," the erstwhile emperor of gangdom was lowered into a grave in the family lot in Mount Olivet Cemetery. There were no bands, no crowds, no politicians. Only his closest relatives and a handful of the old gang—among them Jake (Greasy Thumb) Guzik, Anthony (Don't-call-me-Tony) Accardo, Murray (The Camel) Humphreys and "Golf Bag" Sam Hunt—honored his funeral.

These last, with others of Capone's former friends and enemies, had taken over the empire from America's public Enemy Number One.

THE ALGER HISS PERJURY CASE

Thomas F. Murphy
for the prosecution

vs.

Lloyd Paul Stryker
for the defense

by William Kunstler

Perhaps the most dramatic courtroom struggle of the century took place not between two lawyers but between two private citizens—the urbane, distinguished civil servant Alger Hiss and his brilliant and fanatical nemesis, Whittaker Chambers. In their initial confrontation before the House Committee on Un-American Activities, a little-known congressman named Richard Nixon played an important role. Later, before a federal judge and jury, talented lawyers on both sides wrestled with those notorious pieces of evidence (or were they forgeries?), the "pumpkin papers." But over all the proceedings in Congress and in the courts loomed the huge, irreconcilable presences of the two antagonists, hunter and hunted, Chambers and Hiss.

Whittaker Chambers is dead now, and an aging Alger Hiss, finally out of jail, writes and lectures on the injustice which he claims was perpetrated by his old enemy. In the following selection, William Kunstler, famed defender of controversial political figures, provides us with a concise, dispassionate and readable description of the trials which shook a nation.

A few minutes after eleven o'-clock in the morning of Tuesday, August 3, 1948, a portly little man walked slowly to the front of the Ways and Means Committee Room in which the House Committee on Un-American Activities was holding an open session. After he had been sworn, he sat down gingerly in a wooden chair that was perched directly in front of a raised platform behind which acting Chairman Karl Mundt and five of his colleagues were ensconced. Robert Stripling, the Committee's counsel, began the hearing.

Q. Will you state your full name?

A. My name is David Whittaker Chambers.

Q. Where and when were you born?

A. I was born April 1, 1901, in Philadelphia.

Q. How long have you been associated with *Time Magazine?*

A. Nine years.

Q. Prior to that time, what was your profession?

A. I was a member of the Communist Party and a paid functionary of the party.

The witness asked if he might read a prepared statement. In a voice that was barely audible at the press table, he told of his fifteen years' service as a Soviet espionage agent. In 1939, two years after he said that he had "repudiated Marx's doctrines and Lenin's tactics," he had gone to Washington to report what he knew "about the infiltration of the United States Government by Communists." At that time he had told Assistant Secretary of State Adolph A. Berle, Jr., that there was an underground Communist movement in the government. "The head of the underground group at the time I knew it was Nathan Witt, an attorney for the National Labor Relations Board. Later, John Abt became the leader. Lee Pressman was also a member of this group, as was Alger Hiss, who, as a member of the State Department, later organized the conferences at Dumbarton Oaks, San Francisco, and the United States side of the Yalta Conference."

In New York City, Alger Hiss, who was in the middle of his second year as the president of the Carnegie Endowment for International Peace, had just returned from a month's vacation in Vermont. As soon as he heard of Chambers' charges, he sent a telegram to Chairman Mundt in which he stated, "I do not know Mr. Chambers and insofar as I am aware have never laid eyes on him." He requested permission to "appear before your Committee to make these statements formally and under oath." Hiss suggested Thursday, August 5th, and hoped that "that will be a convenient time from the Committee's point of view for me to appear." Mundt immediately wired back that it was.

On Thursday morning, Hiss had his chance. In the large Caucus Room in the Old House Office Building, he told the Committee that he had never heard of Whittaker Chambers until 1947 "when two representatives of the Federal Bureau of Investigation had asked me if I knew him. . . . I said I did not know Chambers. So far as I know, I have never laid eyes on him, and I should like to have the opportunity to do so." As far as Chambers' accusations were concerned, they were all "complete fabrications." The witness was willing to let his Government service speak for itself.

On Tuesday, Chambers had testified that, before he had broken with the underground, he had tried to persuade Alger Hiss to do the same. In a tearful scene at the Hiss home, his friend had "absolutely refused to break." Hiss denied that any such incident had ever occurred and repeated his statement that, as far as he knew, the name Chambers "means absolutely nothing to me." When he was shown a recent photograph of Chambers, the witness insisted that he "would much rather see the individual. . . . I would not want to take an oath that I had never seen that person. I would like to see him and then I think that I would be better able to tell whether I had ever seen him." When Mundt told him that Chambers was not present in the hearing room, Hiss replied, somewhat sharply, that "I hoped he would be." . . .

After Hiss had denied knowing Chambers, Stripling informed Mundt that "there is a very sharp contradiction here in the testimony. I certainly suggest Mr. Chambers be brought back before the Commitee and clear this up." The chairman agreed and appointed a sub-committee composed of California's Nixon, Louisiana's Hebert and Pennsylvania's McDowell to question Chambers in executive session. Two days later, the sub-committee met in Room 101 of New York's United States Courthouse. With Nixon taking the lead, Chambers was questioned closely about his claimed acquaintance with Alger Hiss and his family. The witness' answers revealed such an intimate knowledge of the Hisses that it was apparent that he had either known them extremely well or done considerable homework.

First of all, Hiss had known him only as Carl, his party name. They had been the best of friends and he had spent a great deal of time at the various Hiss homes in Baltimore and Washington. The witness's knowledge of what Hiss later referred to as "petty housekeeping details" was apparently inexhaustible. He knew that Mrs. Hiss called her husband "Hilly," that the Hisses had a cocker spaniel, and that "they both had the same hobby—amateur ornithologists, bird observers." In fact, he remembered that "once, they saw, to their great excitement, a prothonotary warbler."

MR. McDOWELL: A very rare specimen?

MR. CHAMBERS: I never saw one. I am also fond of birds.

When he first met the Hisses, they owned a Ford roadster which, he remembered, "was black and it was very dilapidated." In 1936, they had purchased a new Plymouth, and J. Peters, the head of the underground organization, had helped them dispose of the Ford through a Communist service station in Washington. He described Hiss as a slender man, "about five feet eight or nine," who walked with "a slight mince"; Priscilla Hiss was "a short, highly nervous, little woman" who had "a habit of blushing red when she is excited or angry, fiery red." Timmy Hobson, Mrs. Hiss's son by a previous marriage, "was a puny little boy, also rather nervous." The boy's father was paying for his education but the Hisses were diverting "a large part of that money to the Communist Party."

MR. NIXON: Hiss told you that?

MR. CHAMBERS: Yes, sir.

MR. NIXON: Did he name the Communist Party as the recipient?

MR. CHAMBERS: Certainly.

MR. NIXON: He might have said simply "the party." Could it have been the Democratic Party or Socialist Party?

MR. CHAMBERS: No.

. . . On Friday, August 13th, J. Parnell Thomas, the regular chairman, sent a telegram to Hiss, asking him to appear before the Committee the following Monday. That same Friday, Donald Hiss [Alger's younger brother] denied at a public hearing "every statement made by Mr. Chambers with respect to me. I am not, and never have been, a member of the Communist Party." He had belonged to nothing more subversive than the Y.M.C.A., the Washington Racquet Club and the Harvard Law School Association. As for his accuser, "I have no recollection of every having met any person by the name of D. Whittaker Chambers nor do I recognize his photograph which I have seen in the public press."

> MR. NIXON: As I understand your statement, you have made an unqualified statement that you have never known a man by the name of Carl who resembled that man?
>
> DONALD HISS: I have never known that man by the name of Chambers, Carl, or any other name, sir.

When he suggested that whoever was lying ought to go to jail, Mundt seconded the motion.

On August 16th, Alger Hiss faced the Committee once more, this time in executive session. Reassured by the fact that the President of the United States had publicly labeled his case as "a red herring," deliberately designed to hide the failures of the Eightieth Congress, Hiss eased himself into the witness chair with a visible air of confidence. Again, it was Nixon who asked most of the questions. The first order of business was to try to determine whether Hiss had ever known Chambers, under one name or another. Nixon handed the witness two photographs and asked him "if you can remember that person either as Whittaker Chambers or as Carl or as any other individual you have met."

This time, Hiss admitted that "the face had a certain familiarity." Although he would still like to see Chambers face to face, he was "not prepared to say that I have never seen the man whose pictures are now shown me." But that was as far as he cared to go until he had the opportunity of "seeing the man, hearing him talk, getting some much more tangible basis for judging the person and the personality."

> MR. NIXON: Would your answer be any different if this individual were described to you as one who had stayed overnight in your house on several occasions?
>
> MR. HISS: I think, Mr. Nixon, let me say this: In the course of my service in the government . . . I have had a great many people who have visited in my house. If this is a picture of anyone, I would find it very difficult to believe that that individual could have stayed in my house when I was there on several occasions overnight and his face not be more familiar than it is.

When the chairman asked him whether he thought he would recognize a man who had spent a week in his house in the past fifteen years, Hiss was sure that he would "if he hadn't had a face-lifting."

> MR. THOMAS: No doubt in your mind?
>
> MR. HISS: I have no doubt whatsoever.

After a brief recess, Hiss announced that "I have written a name on this pad in front of me of a person whom I knew in 1933 and 1934 who not only spent some time in my house but sublet my apartment." The name of this man was George

Crosley and the witness remembered him as a free-lance writer who had occasionally interviewed him when he was counsel to the Nye Committee. As he recalled it, "this fellow was writing a series of articles . . . which he hoped to sell to one of the magazines." In June of 1935, when the Hisses had purchased the P Street house, they had rented their Wardman Park apartment to Crosley and his family which consisted of a "strikingly dark" wife and an infant daughter. Because all of Crosley's furniture hadn't arrived, "we put them up two or three nights in a row, his wife and little baby."

He had also thrown in an old Ford with the apartment. It was an early model A coupe with "a sassy little trunk on the back." He had purchased a new car—a Plymouth sedan—and, since Crosley "wanted a way to get around," he had decided to let him have the Ford.

MR. NIXON: You gave this Ford car to Crosley?

MR. HISS: Threw it in along with the apartment and charged the rent and threw the car in at the same time.

MR. NIXON: In other words, added a little to the rent to cover the car?

MR. HISS: No; I think I charged him exactly what I was paying for the rent and threw the car in in addition. I don't think I got any compensation.

MR. STRIPLING: You just gave him the car?

MR. HISS: I think the car just went right in with it.

No, he had not given Crosley a bill of sale; "I think I just simply turned it over to him." He didn't know whether the writer had recorded the title or not.

He had driven Crosley around Washington in the Ford on

several occasions. Once he had given him a lift to New York "when I was going to make a trip to New York City anyway." . . .

> MR. STRIPLING: You wouldn't say positively George Crosley and this person are the same?
>
> MR. HISS: Not positively.
>
> MR. STRIPLING: You would not say positively?
>
> MR. HISS: I think they are not. That would be my best impression from the photographs.

At one point in the questioning, Hiss stated that both he and his wife were amateur ornithologists. McDowell, who was no mean bird watcher himself, asked him if he had ever seen a prothonotary warbler. The witness replied that he had, "right here on the Potomac." McDowell replied that he once had observed one in Arlington. Hiss, lost in reverie, seemed to forget that he was in a hearing room. "They come back and nest in those swamps," he told McDowell. "Beautiful yellow head, a gorgeous bird. Mr. Collins is an ornithologist, Henry Collins. He's a really good ornithologist, calling them by their Latin names." Nixon brought him abruptly back to earth with a question about the schools his son had attended from 1934 to 1937. . . .

Before Hiss left Washington, he was asked to return at 10:30 A.M. on August 25th when he and Chambers would "have an opportunity to confront one another." The next morning, a member of the Committee's staff telephoned him at his New York office and asked him if he would be able to meet with Mr. McDowell later that afternoon. Hiss replied that he would. Shortly before 5:30 P.M., McDowell called and invited him to come over to Room 1400 of the Hotel Commodore. Hiss asked Charles Dollard, a colleague at the Carnegie Corporation, to accompany him, and the two men walked the few blocks to the Commodore. When they entered the hotel suite, Hiss was asked to sit in a chair facing Nixon and McDowell, the only two members of the Committee present.

A few minutes later, a door behind him opened and Chambers was ushered into the room. Nixon asked the two men to stand and face each other. "Mr. Hiss," he said, "the man standing here is Mr. Whittaker Chambers. I ask you if you have ever known that man before."

MR. HISS: May I ask him to speak? Will you ask him to say something?

MR. NIXON: Yes, Mr. Chambers, will you tell us your name and business?

MR. CHAMBERS: My name is Whittaker Chambers.

MR. HISS: Would you mind opening your mouth wider? Will you go on talking?

MR. CHAMBERS: I am senior editor of *Time Magazine.*

MR. HISS: May I ask whether his voice, when he testified before, was comparable to this?

MR. McDOWELL: I would say it is about the same now as we have heard.

MR. HISS: I think he is George Crosley, but I would like to hear him talk a little longer.

After Chambers had read a portion of a *Newsweek* article about Truman's failure to appoint a new Secretary of Labor to replace Lewis B. Schwellenbach, Hiss announced that, although his voice was less resonant than that of the man he had once known, "I believe . . . that he must be George Crosley." But the man he had known in 1934 and 1935 had had terrible teeth. The teeth of the man he was now asked to identify "look to me as though they have been improved upon or that there has been considerable dental work done since I knew George Crosley." Nixon asked Chambers whether he had "had any dental work since 1934 of a substantial nature." It seemed that he had, "some extractions and a plate."

But Hiss still wasn't certain. Chambers looked "very different in girth and in other appearances—hair, forehead, and so on, particularly the jowls." But it was obvious to everyone in the room that he was beating a slow but steady retreat. After Nixon made him go over his previous testimony about subletting the 29th Street apartment to the "Crosleys," Hiss asked for—and received—permission to question his accuser.

MR. HISS: Did you ever go under the name of George Crosley?

MR. CHAMBERS: Not to my knowledge.

MR. HISS: You did not?

MR. CHAMBERS: No; I did not.

MR. HISS: Did you ever spend any time with your wife and child in an apartment on Twenty-ninth Street in Washington when I was not there because I and my family were living on P Street?

MR. CHAMBERS: I most certainly did.

MR. HISS: Would you tell me how you reconcile your negative answers with this affirmative answer?

MR. CHAMBERS: Very easily, Alger. I was a Communist and you were a Communist.

Finally, Hiss was "perfectly prepared to identify this man as George Crosley." When Stripling asked him if he thought he could produce three people who would swear that they, too, had known Chambers as Crosley, Hiss said that he would try. The only ones he could think of offhand were Stephen Rauschenbush, Robert Wohlford and Elsie Gullender who had worked with him on the Nye Committee in 1935. But he couldn't remember whether Chambers had ever called on any of these people.

McDowell then turned to Chambers and asked him whether he was prepared to identify Hiss as the man "who was a member of the Communist Party at whose home you stayed." He was.

MR. McDOWELL: You make the identification positive?

MR. CHAMBERS: Positive identification.

While Chambers was talking, Hiss rose from his chair and walked over toward him. Livid with anger, he invited "Mr. Whittaker Chambers to make those same statements out of the presence of this Committee without their being privileged for suit for libel. I challenge you to do it and I hope you will do it damned quickly." By the time the had finished hurling his gauntlet, he was so close to Chambers that Louis J. Russell, one of the Committee's investigators, threw himself between the two men. "I am not going to touch him," Hiss exclaimed. "You are touching me." McDowell ordered Hiss to sit down and the hearing was adjourned for a few minutes to clear the air. . . .

The next act in what was rapidly beginning to have all the appearances of a Greek tragedy was scheduled to take place on August 25th in the Caucus Room of the Old House Office

Building. Long before Chairman Thomas gaveled the hearing into being at 10:30 A.M., the chamber was filled to overflowing with more people than it had ever held before. Television cameramen, newspaper photographers, radio commentators, and the less spectacular members of the Fourth Estate crowded every corner of the long room. Thomas welcomed them all in the name of the Committee. "We are glad," he announced, "to have as many representatives of the American public as is possible to crowd into this room today." He was also mighty happy to put Hiss and Chambers on view together before a nationwide audience.

The first order of business was to determine whether anyone but Alger Hiss had ever known of George Crosley's existence. At the Commodore confrontation, Hiss had suggested the names of three former Nye Committee employees whom he thought might have run into Crosley when the latter was scrounging for magazine fodder. Stripling's investigators had discovered that one was dead, another could not be traced, and the third couldn't remember ever having met anyone named Crosley. A search of the records of the Library of Congress, the Copyright Division, and the Public Catalogue had uncovered only two writers by that name—an obscure 1905 poet and a doctor who had published a treatise on the effects of ultraviolet light. If George Crosley had ever existed, he was now a case for the Missing Persons Bureau.

With Crosley out of the way, the Committee turned to Fords and photostats. Hiss had previously testified that after he had purchased a new Plymouth in the Spring of '35, he had either given Crosley-Chambers "the use of the car" or "the car outright." According to the records of the District of Columbia's Motor Vehicles and Traffic Bureau, Hiss had bought the Plymouth on September 7, 1935. If the dates were correct, then Hiss had given Chambers the old Ford *before* he had obtained the Plymouth.

Nixon was obviously fascinated by the business of the cars. Would Mr. Hiss enlighten him as to whether he had sold, or given, the car, to Crosley?

> MR. HISS: I gave Crosley, according to my best recollection . . .
>
> MR. NIXON: Well, now, just a moment on that point. I don't want to interrupt you on that "to the best of my recollection" but you certainly can testify "Yes" or "No" as to whether you gave Crosley a car. How many cars have you given away in your life, Mr. Hiss?
>
> MR. HISS: I have only had one old car of a financial value of $25 in my life. That is the car that I let Crosley have the use of.

When Mundt reminded the witness that, a week earlier, he had sworn that he had "sold him an automobile," Hiss promptly swallowed his words and conceded that, if that's what the transcript said, it must be correct.

After Nixon had read into the record most of Hiss's previous testimony about the Ford roadster, he confessed to the chairman that he was "amazed to hear Mr. Hiss say this morning that he can only testify to the best of his recollection as to whether he ever gave Crosley a car at all, that he is not sure as to whether or not he transferred the car to Crosley, that he might have given it to him for his use only, and that he is not even sure when the transaction occurred. . . ." As far as he was concerned, Hiss ought to "tell us exactly what did happen to that car."

The witness was only too happy to oblige. His testimony, "based upon the best recollection I have, is that I gave Crosley the use of the car, as I gave him the use of the apartment." He thought that the transfer had taken place at the same time as he had subleased the apartment to the Crosleys but it could have taken place "several months after the rental transaction." When Mundt asked him whether he had ever given the Ford "to anybody else in any way besides to Mr. George Crosley," Hiss insisted that he could not answer the question "without consulting the records."

The reason for the Committee's preoccupation with the Ford's disposition became clear when Stripling called Louis Russell, one of its own investigators. Russell testified that he had checked the records of the District's Director of Vehicles and Traffic and that he had discovered that one Alger Hiss had assigned a 1929 Ford automobile to the Cherner Motor Company on July 23, 1936. He identified a photostatic copy of the assignment of title as a copy of the original document which he had seen on file. It was signed by Hiss and notarized by W. Marvin Smith, an attorney in the Solicitor General's office.

After some shilly-shallying about "photostatic signatures," Hiss admitted that "it looks like my signature to me, Mr. Chairman." He was also prepared to go a little further and own that Mr. Smith had indeed notarized his signature. When Stripling produced a sales slip which indicated that the vehicle had been sold by the Cherner Motor Company to one William Rosen a few hours after Hiss had turned it in, that was the last trace of the saucy little car that was carrying the Committee to glory. . . .

In the afternoon, Hiss read a letter he had written to Chairman Thomas the preceding day. After spelling out for the Committee his record as a public servant, he read a list of questions which he wanted Chambers to answer in public. He was informed that Chambers would "take the stand directly after you finish on the stand today." Before he subsided, Hiss challenged Chambers "to make the statements about me with respect to Communism in public that he has made under privilege of this Committee."

It had grown dark when Chambers took the stand, and Thomas ordered the lights turned on. Led by Nixon and Stripling, the portly witness repeated much of his former testimony about Hiss and Communism. Since his predeccessor on the stand had raised a question about the editor's mental condition, Nixon asked him whether he had ever been "treated for mental illness."

MR. CHAMBERS: Yes; I have never been treated for a mental illness—period.

MR. NIXON: You have never been treated in a mental institution?

MR. CHAMBERS: Never.

MR. NIXON: Never. Have you ever been treated for a mental illness or been in an institution during the past four years, which was the charge made?

MR. CHAMBERS: Of course, not; and anyone at *Time Magazine* can tell you that.

Just before eight o'clock, Nixon wanted to know if Mr. Hiss was the witness's closest friend. Chambers replied that he "was certainly the closest friend I ever had in the Communist Party."

MR. NIXON: Mr. Chambers, can you search your memory now to see what motive you can have for accusing Mr. Hiss of being a Communist at the present time?

MR. CHAMBERS: What motive can I have?

MR. NIXON: Yes, I mean do you—is there any grudge that you have against Mr. Hiss over anything that he has done to you?

MR. CHAMBERS: The story has spread that, in testifying against Mr. Hiss, I am working out some old grudge, or motives of revenge or hatred. I do not hate Mr. Hiss. We were close friends, but we are caught in a tragedy of history. Mr. Hiss represents the concealed enemy against which we are all fighting, and I am fighting. I have testified against him with remorse and pity, but in a moment of history in which this nation now stands, so help me God, I could not do otherwise.

The chairman's gavel signified the end of the hearing.

Two days later, Chambers accepted Hiss's challenge to repeat his accusations in public. When he appeared on the *Meet the Press* radio program, Edward T. Folliard of the *Washington Post* asked him, "Are you willing to say . . . that Alger Hiss is or ever was a Communist?" When Chambers replied that "Alger Hiss was a Communist and may be now," Folliard wanted to know if he was "prepared to go to court to answer a suit for libel or slander?" The answer was short and to the point. "I don't think Hiss will go to court."

On September 27th, Hiss proved him wrong by filing a $75,000 defamation suit in a Baltimore federal court. Although Chambers announced that he welcomed the litigation, he became convinced during some pre-trial hearings that, unless he could document some of his charges, he was reasonably sure of losing the suit. However, hidden behind a dumbwaiter shaft in the Brooklyn home of Nathan Levine, one of his nephews, was a bulky manila envelope. In it were forty-seven typed copies of State Department reports, five rolls of microfilm, and four memoranda in Hiss's handwriting. Chambers counted on these to save him from a civil judgment. They didn't fail him.

William Marbury, Hiss's attorney in the Baltimore libel

suit, had asked Chambers whether he could produce "any documentary proof or your assertions?" On November 17th, Chambers complied by dumping the copies of official documents and the Hiss memos on the long conference table in Marbury's office. These, he claimed, Hiss had turned over to him in 1937 after meeting a Colonel Bykov, a Soviet secret agent. Hiss would bring classified reports home for his wife to type. He would return the originals to the files the next morning while the typed copies would be delivered to Chambers for transmission to Bykov.

Hiss immediately directed his attorneys to turn the documents over to the Department of Justice. Alexander Campbell, chief of Justice's Criminal Division, rushed up to Baltimore and took possession of all the papers. At the same time, he ordered John F. X. McGohey, the United States Attorney in New York, to convene the Federal Grand Jury. But, with the exception of a provocative little item in Jerry Kluttz's column in the *Washington Post* that "some startling information" had been uncovered in the Baltimore libel suit, what Chambers was later to refer to as his "lifeline" didn't seem to have made much of a stir.

Bert Andrews of the *New York Herald Tribune* thought that he smelled a rather large rat. He decided to play his hunch and, on December 1st, cabled Nixon, who was on the high seas bound for a Central American vacation, that a "bombshell" had exploded in Baltimore. Nixon ordered Stripling to visit Chambers at his Maryland farm where the latter blandly admitted that he had been less than frank with the Committee. Twenty-four hours later, Nixon, with the help of the Coast Guard, was back in Washington, and Chambers had turned over the five rolls of microfilm which he had cached in a pumpkin in his backyard to William Wheeler and Donald T. Appell, two Committee investigators. Three of the rolls, which had not yet been developed, were still in their aluminum cylinders while the developed rolls were wrapped in oilpaper bags.

On December 3rd, the day before Nixon & Company announced its strike, the New York Federal Grand Jury was called back into session. Its first step was to subpoena both Hiss and Chambers, a step that forced the Committee—most regretfully—to cancel a scheduled public hearing. On December 15th, the grand jurors, by one more than a bare majority, returned a two-count indictment against Alger Hiss. In it, it was charged that he had lied twice in his testimony: once, when he denied that he had turned State Department documents over to Whittaker Chambers, and again when he swore that he had not seen his rotund accuser "after January 1, 1937." According to the grand jury, Hiss had delivered government reports to Chambers in February and March of 1938 and had seen him during those months.

Hiss's trial was originally scheduled for January 24, 1949, but, because of six adjournments, it was not until May 31st that it officially began with the selection of a ten-man two-woman jury. McGohey had entrusted the case for the prosecution to the hands of Thomas F. Murphy, an Assistant United States Attorney noted for the thickest and droopiest mustache in New York County. Hiss had selected Lloyd Paul Stryker, a white-haired veteran of the criminal courts, as his attorney-in-chief. There were others—Thomas J. Donegan, who had been sent by the Attorney General to lend a helping hand, and Edward C. McLean, who used up a chair at the defense table —but it was Murphy and Stryker who carried the biggest swords. The judge was Samuel H. Kaufman, a wizened little man who could hardly see over the edge of the bench without rising from his abundantly stuffed chair.

The jury had been selected in less than three hours. Early on the afternoon of the trial's first day, Murphy heaved his

6'4" bulk out of his chair and opened the Government's case. He was going to prove, he announced, that Hiss had lied as the grand jury charged. Although he intended to corroborate Mr. Chambers's testimony, he admitted, somewhat over-generously, that "if you don't believe Mr. Chambers' story, we have no case under the Federal perjury rule." Stryker was more than willing to do battle on these terms and he assured the jury that he would do everything in his power to prove to their satisfaction that the man who accused Alger Hiss could only be described by the term used "in the southern countries" to warn of the approach of lepers—"Unclean, unclean!"

Chambers was the Government's first witness. Dressed in a baggy blue suit, he wearily repeated the testimony he had given in so many occasions in the past. He described his years in the Communist underground, his intimate friendship with the Hisses, the help the defendant had given him in obtaining secret State Department papers, and his own torturous break with the Party in 1938. This was all old hat to those who had followed the House Committee hearings, but suddenly Chambers added something new. He swore that Hiss had lent him $400.00 in the fall of 1937 to buy a new car for a trip to Florida, a trip that was to mark his disappearance from the Communist scene.

After Chambers had identified the Baltimore documents and the pumpkin papers as having been received from Hiss, Murphy asked him when he had last seen the defendant.

A. I saw Alger Hiss around Christmas, 1938.

Q. And where did you see him?

A. I saw him at his home on Volta Place. . . .

On his last trip to Volta Place, he had tried to convince Hiss to join him in breaking with the underground. His friend had told him that he was sorry that Chambers, whom he knew only as Carl, was leaving the party because he had heard that "a new and more important post was to be given to me." Before they had said goodbye, Hiss gave Chambers a wooden rolling-pin as a Christmas present for the latter's infant daughter. One year later, in a conversation with Assistant Secretary of State Adolph A. Berle, Jr., he had named Hiss "as a member of the Communist Party."

Stryker didn't waste any time beating around the bush when Murphy turned the witness over to him. He wanted to know if Mr. Chambers knew what an oath was. His man did. "An oath is a declaration which a man makes when he promises to tell the truth." He agreed with Stryker that "in our courts it is an affirmation made by a man who calls on Almighty God to witness the truth of what he says." But, Stryker thundered, wasn't it a fact that he had taken an oath in 1937 to "support and defend the Constitution of the United States against all enemies?" He had.

Q. That was false from the beginning to the end, was it not, Mr. Chambers?

A. Of course.

Q. And it was perjury, wasn't it?

A. If you like.

Q. And you did it in order to deceive and cheat the United States Government . . . is that not true?

A. That is correct.

Q. You were an underhanded enemy of this country doing what you could to aid a foreign country and overthrow our Constitution by force and violence?

A. Yes.

Chambers admitted that he had used more than seven aliases between 1924 and 1938 when he was in the underground. Furthermore, he had lied to the Dean of Columbia University, had stolen books from numerous libraries, and had lived with several women including a New Orleans whore with the fanciful name of "One-Eyed Annie." While he was at Columbia, he had written an anti-religious play that was so offensive that he had been expelled from the university.

Chambers was prepared to admit everything—that he had been a liar, a thief, an atheist, a spy, and a cheat. But he insisted tht he had repented when he broke with the Communists in April of 1938. This was the opening Stryker had been waiting for.

Q. Did you have a high, God-fearing man's regard for an oath in August of 1948?

A. Yes.

Q. Did you in October, 1948, testify before the grand jury in this building?

A. I did.

Q. When you testified before the grand jury, you were asked whether there was any espionage and you answered that there was not?

A. I answered I had no knowledge of it.

Q. Was that answer true or false?

A. That answer was false.

Q. Then you admit that you testified falsely and committed perjury before the grand jury in this building, is that right?

A. That is right.

After getting his pliable witness to admit that he had written erotic poetry and that his brother Dick had committed suicide after two previous attempts, Stryker called it a day. Murphy tried to repair some of the damage by asking Chambers to explain why he had perjured himself before the grand jury as late as 1948. The ex-*Time* editor (he had resigned on December 10th) maintained that he had done so "to preseve from injury insofar as I could all individuals in the past in that conspiracy. . . . I was particularly anxious not to injure Mr. Hiss any more than necessary out of grounds of past friendship and because he is by widespread consent a very able man. Therefore, I chose to jeopardize myself rather than reveal the full extent of his activities and those of others." Perjury was never more nobly explained away. . . .

At last, the stage was set for Mrs. Chambers's appearance. A tiny forty-nine-year-old woman dressed in an ill-fitting gray suit, she perched nervously in the witness chair, waiting for the indignities she was sure were in the offing. Under Murphy's gentle questioning, she revealed a wealth of domestic detail about the Hisses that complemented the story told by her husband. The two families had been the best of friends, and she could even recall a wonderul New Year's Eve party at Volta Place in 1937. Alger and Priscilla called her Lisa and her husband, Carl. When the judge asked her what their last name had been during this period of friendship, the witness stated, "We never had a last name to them."

Stryker spent two days trying to destroy a woman who had much more endurance than her frail physique would have suggested. While she admitted that she didn't have "a very good head for figures or dates," she insisted that the Hisses and the Chamberses had known each other intimately and that she had once painted a portrait of Timmy Hobson. The relationship had been so close that Priscilla Hiss had willingly permitted one of her best linen towels to be used as a diaper by one of the Chambers infants. . . .

After Mrs. Chambers had stepped down, Murphy decided that it was time to introduce the State Department documents. Photographic enlargements were exhibited on a platform which was set up on the witness box. Walter Anderson, of the chief of State's records branch, identified the typewritten papers as cables received by Foggy Bottom during the first three months of 1938 from American diplomats scattered from Tokyo to Buenos Aires. They covered subjects as unconnected as Manchukuoan finances, Nazi relations with Austria, and British ship-construction plans. The microfilm documents were, in the main, interdepartmental papers from the files of the Trade Agreements Section.

After a Miss Eunice A. Lincoln, Assistant Secretary of State Francis Sayre's private secretary, had identified four of the Baltimore memos as being in the defendant's handwriting, Murphy called Ramos S. Feehan, an FBI typewriter expert. It was the latter's opinion that all but one of the Baltimore documents had been typed on the same machine as letters written by the Hisses during the thirties. Stryker was not prepared to dispute Feehan's conclusions and conceded their accuracy.

With the documents out of the way, Murphy turned to the task of connecting Chambers with their theft from the State Department. For this purpose, he summoned Henry Julian Wadleigh, an Oxford alumnus, who freely admitted that he had begun "to take out documents and give them to unauthorized people as soon as I jointed the State Department." Although he had not given any of the papers in evidence to Whittaker Chambers, he had turned others over to him. However, he insisted that he had limited his thievery to papers which passed over his desk in the Trade Agreements Section. . . .

It took Murphy three weeks to put in his case. Stryker's defense was confined to showing 1.) that Hiss was a man of sterling character, and 2.) that Chambers was as chronic a liar as had ever lived. To prove the first proposition, he paraded to the stand as impressive a group of character witnesses as ever graced an American court. There was John W. Davis, the unsuccessful 1924 Democratic Presidential candidate, Charles Fahy, a former Solicitor General, Admiral Richard Hepburn, and Supreme Court Justices Felix Frankfurter and Stanley Reed. They all agreed that Alger Hiss's reputation "for integrity, loyalty and veracity" was excellent.

These imposing luminaries were followed by Mrs. Claude Catlett, a rather stout Negress, who had worked as a maid for the Hisses during their early days in Washington. She remembered that Chambers had come to the P Street house once and that he had given his name as "Crosby, like in Bing." When her employers had moved to either Thirtieth Street or Volta Place, they had given her children an old typewriter. But Murphy forced her to admit that "I don't remember nothing about the typewriter." In fact, it hadn't been until 1949 that one of her sons told her that they had received a typewriter from the Hisses.

The Catlett boys, Raymond and Perry, succeeded their mother. Raymond had helped Ed McLean trace the machine —an ancient Woodstock—to one Ira Lockey's house where the lawyer had purchased it on April 16, 1949, for $15.00. Raymond had kept the typewriter for a year or two after the Hisses gave it to him and then he had let his brother's wife take it. She had transferred it to his sister and he lost track of it after that until it had been found in Lockey's house. But he was unable to tell Murphy in what month or year he had received the machine. "I haven't got no papers, no secretary to copy all that stuff down," he explained.

Perry Catlett recalled that the Woodstock had been broken when he first saw it. He had taken it to a repair shop in K Street but some man there had told him that it wasn't worth fixing. He was certain that the typewriter had been given to his family when the Hisses moved to Volta Street on December 29, 1936. But when Murphy asked him, "What if I tell you that the shop on K Street wasn't opened for business until September, 1938?" Perry shook his head and replied, "I don't know the time."

When Hiss, neatly dressed in a tan summer suit, finally took the stand, he denied almost everything that Chambers had said on his direct examination. He said that he had known a man named Crosley between 1934 and 1936 but that he had never, until the summer of 1948, ever associated him with Whittaker Chambers. When Stryker asked him if he had ever been a member of the Communist Party "or a fellow traveler or a sympathizer," he quietly answered, "I am not and never have been." He had never given any "restricted, secret or confidential documents of the State Department of any kind" to Chambers "or any other unauthorized person." Stryker, after taking his client from his birth in Baltimore to the high point of his government career as General Secretary to the San Francisco Conference, wound up with a crescendo.

Q. Mr. Hiss, have you entered your formal and solemn plea of not guilty to the charges here against you, have you not?

A. I have.

Q. And in truth and in fact you are not guilty?

A. I am not guilty.

With a perfunctory "your witness," Stryker returned to the counsel table.

Never once during his cross-examination did the prosecutor refer to the defendant as anything but "Mr. Witness." He took

Hiss through the entire period of his acquaintance with Crosley-Chambers, pointing up, in the process, what he obviously regarded as a bold-faced fabrication—the gift of the Twenty-eighth Street apartment and the Ford. As for the Woodstock typewriter, didn't Hiss tell the FBI agents, who had questioned him on December 4, 1948, that he thought that his wife had given it away "subsequent to 1938"? He might have said that but "my knowledge today is that we gave the typewriter to the Catletts at the time when we moved from 30th Street to Volta Place in December, 1937." Finally, after eight long hours, at the end of which he was trying to make some hay out of the fact that the witness had not insisted on a lie detector test, Murphy was through. . . .

Stryker's last witness was a mysterious man who had been sitting just behind the courtroom's rail making copious notes as Chambers was testifying. At Murphy's request, he had been identified on the trial's third day as Dr. Carl Binger, a psychiatrist. After posing a hypothetical question which included every dereliction in Chambers's past life, the defense attorney asked Binger, "Now, assuming the facts as stated in the question to be true and taking into account your knowledge of his writings and translations, have you as a psychiatrist an opinion within the bounds of reasonable certainty as to the mental condition of Whittaker Chambers?" Before Binger could answer, Murphy stormed up to the bench to remind Kaufman that Chambers's credibility was the central issue of the case and that the psychiatrist's answer would be a usurpation of the jury's function. The judge agreed and the good doctor walked out of the courtroom with the answer to Stryker's question locked behind his beetled brow. . . .

Stryker's summation lasted more than four hours. As far as he was concerned, it was simply a question of Chambers's credibility. Murphy, he reminded the jury, had summed it up best himself in his opening when he had said that "... if you don't believe Chambers then we have no case under the federal perjury rule." And who could believe a chronic perjurer, a fornicator, a confessed spy, an atheist, a pornographic poet, and a blasphemer? "The case comes down to this," he told his twelve auditors, "who is telling the truth? Alger Hiss or Chambers?" There was no doubt as to how he had answered this question for himself. "I would not believe Chambers on a stack of Bibles if the FBI stacked them as high as this building!"

Toward the end, Stryker's face was as red as the hand with which he relentlessly pounded the rail of the jury box. "Ladies and gentlemen," he begged them, "if I have done anything that you don't like, if I have offended you, any one of you, in any way, hold it against me, not against Alger Hiss." Exhausted and shaken, he turned slowly and looked toward the counsel table where his impassive client sat. "Alger Hiss, this long nightmare is drawing to a close. Rest well. Your case, your life, your liberty are in good hands. Thank you, ladies and gentlemen."

Murphy, retreating somewhat from his ill-chosen definition of the federal perjury rule, confessed that he wasn't resting his case on Chambers alone. There were the documents and the Woodstock. If Hiss's contradictions about the apartment and the car he had turned over to Chambers weren't convincing enough, how could the handwritten documents be explained away? Even the defense's location of the missing typewriter was suspect—if the FBI couldn't find it, why was it so ridiculously easy for Ed McLean to trace it to Ira Lockey's house? "I submit that two things must be clear; one, that the typewriter was in the possession of the Hiss family until at least Mr. Chambers's defection, until he left the party; and two, that the Catletts had the typewriter for some time after that. . . ."

"We have shown you here," he thundered at the jury, "the

typewriter, the original State Department documents, the documents in this case—three solid witnesses." The dozen or so character witnesses the defendant had put on the stand couldn't change that. "Mr. Stryker said that he was going to call the shade of Oliver Wendell Holmes and have the ghost of that revered Justice testify on behalf of the defendant. And I said to myself, if he is going to call the shade of Justice Holmes, there are a couple of shades that I would like to call here. One man's name was Judas Iscariot and the other's Major General Benedict Arnold." He paused a moment to let that sink in. "But let me dwell a moment on reputation. I dare say that Judas Iscariot had a fairly good reputation. He was one of the Twelve. He was next to God, and we know what he did. Benedict Arnold came from a fine family. He was made a major general and sold out West Point. He wasn't caught. But, if he had been caught, don't you think he could have had George Washington as a reputation witness?"

He was almost through. "You are the second jury to hear this story," he told them. "The Grand Jury heard the same story. The Grand Jury heard this traitor and Mr. Chambers, and that Grand Jury indicted Hiss. It indicted Hiss because he lied. He lied to them and I submit he lied to you. The Grand Jury said he lied twice on December 15th. And as a representative of 150,000,000 people of this country, I ask you to concur in that charge of the Grand Jury. I ask you as a representative of the United States Government to come back and put the lie in that man's face."

The jury retired at 4:20 on the afternoon of July 7th. Six hours later, after their foreman had informed Kaufman that there was no possibility of reaching a verdict that night, the jurors were sent to a hotel. At noon the next day, they filed back into the jury box to listen to Kaufman's repetition of the portion of his charge dealing with corroborative and circumstantial evidence. Three hours later, the foreman asked a bailiff to deliver a note to the judge informing him that "the jury feels that it cannot arrive at a verdict." At 4:45, he forwarded a similar communication. Kaufman begged them to try once more, but at 8:55 they announced the "the jury finds it impossible to reach a verdict." This was enough for Kaufman who discharged them "with the thanks of the court." The trial was over.

Four months later, the United States of America *versus* Alger Hiss encored, this time with District Judge Henry W. Goddard at the helm. Tom Murphy was still around but Stryker had yielded to Claude B. Cross, a quiet, unassuming Boston elder who looked as if he had never pounded a counsel table in his life. A jury of seven women and five men was quickly selected and, on the afternoon of November 19, 1949, the Government began its second go-round in its attempt to convict Alger Hiss of perjury.

With only minor discrepancies, most of the witnesses who had testified at the first trial repeated their stories. But there were parvenus. Goddard was determined to admit any evidence that was vaguely relevant and several of the witnesses who had been rejected by Kaufman were permitted to tell their once-verboten stories. Hede Massing, for instance, said that she had met the defendant in 1935 at the Washington home of Noel Fields, an erstwhile League of Nations official. Mrs. Massing, an ex-Communist, who admitted that "I have a bad memory," stated that she and Hiss had had a conversation as to which one of them was going to win Fields for his cell. . . .

Cross called Dr. Binger back to the wars. The answer to the famous hypothetical question that Kaufman had blocked in July was about to be delivered with Goddard's blessing. Binger waited patiently until the question was in the record, and then, with his eyes on the ceiling, opined that "Mr. Chambers is suffering from a condition known as a psychopathic personality, a disorder of character the distinguishing features of which are amoral and antisocial behavior." One of the most significant symptoms of this malady was "chronic, persistent, and repetitive lying and a tendency to make false accusations." However, he admitted to Murphy that doctors frequently disagreed on diagnosis and that he had been wrong more than once in his own professional life.

On the trial's last day, Murphy produced his one surprise witness—Edith Murray who had worked as a maid for the Chamberses at their two homes in Baltimore from the fall of 1934 to the spring of 1936. She swore that she had seen Mrs. Hiss there four times and the defendant once. However, when she had first been shown a photograph of Mrs. Hiss by FBI agents, she was not quite sure of her identity. "They asked me did I know this lady, and I said it looks like someone that I know. It looked like—I thought maybe it was an actress or something. I say it looks like someone I know, but I just couldn't remember at that time."

On November 17th, the first day of the trial, she had been stationed in the corridor outside of the courtroom. She was told by the FBI agents who had brought her to New York that "all they wanted to do was bring me up here to see if I could recognize the woman that was in the picture and the man on the picture. . . . I just stood out in the hall and it was a crowd of people. They asked me did I see anybody in the crowd that I know, and I looked around, and I didn't see anyone at this time, and stood there; so then, after a while, in the back of me where I was standing was an elevator, in the back of me, like, and I looked around, and then I see Mr. and Mrs. Hiss come over, and right away I knew them."

The jury filed out at 2:50 P.M. on January 20th. On the afternoon of the next day, it found the defendant "guilty on the first count and guilty on the second." Four days later, Goddard sentenced him to five years on each count, the terms to run concurrently. A few minutes earlier, Hiss had thanked his Honor for allowing him to say a few words. He denied again that he was guilty of the charges against him and promised that "in the future the full facts of how Whittaker Chambers was able to carry out forgery by typewriter will be disclosed."

Goddard set $10,000 bail and paroled Hiss in Cross's custody. In December, the Court of Appeals for the Second Circuit affirmed the conviction. When the United States Supreme Court refused to intervene, the last door was closed. On March 22, 1951, Alger Hiss entered the federal penitentiary at Danbury, Connecticut. What Whittaker Chambers once called "the spectacle of tragedy" had run its course.

THE TRIAL OF REIES LOPEZ TIJERINA

Alfonso Sanchez
for the prosecution

vs.

Reies Lopez Tijerina
for the defense

Reies Lopez Tijerina, the Hispanic leader from New Mexico, is one of those charismatic figures who appear at intervals, like meteors, in the American political sky. Called a Robin Hood by some and a thief by others, a saint and a charlatan, man of the people and madman, he remains something of a mystery even to those who knew him best. This selection, based on firsthand knowledge of Tijerina and his Alianza (land-grant movement), tells the almost incredible story of his trial in New Mexico for shooting up a courthouse, kidnaping and assault. It is the only example in this book of self-defense by a defendant on trial, and one of the most surprising stories in American courtroom history.

On 5 June 1967 a band of armed men swept into a remote northern New Mexico courthouse in search of a hated district attorney. The district attorney was not present, but two officers were wounded, the courthouse shot up, and a newsman and deputy kidnapped. Before nightfall, armored, troop-carrying vehicles of the New Mexico National Guard had fanned out across the vast, mountainous area in search of the "insurrectionists." The date has since become the most discussed and debated in the state's history.

The "courthouse raid," as it is now known, brought national reporters into Rio Arriba County in force for the first time; thus it focused national attention on the land grant issue, on fiery land grant leader Reies Lopez Tijerina, and on the plight of New Mexico's Hispanic[1] population.

Tensions produced by the violent event were to simmer without letup until 13 November 1968—the day the authorities moved the continuing struggle with the Hispanic militants into the the establishment's own arena of the courtroom. There, the mercurial Tijerina—eloquent, but with little formal education, and unversed in the law—confronted the man he had sought to "arrest" a year-and-a-half earlier, District Attorney Alfonso Sanchez. The trial, whether evoking memories of Pancho Villa or Zapata, or capturing the imagination

[1]The issue of what to call New Mexico's Hispanic minority is frequently a hot one in the state. "Spanish-speaking" does not necessarily apply, nor does "Spanish-surnamed." Some prefer "Mexican-American," although others are offended by that term and prefer "Spanish-American." "Hispanic" seems the most adequate, although "Chicano" seems to be gaining favor.

of black separatists and campus revolutionaries, was to become the nonviolent equivalent of the confrontation which never occurred at the courthouse.

To understand what was at stake in the flamboyant trial, it is necessary to have some knowledge of New Mexico history, of the land grant issue, and of Reies Tijerina himself. For the courtroom clash was more than a clash between a dominant, legalistic majority and an unregenerate, radical minority.

Contrary to popular belief, the settlement of New Mexico did not first occur in the 1800s with the westward push of American frontiersmen. When the wagon trains and railroads arrived, they found an already flourishing outpost of European culture. The Catholic Church, a legal system, and agricultural settlements were all ongoing operations, implanted in the vast area by earlier Spanish settlers. Starting with the conquistador Coronado, who moved with his men up the Rio Grande valley in 1540, the stream of Spaniards became sizeable. Santa Fe, America's oldest capital, was founded on the site of an existing pueblo in 1610 to administer Spanish affairs throughout the northern province. Other tiny Spanish towns sprang up—almost always with a Catholic church—along the general route of the Rio Grande. Much of this activity occurred long before the American Revolution erupted in the East.

Indeed, even the early Spanish arrivals found a well-established, civilized, and humane society existing in the numerous pueblos along the Rio Grande. The Pueblo Indians, who had settled in their riverside apartment complexes centuries previous, already possessed an agricultural system, a religion, and amazingly sophisticated forms of art, crafts, and music.

These are not only interesting but pertinent facts, for they illustrate that American frontiersmen[2] were indeed latecomers on the scene. When they arrived, the land ownership issue and interrelated social questions already were becoming confused.

The ordinary difficulties of administering a legal system in a frontier setting, following directions from a distant governing authority in Spain, were made even more complex by two facts: that Indians already claimed substantial acreage in the Spanish domain, and that the newly independent nation of Mexico imposed yet another government over the area before the United States moved in.

Mexico, which gained independence from Spain in 1821, ruled the region which is now New Mexico until 1848, when the United States defeated the fledgling nation and took—under the Treaty of Gaudalupe Hidalgo—the Southwest as new American territory.

That the Indians had bona fide land rights, even as far back as Spanish rule, is clear. Under the 1680 code, *Recopilacion de leyes los Reynos de los Indias,* "not only were the Indians to have full possession of all the area which they used or occupied, but they were also to be given more territory if for any reason their lands were insufficient for their needs," according to New Mexico Archivist Myra Ellen Jenkins.[3] She adds: "Unfortunately, the Laws were honored more in the breach than in the observance. The most influential Spaniard in the area

[2]The question of what to call the "Americans" is likewise at issue, and is most frequently resolved with the term "Anglos." "Americans," of course, cannot be a distinction since all residents involved are United States citizens. "Whites" is not a proper characterization. "English-speaking" can apply to both the majority and Hispanic minority. In this account we will use the term "Anglo" to characterize the non-Hispanic American settlers and their contemporary descendants.

[3]"The Baltasar Baca 'Grant': History of an Encroachment," *El Palacio* 68, nos. 1 and 2 (Spring and Summer 1961): 49.

was generally given the post of *alcalde* mayor for political favor."[4] Miss Jenkins, who has made it her career to study the tortured history of land ownership, also notes that the situation did not improve with Mexican independence in 1821: "The Pueblo Indians suffered even worse abuses under the Republic of Mexico, for now virtually all checks were removed. By the Treaty of Cordoba, Indians were granted citizenship and land rights were continued, but nothing was done to implement this provision by specific legislation or orders to the chief executives. . . ."[5]

The wild and woolly frontier days ushered in by the conquest of Mexico proved to be a fertile time for land maneuverings. Newcoming Anglo frontiersmen proved, for the most part, to be more brash, acquisitive, and land-hungry than the generally placid, rural Hispanic settlers. In addition, the Americans brought with them an entirely new legal system and language—two devices which made it relatively easy for land to be gradually eased away, either illegally or through unethical practices, from the Hispanos. The shady maneuverings, and resultant chaos in land negotiations, has been well documented by officials of the period and by latter-day historians. . . .

The scheming and thievery were not simply the practices of unscrupulous outlaws; indeed, the leading figures of the territorial government were known to have been involved. That this was the case was not lost on the (mainly) defenseless Hispanos of the time. Their resentment festered and was passed down through generations. The Hispanic folklore of a century later was to make it much easier for a firebrand orator like Tijerina to rally supporters behind his land-seeking Alianza. . . .

---

[4]Ibid., p. 53.
[5]Ibid., p. 60.

Some observers are surprised that long-ago excesses by American settlers still have the capability of arousing enmity on the part of mid-twentieth century Hispanos. If it were folklore alone that provoked contemporary wrath, one could rightly be startled. The fact is, however, that current land practices—added to those territorial shenanigans—are also a source of constant irritation to Hispanic residents in the northern part of the state. Specifically, the United States Forest Service—largest landholder in northern New Mexico—has exacerbated old wounds with its frequently changing, little understood, often irritating policies concerning grazing on federal land. The presence of large private ranches owned by Anglos—in contrast to tiny plots held by Hispanos—adds to the feelings of anger and resentment.

> The loss of grant lands . . . has been followed by a tendency toward monopoly of "public" lands by powerful private interests. Much of the jointly-owned range and forest lands of Spanish grants was converted into National Forest lands in the late Nineteenth and early Twentieth centuries. In the subsequent policy of leasing these rangelands, preference for large, corporate leasers as against small stockraisers has all but shut Hispano stockmen out from their ancestral rangelands.[6]

The magnitude of contemporary land ownership is illustrated by the fact that 44 percent, or 33.8 million acres, of New Mexico's total acreage of 77.8 million acres is owned by the federal government.[7] Even an "establishment" publication, issued by the New Mexico State Land Office a few years ago, makes the same point frequently made by Tijerina and his

---

[6]Ibid., p. 309.

[7]Report of New Mexico Land Resources Association, "Land Resources of New Mexico," 1959, p. 75.

followers, albeit in bureaucratic language. The Land Office report asserts that "the present magnitude of ownership of lands by the United States" should be "viewed with alarm." The practice "would not seem to be consistent with our democratic form of government."[8]

State government, too, has been remiss. It should be noted that in addition to the complex land grant problem in the north, there is a highly confused land title situation. In some areas, even county lines are not surveyed with care. The absence of clear property boundaries naturally throws land ownership into doubt, making it impossible for poor residents of the area to secure equity for improvement loans. . . .

Finally, there was the fact that taxes under United States rule were levied against land grants as an entirety. But rights to grants were vested in dozens—perhaps as many as a thousand—of heirs. "Thus," says a state government report, "before the 20th Century was well under way, tax sales, forced sales of land to raise cash in the new money economy, and commercial rather than subsistence use of the [area] had deprived the Spanish-American settlements of much of their traditional range and land resource base. For the first time in centuries, many of the Spanish-Americans were forced to leave their native villages. . . ."[9]

All these diverse elements, along with a myriad of social, economic, and cultural deprivations, combined to make northern New Mexico of the 1960s fertile ground for the militant activity of Reies Tijerina. Although many young men leave the area—for Denver, Albuquerque, Los Angeles—to seek jobs, the predominantly old who remain are susceptible to pleas for direct action, especially if the pleas are as eloquent

---

[8]Ibid.

[9]"Embudo, Pilot Planning Project for the Embudo Watershed of New Mexico," published by the Interagency Council for Area Development Planning and the New Mexico State Planning Office, 1961, p. 23.

as those of Tijerina. However complex the analysis of New Mexico's land issue, it is imperative to review some of these facts in order to understand the rise of Tijerina.

What, then, led to the 1967 courthouse raid and the subsequent courtroom engagement between Tijerina and the New Mexico establishment? What manner of man was able to draw to him an unlikely group of would-be revolutionaries around the unlikely issue of land grant restoration?

"Tijerina's character," writes a journalist who knows him as well as anyone, "contains something of the archetypal Robin Hood style of social bandit. Conflicting with his idealistic platform and his expressed adherence to nonviolence is an obvious pride in his wiles as a fugitive. His statements reveal an enjoyment of contests with the law. In this life-gambling some observers have sensed a fatalism, an embracing of the encounter to have done with it, a desperate leap to unload some private demon from his back. Tijerina says it is the concept of Justice which drives him with such unrelenting force."[10] Tijerina, adds the journalist, "became a catalyst for a variety of frustrations he was never fully to comprehend."[11]

Tijerina was born in Falls City, Texas, on 21 September 1926, one of seven children of poor migrant farm workers. He says he picked cotton himself during the Depression, roamed for a time, and ended up at age nineteen in the Latin American District Council of the Assemblies of God Church at Ysleta, Texas. There, he studied to be an evangelist. The superintendent of the fundamentalist school remembers young Tijerina as being "sincere" but "fanatical."[12]

---

[10]Peter Nabokov, "Reflections on the Alianza," *New Mexico Quarterly,* XXXVII, no. 4 (Winter 1968): 351.

[11]Ibid., p. 349.

[12]These and other details of Tijerina's early life are based on conversations with Tijerina himself and with Peter Nabokov, and on numerous press accounts.

"He was fanatical, more peculiar in his thoughts, I guess," recalls the superintendent. "When he went to school he was a very sincere student. I don't know, when he left school he began to get these rather far out ideas about how people ought to conduct themselves." By 1950 Tijerina's ministerial license and credentials had been revoked because of his "unorthodox attitude." The intense, eloquent young man then wandered around Arizona, Utah, and other states "trying to start up religious movements." During one period in his life he spent some time around the Tierra Amarilla area of northern New Mexico, trying to organize a religious sect and "talking to the old people and learning about their land." Fifteen years later, he was to return with his ideas for a solution to the land problem.

After an attempt to start a utopian religious colony near Florence, Arizona, and several scrapes with the law there, Tijerina says he spent time in Mexico—until 1963—doing research into the laws of the Spanish empire and the background of land grants. New Mexicans first became aware of his presence in the state in 1963 and 1964, when he was organizing the *Alianza Federal de Mercedes* ("Federal Alliance of Land Grants"). This organization, made up of alleged heirs to ancient Spanish grants, later was changed to *Alianza Federal de los Pueblos Libres* ("Federal Alliance of Free City-States"). Most, including Tijerina, simply refer to the organization as the "Alianza."

Tijerina is frequently and accurately described as a "fiery land grant leader." His eloquence, especially in the Spanish language, would be difficult to surpass. He has an intense quality about him, even when relaxed, and his eyes are piercing.

In his attempt to organize the poor Hispanos of northern New Mexico, he seized an ideal issue: land.

Land was only a code word, a symbol, for deeper social

problems facing the Hispanos of northern New Mexico. Governor David F. Cargo told a congressional subcommittee after the raid that "a century of broken promises led to the rebellious act in northern New Mexico." "These people," the governor added, "are losing faith in the democratic process."[13] At another time, Cargo explained: "Contrary to what people have said, the whole thing does not turn around the matter of land grant rights. It involves a hundred other problems . . . from grazing on national forests to disrepair of roads. All he [Tijerina] did was set it off."[14] One of the authors, a Santa Fe journalist at the time, observed: "Underneath, waiting for years to be played upon, were resentments resulting from generations of putting up with unpaved roads, run-down schools, sorry health facilities, and politicians who played upon ignorance.[15]

During 1966 and early 1967 Tijerina and his Alianzans were involved in several confrontations with authorities. Most, such as the attempt to take over a Forest Service campground at Echo Amphitheater and the corresponding "arrest" of Forest Rangers, were designed to dramatize the Alianza's claims to land. Specifically, Tijerina claimed for the Alianza the so-called San Joaquin del Rio de Chama grant in northern Rio Arriba County. As June 1967 approached the Alianza planned a large meeting of land grant "heirs" at the tiny community of Coyote. The night before the meeting, however, a number of Alianza members were arrested on various charges.

As a direct result of the arrest—and also to demonstrate the Alianza's authority in matters of law—members of the organization, including Tijerina, swooped down on the pink adobe

---

[13] *Albuquerque Journal,* UPI, 15 June 1967.
[14] *Sante Fe New Mexican,* 8 June 1967.
[15] Ibid., 16 June 1967.

courthouse at Tierra Amarilla. They sought to "arrest" District Attorney Alfonso Sanchez, who had carried on what they saw as a vendetta against Tijerina.

The courthouse was shot up, its occupants held captive for some two hours, two officers were shot and wounded, and a deptuy and a United Press International newsman were kidnapped. The raiders then fled into the mountainous countryside—all without encountering District Attorney Sanchez, who was in Santa Fe at the time. The "raid" and its aftermath became the biggest story in New Mexico. Reporters from the two Albuquerque dailies, the national networks, and national publications such as the *New York Times* drove into the north, looking bewildered. The National Guard, called out by a jittery Lieutenant Governor E. Lee Francis in the absence of Governor Cargo, swarmed over the region in armored vehicles—most unsuitable for conducting a manhunt in the vast, almost roadless, area. The reaction to the manhunt and to the actions of officers was almost as strong as reaction to the raid itself. While most New Mexicans used terms like "insurrection" and "shocking outlawry," Professor Clark Knowlton, a scholar of Hispanic affairs, shot back the charge that "the National Guard and State Police violated the Spanish-Americans' civil rights . . . when they 'systematically broke into homes, lined the people up, searched them and confined men, women, and children for many hours in a dirty sheep pen.' "[16] In Denver, Hispanic militant Rudolph "Corky" Gonzales said the use of troops was "an act of imperialistic aggression."[17]

District Attorney Sanchez, who all along had been citing "evidence" of "Communist influence" in the Alianza's actions, felt he had been vindicated. Among items confiscated when Tijerina and his colleagues were finally captured were

[16] *Albuquerque Journal,* UPI, 17 June 1967.
[17] *Albuquerque Tribune,* UPI, 8 June 1967.

maps of the area showing "prime objectives for seizure," an organization chart, gas masks, guns, books including *Rise and Fall of the Third Reich* and *Che Guevara on Guerrilla Warfare.*[18]

What the *Albuquerque Journal* called "one of the state's most noted criminal cases" got under way on 12 November 1968, in a paneled, carpeted, heavily guarded courtroom of the Bernalillo County Courthouse in downtown Albuquerque. Reporters, visiting high school classes, hangers-on, and Alianza sympathizers packed the galleries. District Court Judge Paul Larrazolo, a slight, nervous man whose father had once been governor of New Mexico, was plainly ill at ease. He had reason to be. Assembled before him were District Attorney Sanchez and his assistants, Tijerina and nine of his co-defendants, and a diverse array of defense lawyers. In addition to court-appointed New Mexico attorneys, there was legal counsel representing the nation's radical community, whose attention Tijerina had drawn: Beverly Axelrod, one-time friend of Eldridge Cleaver, and bearded, booming, California civil liberties lawyer John Thorne. . . .

Tijerina and the other nine defendants were to be tried on three charges each: kidnapping (which carries a possible death penalty), assault on the Rio Arriba County jail, and false imprisonment of Deputy Sheriff Daniel Rivera. The other defendants were Jerry Noll (self-styled "King of the Indies"); Tijerina's son, Reyes Hugh Tijerina of Albuquerque; Baltazar Martines, Moises Morales, Juan Valdez, Tobias Leyba, and Solomon Velasques of Canjilon; Jose Madril of Velarde; and Esequiel Dominguez of Bernalillo.

One of us talked with Tijerina at his cavernous Alianza

---

[18]Ibid., 7 June 1967.

headquarters in Albuquerque an hour before the trial began. He was plainly nervous, uncertain of what would happen and of his own capability in the new, legalistic arena. He made it clear that he regarded the trial as but one more instrument in the establishment's arsenal. The whole procedure, he said, "was only one more act in the oppression of the Spanish people." Stirring restlessly in his chair, Tijerina seemed alternately remote, distracted, then excitable. He appeared uncomfortable in his green sport coat, green tie, and white shirt. Somewhat incongruously, he also wore slightly scuffed, high-topped black work shoes.

His discomfort appeared to increase once he entered the courtroom. By contrast, his old adversary "Al" Sanchez—the district attorney who regards Tijerina as a Communist and worse—seemed quietly efficient, almost smug. Finally, after more than three years of inconclusive jousting, Sanchez had Tijerina before the bench—required to answer for his militant activities and his continuing challenges of the status quo.

The trial was important beyond the specific charges involved. First, it pitted Tijerina and his archenemy Sanchez in direct battle. Long the most vociferous critic of Tijerina and his Alianza, Sanchez had called loudly and frequently for the land grant leader's detention, and had spread by means of various news media his belief that Communistic influences were at work. Tijerina, for his part, regarded Sanchez (and United States Senator Joseph Montoya) as the Hispano who had "sold out," who had abandoned his heritage to "make it" in the Anglo establishment. Worse, he had turned on *los pobres* ("poor Hispanos") rather than championing their cause.

Second, public opinion throughout the state was enraged by the raid. Editorial writers and citizens in the street called for Tijerina to be "locked up," legal niceties and procedural detail notwithstanding. Tijerina became the target for reactionary denunciations from law officers, public officials, and New

Mexico citizens who were disturbed about urban and campus rebellion elsewhere around the country. He was the local manifestation of hated and feared revolution, the antithesis of law, order, and complacency. Having declined to petition for grievances within normal channels, Tijerina must now submit to the awesome judgment of the law. Thus, the trial became the arena for the protectors of the status quo to assert their full authority over the unregenerate minority.

The trial, then, was for Reies Tijerina a personal confrontation (with Sanchez) and another contest in his continuing struggle against the establishment. Placed in formal, almost austere surroundings, denied the friendly atmosphere of rural Rio Arriba County, denied even his most formidable weapon —the use of fiery Spanish-language rhetoric—Tijerina obviously did not relish the encounter.

The confrontation became direct four days after the trial opened as Judge Larrazolo announced his decision to sever Tijerina's trial from those of nine co-defendants. He acted on the strength of a memorandum from Robert Singer, assistant district attorney in Albuquerque, which concluded that the court could—and should—sever the cases. "The antagonisms developing between prosecuting attorneys and the numerous counsel for the defendants, and among the defense attorneys themselves, seem to foreshadow irreconcilable conflicts at the trial," the memorandum stated. "The situation, if left unaltered, will surely prevent both the state and the defendants from obtaining a fair trial."[19]

Four days of argumentation, motions, and jury selection were thrown out when the announcement came. The Tijerina–State of New Mexico battle was stripped of its distracting elements. "I've given a lot of thought about the manner in

---

[19] *Albuquerque Journal,* 19 November 1968.

which we are progressing on a joint basis in selecting a jury," the judge said. "The court has come to the conclusion that there is a tremendous imposition on court-appointed counsel to continue with this case on a joint basis, that the cost to the State of New Mexico is not justifiable, that even perhaps the interest of all the defendants from the point of view of getting a fair trial all together is not the best."

District Attorney Sanchez declared that the severance was granted "over strenuous objections from the state." But Larrazolo, harassed to his wit's end by the jumble of defense motions, intramural arguments, and disputes over even the most minute points by the battery of lawyers welcomed the opportunity to sever the case.

Tijerina, it should be noted, preferred the severance. Although he did not say so publicly, he indicated indirectly that he was beginning to feel more confident. After four days of watching the powerful legal apparatus of the state become entrapped in a morass of technical confusion, Tijerina appeared to be gaining confidence that he could, just perhaps, beat the state with the force and clarity of his own eloquence.

Two days later, the showdown became even more direct: Tijerina announced abruptly what he had only hinted at before—that he would act as his own attorney in the trial. The announcement came after more than a week of desultory maneuverings, and yet before jury selection had been completed. It obviously caught Tijerina's attorneys by surprise. "The job of a lawyer is to represent his client and I want time to discuss this with Mr. Tijerina," attorney Thorne told Larrazolo. The judge agreed to allow Tijerina to defend himself, but ordered that court-appointed attorneys Beverly Axelrod and Gene Franchini remain as advisers. The ever-more-confident Tijerina objected to this, too. He said he was "reserving my right to dismiss these attorneys at any time." The one-time migrant cottonpicker and wandering evangelist obviously was regaining his composure, losing his fear of the formal surroundings, and finding himself eager to test his powers of oration in the courtroom. Severing of the trial, he announced, had made his attorneys "obsolete." But he insisted that he needed "a few days" to prepare his case.

Larrazolo, growing increasingly impatient with the slow pace of the exasperating trial, told Tijerina sharply: "I don't want to hear any speeches from you. I just want to know if you want to represent yourself." When Tijerina said he would "give my answer in a few days," Larrazolo retorted that the land grant leader would have exactly thirty minutes to respond. Added prosecuting attorney Jack Love, assistant to Sanchez: "We can't wait until Tijerina learns how to conduct a criminal case."

Surprisingly, Alfonso Sanchez did not seem to jump at the chance of meeting his old adversary face-to-face in his, Sanchez's, own arena. During most of the trial, in fact, Sanchez sat quietly, making notes and conferring with E. E. Chavez and Jack Love, his assistants. Love, indeed, carried most of the load in arguments and cross-examination. Sanchez perhaps was reluctant to meet Tijerina in a test of oratorical ability; or perhaps he simply was so confident of victory that he preferred to sit quietly and not rock the boat. In such a way, the drama between Tijerina and Sanchez actually was heightened: Tijerina, self-assertive, growing more confident—perhaps cocky—pacing, using the rhetoric that evoked images of tent revivals and migrant farm camps; Sanchez, quiet, with an air of condescension, making his little notes and appearing serene, no matter what was happening within. One thing he did not attempt to hide was his ever-prevalent, intense personal dislike of Tijerina. . . .

After the stage was set for direct battle, the trial took a meandering course. Reporters, including one of the authors, found it extremely difficult to predict a possible outcome. As Peter Nabokov wrote, Judge Larrazolo "apparently felt his court sinking into a legal bog." Tijerina surprised almost everyone with his adroit handling of the case—aided, to be sure, by Thorne, Miss Axelrod, and close legal adviser William Higgs. But it was Tijerina himself who, through shrewd cross-examination, succeeded in making the state's case appear a bit shaky. Sanchez and Chavez, probably more familiar than any lawyers with the entire case, never seemed to get the prosecution rolling. Jack Love, the bright and able assistant who had recently joined the case, was not as well prepared as he should have been.

One of the prosecution's main witnesses was Pete Jaramillo of Expanola, now sheriff of the county, the deputy who was held hostage during the raid. Jaramillo, in his testimony, placed Tijerina at the scene. He said Tijerina held a rifle to his ribs and gave orders to other armed men at the courthouse. "Reies Lopez Tijerina came behind me and put a gun in my ribs and said 'Where's Alfonso Sanchez? Tell me, you son-of-a-bitch, or I'll kill you,' " Jaramillo testified.

But Tijerina, throughout the days of testimony, sought to place doubts about the time he actually arrived at the courthouse (he said it was after the raid had begun), and whether he was—beyond doubt—guilty of the specific charges brought by the state.

In a more interesting tactic, he continually advanced the notion that citizens may make "arrests" of guilty persons—even authorities themselves (such as Sanchez). His deeper point was not missed by the intent Hispanos who sat in the gallery: that, in the land grant areas, the Alianza—not the state—is the law. If men got shot and a courthouse damaged in the process of making a legitimate "arrest" that was too bad.

Tijerina drew out this contention further when cross-examining State Policeman Juan Santistevan. The officer had testified he was approaching the courthouse on 5 June when men started shooting at him. A bullet hit the windshield of his car; he backed the vehicle behind a house and ran for cover.

"Did you know that citizens of the United States could arrest an officer if they believed they had a grievance against him?" Tijerina asked. "No," replied Santistevan. "Isn't it possible," asked Tijerina further, that "these people, pushed to the brink of desperation, had to teach you a lesson, teach you what you were not taught by your superiors?"

Undaunted, Tijerina did not miss an opportunity to pursue this point throughout the trial. He knew that if the "citizen's arrest" theory could be vindicated, it would have the short-range practical effect of making the raid—in search of Sanchez—plausible. Further, it would secure him a valuable legal weapon in his efforts to secure Alianza hegemony over territory within the "free city states." As every witness ascended to the paneled witness stand, he hammered home his point as to the plight of a people "pushed to the brink of desperation" and using the common law right available to every citizen to obtain redress.

To make matters worse for Sanchez and the prosecution, witnesses at the courthouse failed to come through with the clear-cut, dramatic testimony that was expected. On 3 December, in fact, when the state rested its case, a Rio Arriba County under-sheriff seemed to take the steam out of an already sputtering prosecution case. The undersheriff, sixty-eight-year-old Daniel Rivera, told the jury he had not heard Tijerina order him to be pistolwhipped. "I'm not blaming you for anything, sir," he told Tijerina.

As the trial proceeded into December and neared a close, it became even more difficult to predict the outcome. National attention was focused on the trial. The state press, particularly the Albuquerque dailies and television stations, provided extensive and daily coverage. Although editorial comment was not forthcoming, those familiar with New Mexico newspapers knew there was strong sentiment among editors for a conviction on all three counts. If halfway talk was a fair indication, New Mexico reporters at the scene seemed to feel the state could get a conviction on only one or possibly two charges—not all three. Meanwhile, the nation's underground and left-wing press were keeping a close watch on Albuquerque. The *National Guardian,* a leftist publication, wrote on December 14: "The trial of Tijerina for crimes supposedly committed in the Tierra Amarilla Courthouse 'raid' of 5 June 1967, finally got down to the real issues: the oppression and exploitation of the Indo-Hispano people. At the same time, Tijerina's legal chances also seemed to be improved."

The *Guardian* also cast aspersions on District Attorney Sanchez's refusal to take the witness stand himself, at Tijerina's request. It noted with approval this vignette, which occured on 5 December: "A group of young people including members of Los Comancheros del Norte (a rural version of the Brown Berets) picketed outside the courthouse with signs saying 'Sanchez is afraid of Tijerina.' These signs were seized by the state to be entered as evidence. Then, in a dramatic courtroom scene, a Comanchero strode up to the judge to demand their return—and got them."[20]

Finally, on Friday the thirteenth, after a month of seemingly inconclusive testimony, Judge Larrazolo prepared to instruct the jury. His instructions, although perhaps not directly affecting the jury's verdicts, certainly were regarded with amazement by New Mexico legal practitioners, and with delight by Tijerina and his sympathizers in the state and around the coun-

[20]*National Guardian,* 14 December 1968.

try. The instructions seemed to give particular sanction to the concept of "citizen's arrest."

Those instructions read:

> The Court instructs the jury that citizens of New Mexico have the right to make a citizen's arrest under the following circumstances:
> (1) If the arresting person reasonably believes that the person arrested, or attempted to be arrested, was the person who committed, either as a principal or as an aider and abettor, a felony; or
> (2) If persons who are private citizens reasonably believe that a felony has been committed, and that the person who is arrested or attempted to be arrested was the person committing, or aiding and abetting, said felony.
> The court instructs the jury that a citizen's arrest can be made even though distant in time and place from the acts constituting or reasonably appearing to constitute the commission of the felony. The Court further instructs the jury that a citizen's arrest may be made whether or not law enforcement officers are present, and, further, may be made in spite of the presence of said law enforcement officers.
> The Court instructs the jury that anyone, including a State Police Officer, who intentionally interferes with a lawful attempt to make a citizen's arrest does so at his own peril, since the arresting citizens are entitled under the law to use whatever force is reasonably necessary to defend themselves in the process of making said citizen's arrest.[21]

[21]Quoted in full, *The New Mexico Review and Legislative Journal,* 30 January 1969, p. 3.

These words were startling enough to the courtroom observers, but in a few hours they were overshadowed by the surprise verdict: "not guilty" on all three counts. . . .

Later, in a talk with one of the authors at a Santa Fe cafe, Tijerina talked further about his court victory:

"First, it was a great example for a terrified people who had been in captivity for more than 470 years." The state, he said, "threw all the organized power that the taxpayers have built up to crack the people of the mountains. They got me into court. I took it on myself to beat them in their own game. Now everyone knows that the cops are subject to citizens' arrest, just like criminals. The establishment is cracked already—it's like the Liberty Bell. They thought I was going to break down under court entanglements, court threats, court action. But I didn't. I go for court action now. I love it."[22]

He vowed to carry on with his land grant activities, claiming his (almost) single-handed victory in the courts had increased his popularity among northern Hispanos. He gleefully told the *New York Times:* "My philosophy is that of the cricket against the lion. The cricket is the king of the insects and the lion is the king of beasts. The cricket had no chance against the lion, so he jumped into the lion's ear and tickled him to death. That's what we're going to do to the United States—we're going to tickle him to death."[23] . . .

If there was jubilance among the militants, there was consternation among New Mexico officials and middle class citizens. Reporter Ed Meagher, who covered the trial for the *Los Angeles Times-Washington Post* service, wrote: "New Mexico was in a state of shock . . . following the acquittal . . . of Reies Lopez Tijerina."[24] The *Washington Post* account read: "The

[22]Interview with Carrol W. Cagle in Santa Fe, New Mexico, 27 May 1969.

[23]*New York Times,* 19 December 1968.

[24]*San Francisco Sunday Examiner & Chronicle,* 22 December 1968.

acquittal of Reies Lopez Tijerina . . . has stunned New Mexico's officialdom."[25]

The *New Mexican,* a Santa Fe daily, editorialized: "The recent trial . . . was a travesty on our New Mexico system of law enforcement. The lengthy and costly trial did little, if anything, to uphold law and order in New Mexico.

And, perhaps worst of all, it will lend encouragement to men like Tijerina to stir racial unrest and hatred."[26]

Alfonso Sanchez was a beaten man, and did not hide it. The previous August, he had been defeated in the Democratic primary election; thus he knew that the Tijerina case would be his last one as district attorney. Voters apparently were strongly dissatisfied with Sanchez's poor performance in a highway scandal case (he lost on a legal technicality), and with his intemperate but incompetent attack on the Alianza. Rather than lash out bitterly, Sanchez remained quiet, as if in a state of shock. About the only public comment he made was to tell the Associated Press a few days later that the state should have the right to appeal questions of law in criminal cases. Speaking of the defendants, Sanchez said: "Law forces us to give everything to them and they don't have to reciprocate."[27]

Sanchez, in a later interview with one of the authors after leaving office, went into further detail on the trial. "Everything is over-balanced in favor of the defendant," he said. He cited what he called "sympathy" for Tijerina on the part of the jurors.

Then he detailed his contention that the Tierra Amarilla raid did not have to occur in the first place. He recalled that, before the raid, Tijerina already was wanted on another war-

[25] *Washington Post,* 16 December 1968.
[26] *Santa Fe New Mexican,* 16 December 1968.
[27] *Albuquerque Journal,* 18 December 1968.

rant, but had not been picked up. "I knew that as long as Tijerina was out, that someone was going to do something," Sanchez said. "I could just tell that man had a one-track mind." Sanchez explained that he had learned the morning of 5 June that Tijerina was at the home of Tobias Leyba in Canjilon. He called State Police Chief Joe Black and urged an arrest to be made.

Black replied, according to Sanchez, that he would have to have search warrants to go to Leyba's house. The warrants were ready by noon, but never were picked up, Sanchez said. "That's where Cargo came in, you know. They were wheeling and dealing," Sanchez declared. He refused to elaborate, but indicated that the governor—who had long disputed Sanchez's tactics concerning the Alianza—refused to enforce the law strictly, and instead intervened to try to "cool things off." Such tactics, Sanchez said, do not work with Tijerina.

"History proves I was right," said Sanchez. "Tierra Amarilla shouldn't have happened, really. This guy is crazy and I've said that all along." He said he told Governor Cargo the morning of 5 June: "Look, you're dealing with a crazy man. You don't know what you're dealing with."

Asked what he sees next for Tijerina, Sanchez replied: "A guy like that has got a one-track mind. He's built a monster and doesn't know how to handle it."[28]

Although Tijerina took the "citizen's arrest" instructions of Larrazolo to heart (in June 1969 he tried unsuccessfully to arrest Cargo, Los Alamos atomic scientists, and Chief Justice Warren Burger), there is evidence that the jurors themselves paid little heed to the instructions as such. Instead, the majority seemed to feel that the state failed to prove beyond doubt that Tijerina was guilty of the specific charges involved.

---

[28]Interview with Carrol W. Cagle in Santa Fe, 15 June 1969.

Only one juror indicated that the state absolutely proved its case, but said it was impossible to try to convince his colleagues. These comments were published 22 December 1968, in the *Albuquerque Journal.*

Jury foreman Charles Burand was quoted as saying: "I think the general consensus of the jury . . . was that there was not enough evidence and so much of the evidence was in conflict, that we thought we could not convict him beyond a reasonable doubt."

Another juror, Mrs. Willard Tennison, said, "We read the instructions over and over. We discussed each one and finally all decided there was not enough evidence to convict." She added that no one seemed to arrive at his or her decision on the basis of "fear." "A lot of people think that we did it because we were afraid," she said, "but none of us felt that way at all." Three jury members, said the *Journal,* believed Tijerina was completely innocent. But most, the newspaper said, shared the feeling of Mrs. Andrew Johnson: "We thought he was behind it, but there was nothing we could do about it. We tried awfully hard but couldn't come up with a thing as far as the charges on which he was tried were concerned. That's what made us so sick."

Many agreed that Tijerina was a "pretty good" attorney for himself. Mary Hochstatter put it this way: "The man has a fantastic mind, and he did an unbelievable job for not being an attorney."[29]

The acquittal seemed, at first, to provide a much-needed boost for the Alianza and for Tijerina personally. The land grant issue had begun to drag, and Tijerina spent much of his time involved in numerous state and federal court proceedings

[29]*Albuquerque Journal,* 22 December 1968.

stemming from several minor confrontations. But the surprising acquittal seemed to give the land grant leader new strength. Smiling broadly, pacing frantically, he tossed out ideas for new Alianza programs. In addition to announcing plans to organize garbage collectors and sue the board of education, he was sharply critical of the 1969 Legislature for forcing New Mexico out of Medicaid, the health care program for the poor.

Still, Tijerina seemed to lack enthusiasm for these more "acceptable" goals. He seemed to yearn to get back to the land grant issue, but months went by before the Alianza returned to the north in numbers.

Then, on 5 June 1969—the second anniversary of the raid—some one hundred Alianzans began a camp-out near Coyote in Rio Arriba County. Signs appeared on boulders near roadways and on makeshift signboards proclaiming "San Joaquin: A Free City State." Armed members of the Brown Berets, a militant band of youthful Hispanos, guarded the entrance to the secluded campground. Tijerina and a few others sported big, colorful, Zapata-style sombreros. Shotguns and pearl-handled revolvers were in evidence.

One of the authors camped with the Alianzans, and heard Tijerina explain his summer goals: a cattle drive across Forest Service land to dramatize Alianza land claims, construction of a "municipal building" for the San Joaquin Free City-State, organization of a private "security force" to enforce Alianza laws within the area. He warned that interlopers could be treated "severely." "There's no way," he said, "the government or the state can interfere with our police. Any state policeman interfering or questioning our police will be in violation of the law. He will be considered a threat. . . . These guys will be subject to immediate arrest. We're serious. We will act immediately and severely. We're not going to start any trouble, but we're not going to stand for any foolishness either." Underscoring his claims to the land, he declared: "If you have private land, you have the absolute right to protect it."[30]

Still, there seemed to be an irresolute, desultory atmosphere about the gathering. Tijerina and those close to him kept intimating that "something" would happen, without specifying what. The much-mentioned cattle drive never became reality.

Finally, on Saturday afternoon, 7 June, there seemed to be a rapid change of mood. Apparently tiring of doing nothing, and realizing that the news play of his camp-out was dropping off, Tijerina announced abruptly that the Alianza would make "arrests" of Governor Cargo and an unspecified number of atomic scientists at nearby Los Alamos. Tijerina was angered by Cargo's criticism of a Presbyterian national council plan to give sizeable acreage in northern New Mexico to "recognized" Hispano organizations (not the Alianza). Tijerina's logic was unclear; he seemed merely to be searching for an anti-Cargo issue. The scientists would be arrested, Tijerina explained, for their part in devising "instruments of destruction."

Thus began a tumultuous, confusing sequence of events. The two reporters on the scene telephoned the story to their Albuquerque offices; Tijerina's announcement was being broadcast and published within an hour. State Police whisked Cargo—who was not even at the state capital—away by airplane to an undisclosed place. Los Alamos authorities prepared for trouble. As the twenty-five-car Alianza caravan pulled out of the camp-ground, the situation began to develop aspects of a slapstick comedy. First, Tijerina's car radio picked up the news that Cargo, their first target, had been spirited

[30]Interview with Carrol W. Cagle near Coyote, 7 June 1969.

away. So the caravan pulled over while discussions took place as to what to do next. It was decided to go instead to Los Alamos to arrest the unnamed "scientists." When the caravan stopped temporarily because of car trouble, one of us asked Tijerina how he expected to find atomic scientists and to know who they were. "We'll just have to go door-to-door, I guess," he replied.

It sounded like a joke, but it might not have been. Upon arriving in the scientific research town, the curious-looking caravan wandered aimlessly for a time and then ended up at the laboratory's museum. Tijerina was met by the chairman of the county council, Del Sundberg, who explained that he would like to help but there were no scientists around. It was, after all, a Saturday afternoon, he explained.

Tijerina told Sundberg he had a "warrant" for the arrest of scientists, but didn't know who should receive it. Sundberg told Tijerina the director of the laboratory, Norris Bradbury, would be the logical person, but that he did not know where to find him. With that, Tijerina and his ragtag caravan drove off, searching for a telephone booth and a directory to ascertain Bradbury's address. Once this was accomplished, the Alianzans discovered they had no idea where the address was located, so a helpful group of curious Los Alamos teenagers agreed to lead the caravan. The situation did not improve once the caravan and its entourage of hangers-on reached Bradbury's residence. Tijerina strode to the door, knocked purposefully, and waited confidently while news cameras whirred. No one answered. He knocked again. Still no one. He rang the door bell. It was obvious that if anyone were home, the door was not being answered. With that, Tijerina was reduced to placing the "warrant" in Bradbury's mail box and leaving. The caravan dissolved. "Ludicrous," reporters said. Neighbors shook their heads in wonderment.

Before the weekend ended, Tijerina was arrested on a minor charge when his wife, Patsy, set fire to a Forest Service sign. And he ended in federal detention, at least temporarily, when bond for a previous offense was revoked. There were signs that the movement was losing steam, and worse, credibility. Tijerina seemed to recognize this, but did not know how to cope with the flagging effort. It would be a mistake, however, to count the fiery orator out as a bona fide leader of the poor Hispanos of northern New Mexico. Those who love him really love him. And he is a magnetic, engaging man with many appealing qualities. The question now is whether he can translate his personal strength into a viable, vital movement. Land is his dream, and the dream of his followers. His slogan, starkly presented on posters, may someday become reality. The posters say: *"Tierra o Muerte,"* "Land or Death."

THE COURT-MARTIAL OF BILLY MITCHELL

Allen Gullion
for the prosecution

vs.

Frank R. Reid
for the defense

by Joseph Di Mona

American courtrooms have often been the forums for debates addressed more to the country at large than to the judge and jury. This is also true—although instances are more rare—of military courtrooms. In the justly famous court-martial of Billy Mitchell, brilliantly described below by Joseph Di Mona, the famous World War I air ace virtually forced his own trial for "conduct of a nature to bring discredit on the military service" in order to bring the case for air power before the American people. His defeat in court was foreordained; but so, perhaps, was the ultimate victory of his military philosophy.

The dirigible *Shenandoah,* the most beautiful of the Navy's lighter-than-air craft, rose gracefully above the Lakehurst, New Jersey, Naval Air Station, beginning a goodwill flight over cities, towns, and state fairs in the Midwest. As the ship took to the air, one man, Zachary Lansdowne, the *Shenandoah*'s commander, did not share in the satisfaction of the smooth takeoff. He was worried. Squalls and storms had been reported over the Great Lakes area, and in 1925 there was no meteorological service to advise pilots which way storms were moving. Lansdowne, experienced in dirigibles, knew that it was murder to take one even *near* a squall. He had protested to his superiors but had gotten nowhere—in the opinion of the Navy brass the route of the *Shenandoah* would not cross the path of the storm. His protests disallowed, Lansdowne had given the orders and the great helium-filled ship had soared from her resting place and headed west.

It was, by later accounts, a lovely evening. Down below, people on farms and streets could see the running lights of the *Shenandoah* passing overhead like a grand constellation. But the *Shenandoah* was not a constellation, it was a flying machine. And the machine was not perfect. A few months before she had been partially disabled in an accident and many of her safety valves had been carried away. They had not been replaced. Furthermore, one of her engines, over the bitter objections of her designer, Jerome Hunsaker, had been removed completely. Yet as long as the air was smooth, all was serene. Lansdowne gave final instructions to the lieutenant at the controls and went to bed.

About three in the morning one of the crewmen on watch

saw lightning to the east. By the time the commander had been called, lightning was flickering on both sides of the ship and the *Shenandoah* was bucking stiff headwinds. From their altitude of about 3,000 feet, Lansdowne directed the ship to 2,000 feet, but even with engines full ahead, the ship made little headway. Suddenly, the ship rose in the freshening winds, her nose pointing down. Lansdowne ordered safety valves opened to bleed off the gas which distended at higher altitudes. But despite the engines, the safety valves, and the frantic efforts of the men at the controls, the ship continued to rise.

The safety level for helium-filled dirigibles was 3,800 feet. Above that the gas expanded so much that a ship could burst. Helplessly the *Shenandoah* rose past that altitude, and even higher. To 5,000 feet. To 6,000 feet, and the center of the squall. Then the ship suddenly dropped like a rock, 3,-200 feet in a minute and a half. Lansdowne was prepared; his men emptied water ballast and saved the ship from crashing.

Hearts hammering, the men looked down from the bucking, pitching cabin to the stormswept countryside below. The ship nosed down, then rose again. And suddenly the controls were useless against the strength of the squall. The ship rolled, turned, spun, throwing everyone in the cabin about. Rising once more breathtakingly, the ship, with a terrible noise, suddenly split. Girders tore, the skin pulled apart, and the men spilled out to the ground, 6,200 feet below. The ship literally tore in half, the tail section floating in great circles to the earth, with men leaping through holes as the fragments approached the ground. The bow section came down minutes later, bearing a cargo of death. Some men miraculously survived the terrible fall. But not Commander Lansdowne.

In the aftermath of the tragedy, Secretary of the Navy Dwight Williams in Washington had soothing words. The accident had proved, he announced, that the nation need fear no attack from enemy aircraft. Flying was simply too hazardous.

In San Antonio, Texas, another high official had a quite different reaction. General William ("Billy") Mitchell, air ace of World War I, apostle of air power, and gadfly to generals wedded to infantry and admirals infatuated with battleships, had finally had enough. The *Shenandoah* disaster followed closely on another ill-conceived program in which three totally unsuitable craft had been sent on a flight from Los Angeles to Hawaii. All three had crashed, proving to the Navy that airpower was a myth and flying suitable only to stunt men and maniacs. Mitchell had been fighting this attitude for years, and the *Shenandoah* became his Rubicon. He called a press conference and handed out the following release:

"I have been asked from all parts of the country to give my opinion about the reasons for the frightful aeronautic accidents and loss of life, equipment, and treasure that has occurred during the last few days.

"My opinion is as follows: These accidents are the direct result of the incompetency, criminal negligence, and almost treasonable administration of our national defense by the Navy and War Departments."

The words burst on Washington like a star shell and illuminated officers who had hated Mitchell for a long time. Now, at last he was in their hands. A court-martial was ordered.

Billy Mitchell came from a famous family. His grandmother had founded one of the great banks in the nation; his father had been a U.S. senator. But it was not banking or law to which the young Mitchell was drawn. He became enchanted with the wooden crates which daring men were attempting to fly and saw in them possibilities so vast they frightened him.

When World War I came along, he volunteered to lead America's small group of flying men.

To make certain he got the assignment, Mitchell went to Paris even before America entered the war. He studied the French and English aircraft and worked out possibilities for their use. The Allies had used aircraft merely as observation planes for artillery spotting and intelligence. Mitchell felt they could attack with bombs and machine guns.

General Pershing did not agree, but he was too good a general to pass up new ideas. As Mitchell's constant badgering bothered him, he placed another officer over Mitchell to keep him in line and to exploit whatever good notions he had. And so Mitchell got his chance. In the battle of Saint Mihiel he sent over waves of aircraft, 1,500 of them, so many they literally "blackened the skies" according to an awed infantryman. Strafing and bombing, they helped to make the battle a stunning success. Pershing graciously gave credit to the airmen.

Mitchell came back from the war a hero. He had been the first American officer under enemy fire, the first to fly over enemy lines, the first to be given a *Croix de Guerre.* He was the very model of the gay, insouciant, reckless pilot, and the American people took him to their hearts. His face became as well known to them as any movie star's, and he was always referred to as "Billy."

But the war was over—and it had been the war to end all wars. America had not an enemy in sight and no desire to keep millions of men in uniform or spend millions of dollars on defense. When Mitchell arrived in Washington, he found that his fledgling air force, part of the Army, was the first to feel the effects of cutbacks. He soon had just a few pilots and airmen, and only a small scattering of planes, all left over from World War I.

The entrenched powers in the military were the old-line generals and admirals. The generals tolerated him for a time.

But the admirals soon developed a bristling feud. What brought it on was Mitchell's brash statement to the public and to Congress that the battleship was useless against air power. The thought that a flimsy wooden crate in the air could challenge a great steel battleship was anathema to any right-thinking admiral.

So an epic test was arranged. Great steel ships, captured from the Germans, were to be moored off Norfolk, Virginia, and attacked by Mitchell's air fleet. Mitchell set to work with a fury. First he needed bombs, bombs bigger than any that had ever been manufactured. He got them designed and built in three months. Then his pilots had to be trained. No aircraft had ever attacked a battleship before. Should you attempt to hit the ship squarely? Or burst the bombs in the water beside her, hoping to open the seams? Mitchell planned both.

For weeks the newspapers heralded the coming test, and the admirals supplied every delaying tactic and restrictive rule they could muster. But when the day came, and the flimsy little planes staggered into the air with their dangerously heavy loads of bombs, Mitchell won the challenge completely. Every ship was sunk, including the *Ostfriesland,* one of the strongest ships ever built by the Germans and considered almost unsinkable by naval experts.

When the great battleship started to sink at the stern, her bow pointing helplessly toward the skies, some admirals cried openly. They were, all unknowing, watching the future in miniature.

But instead of looking to the future, they turned to a bitter attack on Mitchell. The tests they explained away. After all, the ships had been unarmed and not moving. Antiaircraft guns would have driven the planes off. Nothing had been proved.

But they suffered. And their Army counterparts suffered, too. For Mitchell was the delight of the press. His every statement seemed to make headlines while an opponent would be buried in the back pages. And Mitchell was now carrying his fight for air power to his own superiors. He wanted more aircraft, more trained men, more air bases. He wanted a complete meteorological system set up for the United States. He wanted bombsights, armaments, bombs.

Time and again he went before Congress to plead his case and stir up a storm which usually broke over the head of the Secretary of War. He outlined his vision of the future in chilling terms: cities and manufacturing plants bombed; planes attacking not only infantry but the home front, destroying industrial capacity and the will to fight. He pictured New York City in ruins, skyscrapers tumbling, stone falling to the pavement, sewers bursting, fires spreading.

The War Department had enough problems. It could barely get enough funds to equip its ground troops and Mitchell was urging them to divert some of these precious funds to his air force. It was absurd. Europe was thousands of miles across the ocean and Asia farther yet. And here, now, Mitchell wanted money to combat a future threat which sounded as likely as an invasion from Mars.

The Secretary of War thought he knew how to deal with the situation. It was in the familiar military tradition, still followed to this day. He transferred Mitchell from his spotlight post in Washington to an outpost—San Antonio, Texas.

Then the two ill-conceived air accidents happened. Mitchell knew his career was on the line but he determined to chance it. He called his press conference, and awaited the summons.

His was to be the most celebrated American court-martial of its day. Beginning in October, 1925, it had the full attention of the press, but the press was divided. Some reporters thought Mitchell a "screwball"; others thought him a visionary held back by crusty, unimaginative generals. But whatever he was, he was fascinating. Handsome, tall, trim, with a ready smile, he was in the image of the American hero. Indeed, his civilian attorney Frank R. Reid told reporters at the trial, "Rome endured as long as there were Romans. America will endure as long as there are Mitchells."

Mitchell was to be brought to trial under the 96th Article of War, known as the "catch-all" provision, which read: "Though not mentioned in these Articles, all disorders and neglects to the prejudice of good order and military discipline, all conduct of a nature to bring discredit upon the military service" would be subject for a court-martial. Under this provision, Mitchell once said, an officer could be tried for tickling a horse.

Mitchell's press statement, if nothing else, had certainly brought "discredit upon the military service," and under the article, the general had no chance. Friends in the service urged him to plead guilty. But Mitchell and his attorney were adamant. They saw one chance. They planned to prove that every one of his statements about the military was true.

The court-martial was held in a converted warehouse in Washington, D.C. In view of the pretrial publicity, the public and the press had expected some sort of indoor coliseum; the choice of a shabby warehouse was seen as a direct slap at Mitchell.

But Mitchell and his attorney, Congressman Reid, could slap back—and they started in fine fettle by challenging the august panel of generals who would hear the case.

The panel, with Major General Charles P. Summerall presiding, comprised four major generals (including Mitchell's boyhood friend Douglas MacArthur) and six brigadier generals. From these eleven officers six would be selected; the Army, anticipating challenges by Mitchell, had chosen extra panelists. They had not anticipated the object of the first challenge: the President of the Court.

General Summerall had commanded the Hawaiian Islands some years earlier, when Mitchell had made a highly publicized inspection trip there. From this inspection Mitchell had made a prediction. In the next war, he warned, the Japanese would attack Pearl Harbor with aircraft and submarines and he predicted that the attack would center on Ford Island. The report was considered so silly it was not even read by most of the Army's hierarchy. Also in that report, Mitchell had delivered a stinging attack on Summerall's defense plans, and now Reid quoted some of Summerall's rebuttal: "The public is being misled by fanciful and irresponsible talk emanating from a source either without experience or whose experience in war is limited to the very narrow field of aviation."

Summerall, furious, told Mitchell's attorney: "I regarded the report as untrue, unfair . . . and ignorant." Later, after he left the panel, he told reporters, "We're enemies, Mitchell and I." Two other generals were challenged on similar grounds. They departed and the trial began.

Reid then asked for dismissal on grounds that foreshadowed the trials of the 1960s and 1970s—that the court had no jurisdiction. He argued that the offense was in the category of the First Amendment, freedom of speech. But the Army Judge Advocate, Colonel Sherman Moreland, argued that a man who enlisted gave up his civilian status and its corresponding personal liberties. The court decided that it did, indeed, have jurisdiction.

In his opening statement, Reid announced that Mitchell would prove that his statements about the flights to Hawaii and the *Shenandoah* "were true, as a matter of fact." In addition, he said, "We will prove by evidence that Mitchell, after exhausting every usual means to safeguard the aerial defense of the United States, without result, took the only way possible that would cause a study of true conditions of the national defense to be made."

In other words, this was to be not a trial of one man for one offense, but an examination of the whole defense posture of the United States. The generals on the panel, who had expected a quick trial, were taken aback, especially when the defense demanded that seventy-one witnesses be heard.

The first witnesses were called to establish the fact of Mitchell's announcement. Newsman A. A. H. Yeager of the San Antonio *Light,* for example, testified that on September 5, 1925, he and other reporters had been invited to Mitchell's office where they were handed a mimeographed statement.

These facts were not challenged and the defense began its parade of witnesses—and immediately established the theme which was to make this trial memorable: The wars of the future would be dominated by air power.

The first defense witness to take the stand was Major General Amos J. Fries, Chief of the Chemical Warfare Service. His testimony at first seemed irrelevant, and the prosecution launched a storm of objections.

"I want you to tell us what mustard gas was, how it was used [in World War I] and what its effect is on the occupation of territory."

"It burns the skin . . . goes through clothes as though you had none on. It affects the eyes and lungs likewise. . . ."

"Now tell us what other kinds of chemicals and gases were used?"

"We used pure chlorine . . . released only as a gas on the front lines and allowed to drift with the wind. . . . We also used phosgene, a chemical combination of chlorine and carbon monoxide . . . about ten times as poisonous as chlorine.

"Now can you tell us what amount of gas will be necessary to effectively gas an area the size of the *District of Columbia?*"

At last the prosecution grasped the real drift of the questions and objected even more vehemently. To quell the storm the defense counsel nimbly shifted ground—and still made his point.

"So an airplane could carry a ton of this?"

"Airplane bombs would carry gas in the same way as high explosives."

So the defense counsel had neatly started off the trial with a whiff of mustard gas in court, capable of being delivered from airplanes over the District of Columbia, where the trial was being held. While the prosecution was still reeling from this unexpected testimony he brought in a witness from another angle of the case, demure—and angry—Mrs. Peggy Lansdowne, widow of the *Shenandoah*'s commander. Mitchell had predicted in his statement that the Navy would try to "whitewash" the *Shenandoah* tragedy. Mrs. Lansdowne had been asked to testify at the hearing into the catastrophe. The day before the hearing the Navy had sent an officer to her with a statement it wished her to read in court as if it were her own statement.

"Have you a copy of this communication?"

"I have not."

"What was done with it?"

"I tore it up."

"Can you state in substance to the court here what was in that communication. . . ?"

"Irrelevant!" the prosecutor objected, but Reid was now upset.

"Colonel Mitchell in his statement for which he is on trial charged that the Navy would proceed to whitewash the *Shenandoah* accident, and in pursuance of that would do certain things. We expect to show that they absolutely did that by trying to get this witness to give false testimony in regard to the accident."

The court ruled for Reid, and he proceeded:

"Was that statement false?"

"False . . . the main point in which the statement was false was my husband was willing to take the *Shenandoah* anywhere at any time regardless of weather conditions. It was an insult to his memory to insinuate he would do such a thing. . . . My husband was very much opposed to this flight and protested as vigorously as any officer is allowed to do to his superior."

"Did you finally appear before the *Shenandoah* Board?"

"I did."

"Did you make a statement in regard to it?"

"I did."

She read the statement: "Immediately after the wreck of the *Shenandoah* and the death of my husband, I stated to the newspapers that my husband was ordered by the Navy Department to proceed upon this flight to the midwest in spite of protests made by him to the department, and that the flight was made solely for political purposes. Secretary Wilbur was quoted in the press as saying that my husband had made no protest aginst going at this time and one of my principal reasons for appearing before the Court is to emphasize the fact that my statement has been substantiated by official correspondence read into the Court record."

Mrs. Lansdowne's testimony was effective. Her husband had been killed in an accident he had foreseen—and the Navy had tried to persuade her to sign a statement denying his warnings. The next day some newspapers called for the resignation of Navy Secretary Wilbur.

Meanwhile in court the bemedaled veteran pilots of Mitchell's World War I cadre began to take the stand to prove another part of his argument: the systematic denigration of the air service. Major Carl "Tooey" Spaatz, later to become one of the great airmen of World War II as commander of the U.S. Strategic Air Forces, now took the stand to tell—in a nutshell—the story of the tiny air force's problems in 1925. The total U.S. air power which could be gotten into the air in case of attack in that year was twelve to fifteen planes—and even to do that he would have to use some administrative officers as pilots.

Spaatz went on: "The bulk of equipment in the air service is very obsolescent or obsolete."

What was holding it up? The Army chiefs who did not believe in air power were not appropriating any money. The argument seemed to Spaatz to be reduced *ad absurdum* when "we tried to get the War Department to appropriate *one dollar* to rent a field. . . . It required a long time for us to reach a consummation."

The next defense witness was another major destined to become a World War II leader, H. H. "Hap" Arnold. He said that distance as a military factor no longer existed. On cross-examination, the prosecutor implied that Arnold was speaking only of war between France and Germany. They were next-door neighbors; America was thousands of miles away. Arnold replied, "I think that makes no difference in an aerial war, where time is annihilated to a few hours."

This was too much for the prosecutor who asked sarcastically, "Is thirty-five hundred miles of salt water annihilated?"

"Yes, sir, it is today."

Who could believe it in 1925? The prosecutor shrugged expressively; apparently madmen were appearing as witnesses, to his line of thinking. The court, he was sure, would agree.

As the trial proceeded, some generals on the panel became miffed at the defense witnesses' implied comparison between the air and the ground troops. They seemed to be saying that aerial combat was more hazardous. The ground officers didn't like that and one of them asked: "Do you consider service or duty in the air service more dangerous than serving in the line in the infantry, in wartime?"

Arnold countered with the General Staff's own figures that showed twenty-three percent replacements in the air service as against seven percent in the infantry.

After other witnesses were heard, the nation's leading air

ace in World War I, Eddie Rickenbacker, approached the stand.

"You have the title of 'ace of acres,' have you not?"

"Correct."

"And for what was that?"

"The greatest number of enemy planes shot down by any American pilot . . . twenty-six planes and balloons."

"Approximately how many hours were you in the air over there?"

"Approximately three hundred."

"How many hours exposed to enemy antiaircraft fire?"

"Approximately three hundred."

"Were any of your planes ever shot down by antiaircraft fire?"

"No, sir."

This was a point Mitchell dearly wanted to bring out. Most of his superiors in the Army contended that antiaircraft fire would be sufficient to deal with any attack from the air. And on cross-examination, Major Francis Wilby, one of the prosecuting attorneys, moved to give increased stress to the Army's contentions.

"Did you ever hear of a German ace by the name of Baron von Richthofen?"

"He was exceptionally good—their best."

"How did he come to his death?"

"My understanding is that he was brought down by machine-gun fire from the ground in trench strafing during the advance on Paris."

"He wasn't as fortunate as you in avoiding machine-gun fire?"

"No, sir."

But Rickenbacker nevertheless had the last word. The prosecutor asked him whether he was aware that in World

War I our Twenty-Third Antiaircraft Battery had officially brought down nine planes with only 5,092 shots.

Rickenbacker asked: "Were those all German or some American?"

The exchange evoked bitter smiles from veteran American pilots who had sometimes spent many minutes frantically dodging their own ground fire.

To bolster the testimony about the impotence of antiaircraft fire, the defense now brought witnesses who had participated in tests the Army had run the previous year. One pilot testified that he had towed a target for an hour without any hits from below. He finally got tired and came down and asked how things were going. The colonel in charge told him that he had quit long ago. Trying to operate the gun, he said, was like trying to pat his head with one hand and rub his stomach with the other. Other pilots testified to the same results. The antiaircraft guns simply couldn't hit a big target towed slowly across in front of them.

One of Mitchell's more flamboyant witnesses was a congressman who would later become Mayor of New York City, the peppery and outspoken Fiorello LaGuardia. LaGuardia had a way of creating a sensation wherever he went, and this appearance was to be no exception.

A long-time supporter of Mitchell, LaGuardia was convinced that the officers on the panel had been instructed to bring in a guilty verdict, and before appearing in court he told newsmen so in his usual blunt and colorful way. To no one's surprise, his words made headlines and before he appeared in court the papers had put out extra editions.

The members of the court, who had seen the headlines, were not pleased with the witness, who began his testimony with a comic reenactment of some disastrous antiaircraft test at Fort Tilden, New Jersey, in which not a single target had been hit. When he was finished, the prosecutor ignored that issue to hold up a paper proclaiming, over LaGuardia's name: "Billy Mitchell is not being tried by a jury of his peers, but by nine beribboned dogrobbers of the General Staff."

"Were you correctly quoted?"

"I did not say 'beribboned,' " was the answer.

When pressed for an explanation of his remark, LaGuardia stated, "I do not think I am called upon to do that, but I'll be glad to do it. . . . From my experience as a member of Congress and from my contact with the General Staff, I am convinced that the training, the background, the experience and the attitude of officers of high rank of the Army are conducive to carrying out the wishes and desires of the General Staff."

Then, looking at a controversial officer on the panel, LaGuardia added with a smile, "I want to say that at that time I didn't know that General MacArthur was on this court."

The trial continued week after week. Seemingly every member of the small but elite air fraternity came to lend their support to the man whose career was on the line. Ordinary citizens came, too, including Mitchell's good friend, Will Rogers, who showed up just to sit at the defense table for a few days.

But the real drama of the courtroom was ahead. Billy Mitchell was about to take the stand. Handsome, erect, he strode quietly to the witness chair, and the court was hushed. Reid led him through an account of his war service, and then asked him to describe his troubles during the postwar years; in effect a profusion of recommendations which had been rejected. A radio network, a meteorological service, trained mechanics, all-metal bombers, air units around the world, four-engine bombers, aircraft carriers at sea, airborne torpedoes, "gliding bombs" which could be launched from aircraft at targets miles away.

Every one of these, of course, eventually came into being. But in 1925, and before, Mitchell couldn't get anyone to take them seriously. Now he tried again. He had a vision of the future, and the future was as he saw it. For example, years before the invention of radar, he outlined exactly what was going to come.

"First, you must have listening posts and places in suitable positions for determining the aircraft that are coming, what their numbers are and their position and their probable intentions. . . .Without going into detail, they have to be far enough out as to enable our own forces to get into the air at any altitude both by day and night, and meet the attack. . . . The scheme must be completely worked out for day and night attack because an attack is not made simply by a ship flying over a place. Feint after feint is made and everything is done to confuse the defense. . . . You might say we have never been able to get a study of a thing like that in this country."

On and on the recommendations went; instruments for flying in bad weather, self-starters for aircraft, bomb-loading machines, variable-pitch and reversible propellors, amphibious planes. And as Mitchell spoke, the generals on the panel could only stare and shake their heads. Two years before Lindbergh piloted his tiny plane across the Atlantic, this acceptance of an era of fleets of sophisticated bombers striking across the world seemed fantastic.

When Mitchell's direct testimony ended, one of the prosecuting attorneys, a brilliant, sarcastic courtroom veteran, Major Allen Gullion, went immediately to the attack.

Under the whiplash of his questions, all delivered with the contemptuous tone of a sane citizen of 1925 speaking to a mad visionary, Mitchell did not make an effective witness until the end of the cross-examination.

Gullion's first question startled Mitchell and the Court.

"Colonel Mitchell, have you any idea of the estimated wealth of the United States?"

"No."

"The World Almanac, page 754, 1923 edition states that the estimated wealth of the U.S. in 1922 was $302,803,-862,000. Now I would be much obliged to you if you would keep that figure in solution, and the relevancy of questions will appear later." Gullion then went on to quote from Mitchell's criticism of the Pacific Fleet operations of the past summer. Mitchell had predicted an attack on Pearl Harbor by a Pacific power. He had said that mines would be used as part of the attack.

"Would you mind telling us what Pacific power you had in mind?"

"Japan."

Later, he asked, "Do you know of any instance in the World War where one—just one—ship was ever sunk by a mine?"

"Yes. . . . The *Audacious.*"

"Are you familiar with Corbett?"

"Jim Corbett?"

"No, not Jim Corbett." The assured attorney was momentarily flustered. "Don't think I'm trying to make a hippodrome out of this. I certainly didn't mean Jim Corbett. I have reference to the naval authority Corbett."

"No."

"In his book *Naval Operations of the World War,* Volume I, page 442 he says that the *Audacious* was not sunk that way."

"I have heard others say she was."

"Then you take what you have heard other people say over what is laid down in serious history, do you?"

"I have heard people as serious as anybody could be say that."

Gullion finally got around to his reason for bringing up the figure of the national wealth. Mitchell's criticism had included the prediction that enemy submarines would be assigned to areas all over the Pacific to intercept shipping. Gullion calculated that the Japanese would have to send out 12,500 submarines to adequately cover the Pacific Ocean. Each submarine cost five million dollars. Since a nation would only be able to keep ten percent of its submarines on station at one time, the total cost of such a submarine fleet, according to Gullion's calculations, would be $625 billion. And the wealth of the United States was less than half that.

This mathematical juggling only seemed to amuse Mitchell, but that afternoon he slipped badly. Gullion was questioning one of his prophecies in the report he had submitted after touring the Pacific. Mitchell had said that submarines might some day carry large guns or gas rockets or other missiles, he did not know what but he did know submarines would be a fantastic weapon of the future capable of challenging battleships. Gullion thought this was absurd, and said so. Mitchell said, "That was my opinion."

Gullion: "That was your *opinion?*"

"That was my opinion."

"Is that your opinion now?"

"Yes."

The trap was ready to snap shut—but Gullion seemed almost amazed by his good fortune. For once, he stammered: "Then, any statement—there is no statement of *fact* in your whole paper?"

"The paper is an expression of opinion."

Gullion wanted that to sink in. He repeated, *"There is no statement of fact in your whole paper?"*

"No."

Defense counsel winced, and from then until the end of the cross-examination Gullion would begin every question about the statement with the words: "In this statement which contains not one item of fact you say . . ."

But Mitchell was to make his points, too. Gullion, quoting from the statement, read: " 'In the development of air power one has to look ahead and not backward. . . . That is why the older services have been psychologically unfit to develop this new arm to the fullest extent practicably. . . .' Isn't it a fact that air officers in the development of air power look backward for lessons to guide them?"

Mitchell's answer to this question perhaps summed up the problems of the air service better than any other exchange at the trial: "They have so little to go on in looking backward, they have to look forward in order to meet the conditions in air arms."

Gullion then turned to the heart of Mitchell's criticism. He quoted: "These accidents are the direct result of incompetency, criminal negligence and almost treasonable administration of the national defense by the War and Navy Departments." Gullion looked at Mitchell. "Well, what is treason?"

"There are two definitions of treason, one is that contained in the Constitution. That is, levying war against the United States, or giving aid and comfort to its enemies. The other is to give up or betray; betraying of any trust of confidence; perfidy or breach of faith. I believe that the departments, the system, is almost treasonable . . . in that it does not give a proper place to air power in organizing the defenses of the country, which is vital as an element. That is what I believe. It is a question of the system, and not the individuals, entirely."

Under further questioning, Mitchell elaborated: "I think officers in the air service who are subjected to the command of people who know absolutely nothing about aviation, who come and inspect their outfits without knowing anything about them whatever and ask foolish questions—I think that is repugnant in every way to a man who has given up his life to this duty and is constantly exposed to danger in the air in that way."

After more questions, most of them delivered in sarcastic tones and filled with allusions to "exaggeration," "dreams," and "visions," Michaell's ordeal was over. But his testimony had overcome all of Gullion's efforts to discredit it in the eyes of the public; newspapers carried Michell's philosophy to every corner of America.

The prosecution tried to counter this impression with a range of witnesses varying from dirigible designers to Admiral Richard Byrd, the famous explorer. Reid, too, was a brilliant cross-examiner, and also a master of sarcasm. Finally, his tactics became too much for at least one general on the panel. After one question by Reid, General Edward A. King suddenly burst out, "Damned rot!" As a clue to the general's impartial attitude this was revealing. King apologized but as Reid told reporters later, "You all know that if this was a civilian court, this case would be thrown out immediately."

Perhaps Mitchell's greatest enemy in the military service was Major General Hugh A. Drum, the Assistant Chief of Staff G-3 (Operations). Drum was a belligerent, testy witness who thought that aviation as a military factor was next to nonexistent. With a few antiaircraft guns, he could keep any bombing fleet away from a target. If the planes flew high enough to avoid the guns, they would be unable to bomb effectively. When Reid tried to question him, Drum retorted, "Will you tell me what *your* war experience was, and we can judge."

Lieutenant Colonel Lesley J. McNair of the General Staff ridiculed Mitchell's prediction that the oil tanks at Pearl Harbor were vulnerable.

"Would you say that they are noncombustible?"

"I can explain that, but I would prefer not to."

Time and again taking refuge in "confidential" matters, the colonel did not admit the defenses of Hawaii were not actually in being. But they were planned, and they would take effect when war came.

And so it went. Leaders of the antiaviation group, by far the majority in the military, came forward one by one to counter the testimony of the small clique of men whom Mitchell called "the air fraternity."

As Mitchell said, when he rose to make his closing statement: "The truth of every statement which I have made has been proved by good and sufficient evidence before this court, not by men who gained their knowledge of aviation by staying on the ground . . . but by actual flyers who have gained their knowledge firsthand in war and peace.

"The court has refrained from ruling whether the truth in this case constitutes an absolute defense or not.

"To proceed further with the case would serve no useful purpose.

"I have therefore directed my counsel to entirely close our part of the proceedings without argument."

The Court was stunned. In the silence, Gullion jumped to his feet and announced loudly that he did not propose to give up *his* part of the proceeding. He well knew of the country's fascination with Mitchell. But Gullion, who was later to become Judge Advocate General of the Army, knew military justice—and how to win the votes of the officers on the panel. Clutching a newspaper, he pointed to its headline and read, *" 'The people are behind Mitchell. . . .'* Who are the people?" he asked. Then looking at the generals on the board he said, "Are you not *people?* You who served your country in war and risked your lives, are you not people, too? I say that you are the real people, the real citizens, and that what you believe is what matters!"

In one of the more obvious appeals to a jury ever heard in a military or a civilian court, Gullion expounded on this argument for ten more minutes, flattering the "distinguished" officers on the panel. But then he turned, almost reluctantly, it seemed, to his main target, Billy Mitchell.

"Is such a man a safe guide? Is he a constructive person or

is he a loose-talking imaginative megalomaniac cheered by the adulation of his juniors who see promotion under his banner . . . and intoxication by the ephemeral applause of the people whose fancy he has for the moment caught?

"Is this man a Moses, fitted to lead the people out of a wilderness which is his creation, only? Is he of the George Washington type, as counsel would have you believe? Is he not rather of the all-too-familiar charlatan and demagogue type—like Aleibiades, Catiline, and except for a decided difference in poise and mental powers in Burr's favor, like Aaron Burr? He is a good flyer, a fair rider, a good shot, flamboyant, self-advertising, wildly imaginative, destructive, never constructive except in wild nonfeasible schemes, never overly careful to the ethics of his method.

"Sirs, we ask the dismissal of the accused for the sake of the Army whose discipline he has endangered and whose fair name he has attempted to discredit . . . we ask it in the name of the American people whose fears he has played upon, whose hysteria he has fomented, whose confidence he has beguiled, and whose faith he has betrayed."

Gullion sat down in the silence of a momentarily stunned courtroom. In that silence, a friend came to Mitchell's side and patted him on the back. Will Rogers was telling Mitchell that the people were with him.

The prosecution rested, and the panel withdrew to consider its verdict. The voting in that panel has never been resolved. One of Mitchell's biographers said that a paper in MacArthur's handwriting had been found which voted for the dismissal of Mitchell. MacArthur in his own autobiography stated:

"When the verdict was reached, many believed I had betrayed my friend. . . . Nothing could be further from the truth. I did what I could in his behalf."

But when the panel of generals filed back in they read their verdict: Guilty to all charges and specifications.

The sentence: "The accused to be suspended from rank, command, and duty with forfeiture of all pay and allowances for five years."

Billy Mitchell had lost. Within a few months he resigned from the Army and retired to Virginia, cut off from the air service which he had done so much to create.

But the air arm lived on and grew and fulfilled all of Mitchell's predictions. As Reid told reporters immediately after the trial: "They may think they have silenced Mitchell, but his ideas will go marching on, and those who crucified him will be the first to put his aviation suggestions into practice.

"He is a 1925 John Brown."

EPILOGUE

Although Mitchell's lawyer raised the question of the First Amendment, the court disallowed it, and it would be a long time before it would be raised with success. But another legal irritation to constitutional lawyers was raised with somewhat more success. This was the "catch-all" or "horse-tickling" provision.

The provision, Article 96 of the old Articles of War, now for the first time came under attack in Congress. Fiorello LaGuardia submitted a bill at the end of the trial that would drastically reduce the penalties a court-martial could mete out under this article. The bill died, but showed its impact, as the provision has been downgraded in revisions of military law and more and more specific offenses have been included instead.

(In the Uniform Code of Military Justice, however, the provision is still there, although a revision proposed by Senator Mark Hatfield would eliminate courts-martial under this article.)

But this was a court-martial that was of much greater importance than any legal impact it might have had. It was a court-martial that had the world in attendance. Military men in Germany, France, England, and the Far East took heed of the testimony that had been heard in the courtroom and Mitchell's predictions about the future of air power helped mold their plans. Only in his own country was Mitchell a prophet without honor.

Throughout the Twenties and Thirties, American military men based their appraisal of air power on the statement of French General Ferdinand Foch. Air power, he had said, was "pour le sport." It took the reality of one of Mitchell's most fantastic predictions to wake them—and when the Japanese attacked Pearl Harbor with airplanes and submarines it was almost too late.

THE TRIAL OF ADOLF EICHMANN

Gideon Hausner
for the prosecution

vs.

Robert Servatius
for the defense

This is a remarkable trial description for several reasons. First, the Eichmann case was the major international trial of the post-Nuremberg era, an unparalleled example of how a great courtroom battle combines dramatic form with issues of importance to all mankind. Second, the author is a distinguished American jurist who was a key witness at the Jerusalem trial; he gives us an idea of what it is like to take the witness stand in an historic courtroom confrontation. The story begins in the gloomy corridors of the Nuremberg prison. . . .

The Nuremberg prison, 1946. Formidable, forbidding, fortresslike. An ominous and sinister mood pervades the atmosphere as hollow echoes rise from the boots of soldiers as they tramp through the long cell blocks wrought of iron, steel, and concrete. Other soldiers stand guard at the entrances and still more peer through grilled apertures in the thick oaken doors. Each cell has its own sentinel whose assigned duty it is, not only to prevent any endeavor at escape, but also to safeguard the prisoner himself from a possible attempt at suicide or self-injury. The blood-speckled dust of World War II has only recently settled, but many of those who blasted history into that red powder are within these deep, dimly lit dungeons.

As I move through the somber passageways, a companion at my side, I think of Dante and Virgil pacing their wonder-stricken way through Il Inferno. The allusion may be excessive but here indeed are the men who stoked, fueled, and kept blazing the fires not of an imaginary Hades, but a living hell —each one now in a fireproof chamber. Here is Hermann Goering, Pluto to Adolf Hitler, the Nazi Lucifer. There is Field Marshal Wilhelm Keitel, Chief of the High Command that planned the satanic invasions, transforming into a purgatory of agony and torment a dozen countries that had theretofore known the paradise of peace. Keitel was the man who had proclaimed that the life of civilians in a conquered land meant "nothing" In another dungeon I see Colonel General Alfred Jodl, Chief of Operations, who directed the iron-helmeted, jack-booted hordes which spread disaster, wrack and ruin in thousands of cities, villages, and hamlets. Watching at his own little grated window of what is left of his world stands Admiral

Karl Doenitz, who commanded the underseas fleets which plummeted ships, men, women, and children to the bottom of the sea.

And there are many others whose names in flaming letters spelled misery and death: Hans Frank, the butcher of Poland; Ernst Kaltenbrunner who commanded the slaughterous SD; Julius Streicher, the "venomous vulgarian," Hans Sauckel, the slave-driving Pharaoh of Naziland. . . .

My companion is Captain G. M. Gilbert of the United States Army, attached to the Intelligence Corps, but now prison psychologist in constant attendance on these high-ranking German officers. Hitler is not present and I am inquiring into the reasons for his absence. Is he really dead? The Russians first announced they had proof of the Fuehrer's death and then denied possession of such evidence. They seemed prepared to adopt either position—that Hitler is alive or that he is dead—depending on which story may better suit their propagandistic purposes.

I am exploring the corridors of this prison, as I have been searching through much of Germany, seeking evidence which is trustworthy as to whether Hitler has escaped to another continent or lies a nameless cadaver among the ruins which are his monument. As a Navy officer I have been directed by my military superiors to investigate and report on the conflicting claims regarding Hitler's survival. Obviously, if the continent-smashing dictator is alive, the war has not truly ended; and if he is dead, but Germany still believes him alive, continuing ferment is inevitable as his fanatic supporters mark time until his return. . . .

At Potsdam, Josef Stalin informed President Truman he thought Hitler was hiding in Spain or Argentina. Behind his huge mustaches the Communist chief kept concealed his plan to accuse the Allies, when it would be to his advantage to do so, of harboring the Fuehrer. It developed later that Stalin knew even then that the jawbone of that erstwhile fellow gangster had been recovered in the Reich Chancellery garden and was now in the Kremlin vaults.

But none of this was known in the early days of my investigation. Obviously, the persons who might best be familiar with Hitler's intentions, plans, and movements in the final days of the crumbling Reich are those who intimately worked with him up to the time of the collapse. And so I am questioning the twenty-one defendants accused of being Hitler's major accomplices.

The first prisoner I interview is Hitler's alter-ego. Captain Gilbert introduces me to Field Marshal Hermann Goering, who is clad in a double-breasted pearl gray uniform and the inevitable habitude of his ostentatious past. Captain Gilbert translates my English into German and Goering's German into English.

I ask the huge and pompous field marshal what he knows about Hitler's disappearance, and he says he last saw the Fuehrer on April 22 when he (Goering) departed from Berlin to carry on the battle further south. He emphasizes the word "battle," but the real reason why Goering shook off the dust of Berlin from his yellow-top boots, which he still wears, was not to carry on the battle, but to avoid being hooked by the Russian pincers then inexorably closing in on the Reich Chancellery. He explains that, considering the messages he received and the circumstances of those final days, there can be no doubt that Hitler is dead. He emphasizes that Hitler would not have written his last will and testament and certainly would not have released it to the world had there been the slightest chance he could have slipped through the encircling Russian divisions.

We discuss that portentous last will and testament, in which Hitler blames the Jews for Germany's defeat, and this causes me to ask the field marshal how it was that so cultured and enlightened a country as Germany could have perpetrated the incredible atrocities and the mass killings of Jews, incontrovertible evidence of which has been uncovered by United States Congressional Committees. He replies that he was unaware that the massacres had reached the proportions reported, but that the men chiefly responsible for what happened were Hitler, Bormann, Goebbels, Himmler, Heydrich, and Eichmann. I have never before heard the name Eichmann, so I inquire about him. Eichmann, Goering replies, was the man who headed the entire Jewish program. And then, as if to shake himself loose from any possible involvement in the "program," he adds hurriedly that he didn't find out the whole truth about this until the war ended. He then proceeds to say that Eichmann was the man who determined in which order the conquered nations should deliver up their Jews, that Eichmann arranged the schedules for the trains which were to take the Jews to the extermination centers, and generally supervised the whole anti-Jewish operation.

After our conversation with Goering, Captain Gilbert and I call on Admiral Doenitz who speaks English, so that Gilbert does not remain to interpret. Since Doenitz was Hitler's successor to the Fuehrership, there can be no doubt in his mind of his predecessor's death. He knew Hitler too well to assume for a moment that he would relinquish his grasp of the scepter of absolute dominion unless and until the scepter slipped from his lifeless hand. Doenitz tells me in many words that Hitler is dead and that he, Doenitz, had nothing to do with the Jewish extermination program. Gilbert takes me to other defendants. Later, other interpreters accompany me to those who converse only in German.

One with whom I needed no interpreter was Joachim von Ribbentrop, former Nazi foreign minister, who spoke fluent and voluble English. As Goering was the most glittering of the frauds among the Nuremberg defendants, Ribbentrop had to rank as their most distinguished poltroon.

His training for diplomacy had consisted mostly of wine-selling, in which he had achieved such proficiency that even after acquiring cabinet rank he continued to vend champagne to both friend and foe. He had been so certain of Nazi world-supremacy that when he was presented to the King of England he greeted the monarch with a stiff-armed Hitler salute!

Ribbentrop clings to the image of Hitler's infallible greatness. When I indicate to him the possibility that Hitler is still alive, his voice soars with excitement. "Do you think so? Please tell me? Where is he?" I tell him I have nothing to support the rumors, and that my reason for being there is precisely to learn from him just what he knows about Hitler's disappearance. The luster in his face fades away as he now lugubriously relates his last visit to the Reich Chancellery underground on Hitler's birthday when he heard the Fuehrer say he would never allow himself to be taken alive.

As he breaks into another impassioned eulogy of his chief, I ask him how he, "a person of supposed normal impulses, could justify Hitlers's decree for the annihilation of wholly unoffending, unarmed peoples?"

"If you are referring to the Jews," he quickly rejoins, "let me tell you that the Fuehrer was entirely under the influence of others."

" 'Of others?' Who could possibly influence Hitler?"

"Well, for one, Adolf Eichmann."

"You're the second person of the defendants who has advanced the name of Eichmann," I say. "Goering also charged Eichmann with directing the operation against the Jews."

"Goering is right. Hitler did put the program of curbing the Jews into Eichmann's hands, but Eichmann went too far. I resented his trying to tell my foreign ministry what it should and should not do in Jewish affairs."

I call on Hans Frank, who had been Bavarian Minister of Justice under Hitler and then Governor-General of conquered Poland. I had learned that Frank, through study or by sojourning in Italy, spoke Italian, so I address him in that language. *"Mi piacerebbe se Lei mi dicesse qualche cosa riguardante la sorte di Hitler. E' morto o vivo?"* (I would like you to tell me something about the fate of Hitler. Is he alive or dead?)

"E' morto, grazie a Dio, ma e' morto troppo tardi!" he explodes in reply. (He is dead, thank God, but he died too late!) . . .

He speaks of the massacre of the Jews and relates how toward the end of the war he couldn't wade in blood any more, so he went to Himmler and protested to him. Himmler told him that he was too busy at the time because of a military assignment given him by Hitler, and that he should talk to Eichmann. He says, "I went to Eichmann, but I got nowhere with him."

Again Eichmann.

The next defendant to speak of Eichmann is Ernst Kaltenbrunner. Tall and horse-faced, with scars crossing and criss-crossing his elongated countenance like the markings of an irrigation canal, Kaltenbrunner had headed the portentous Reich Security Main Office (RSHA), which directed the Gestapo and the murder mills. He says he has no personal knowledge of Hitler's eventual fate, but from everything he has learned, the Fuehrer has to be dead. He drops his voice funereally as he pronounces these words. Then, as if another matter has been occupying his mind, he blurts out that the persons mostly responsible for the terrible things which happened to the Jews, and about which there was much discussion at the time, were Himmler, Borman, Heydrich, and Eichmann, acting under Hitler, all of whom, together with Hitler, are unquestionably dead.

While still engaged in my investigation into Hitler's death, the Navy assigned me to cover the trial of the Nazi military and political leaders and to report on the evidence presented against the German admirals Karl Doenitz and Erich Raeder, accused of aggressive war, war crimes, and crimes against humanity. Thus I became an official observer at the first international trial, as the United States, Great Britain, France, and Russia reckoned the guilt or innocence of twenty-one defendants, including those I had interviewed.

As the trial progressed and the whole gruesome panorama of the Third Reich unfolded in the light of evidentiary revelation, I felt a deep sadness pervading my being. What had happened to the human race that such unspeakable slaughter of the innocents and such terrible atrocities could have been committed in this supposedly enlightened age? But one day I was to stagger under the impact of evidence which simply defied imagination. Rudolf Hoess, who had been commandant of the Auschwitz Concentration Camp, testified from the witness stand that, during the time he headed the camp, the number of people gassed to death, and their bodies cremated in specially built crematoria, reached the total of two and a half million!

Casually he related how in June of 1941 he had been called to Berlin where Heinrich Himmler, supreme police officer of the Reich, informed him that Hitler had ordered the extermination of the Jews. Himmler said further that he had chosen Auschwitz for the major killing site and that Sturmbannfuehrer Adolf Eichmann would call on him at Auschwitz to give him instructions as to the modus operandi.

Four weeks later Eichmann arrived at Auschwitz and discussed with him the "details" for carrying out the project. Hoess added that from then on, in "carrying out" the extermination project described by Himmler, he received all his orders from Eichmann.

Eager to make good at his job, Hoess decided to introduce the most efficient and modern methods of killing. He found that Zyklon B gas was a decided improvement over monoxide gas, which had been employed at the Treblinka extermination camp where they killed 80,000 Jews in a half year. In Auschwitz, Hoess built a gas chamber which could accommodate 2,000 people at a time, a decided numerical advance over Treblinka whose ten gas chambers could hold only 200 people each.

He related that with Zyklon B gas, it took only from three to fifteen minutes to kill people, although, he added, in order to be precise, much depended "upon climatic conditions." He explained that "we knew when people were dead because their screaming stopped." After the bodies were removed "our special Kommandos took off the rings and extracted the gold from the teeth of the corpses."

He described how selections for the gas chambers were made. The prisoners marched past two doctors who decided then and there who were fit to work and who should die. "The children of tender years were invariably exterminated," he explained, "since by reason of their youth they were unable to work." The candidates for death were told that no harm awaited them because they were merely being sent into the large bathing accommodations for cleansing showers. Of course it would happen that some of the victims saw through the deception and then, Hoess said, "we sometimes had riots and difficulties." There were also difficulties with mothers because they "would hide their children under the clothes," but, Hoess said, this did not avail them anything because "when we found them we would send the children in to be exterminated."

Another difficulty Hoess encountered was that, although he was required to carry out the exterminations in secrecy, "the foul and nauseating stench from the continuous burning of bodies permeated the entire area and all of the people living in the surrounding communities knew that exterminations were going on at Auschwitz."

Occupied with all these troubles, Hoess could not find time

to keep an exact record of the number of human beings he had finally dispatched into eternity on the clouds of gas and smoke. But Eichmann relieved Hoess of this worry because he was well equipped with adding machines and he informed Hoess that he, Eichmann, had organized, assembled, and sent to Auschwitz, and that Hoess had, in consequence, exterminated, "a total sum of more than two million Jews."

Hoess's testimony threw a panic into the defendant's dock and Goering expostulated to Captain Gilbert, who had interviewed Hoess before he testified, that it was technically impossible to exterminate two and a half million people. When Gilbert questioned Hoess about this, the latter drew a diagram and showed how his plant operated twenty-four hours a day. By using six extermination chambers, two of the larger ones containing 2,000 each and the four smaller ones up to 1,500, he could and did kill 10,000 persons a day. Appalled by what Hoess said, Gilbert tried to make the calculations himself, but Hoess chided him: "You don't figure it right. The killing itself took the least time. You could dispose of 2,000 head in a half hour, but it was the burning that took all the time. The killing was easy; you didn't even need guards to drive them into the chambers; they just went in expecting to take showers and, instead of water, we turned on poison gas. The thing went very quickly." . . .

Although Eichmann was not in the defendants' dock, nor was he indicted, like Martin Bormann, in absentia, his name kept recurring in the testimony like the sighing of the wind through a deserted empty house, and the rustling of tree branches against the roof suggesting supernatural visitations. One day considerable questioning arose over documents which had to do with the request of a Professor Hurt of the Strassburg Anatomical Institute for 150 skeletons, to use in connection with anthropological research he was conducting. The professor did not ask for bodies gathered from one of the numerous battlefields where soldiers were being killed every minute, or from any city of the many that were under air bombardment. He wanted *fresh* skeletons. Living persons had to be killed and their bony structure extracted. He directed this grisly request to Adolf Eichmann, in charge of Department IVB4 of the Reich Security Main Office. Considerable correspondence developed around the macabre project and finally came a letter from Himmler's adjutant, Brandt, directing Eichmann to make arrangements "with regard to straightening out the details."

Eichmann's functions as head of the Department of Jewish Affairs in the Gestapo covered such a vast scope of activity that he operated from a four-story building all his own at 118 Kurfuerstenstrasse, Berlin. In each of the German-occupied countries, he had a deputy, who, working with the government officials in that country, rounded up the Jews and, through Eichmann, obtained trains and freight cars for the shipment to the death camps. The deputies reported regularly to Eichmann, who sat at the center of a vast network of telephone and telegraph wires reaching into the uttermost reaches of his far-flung territorial command. He moved in airplanes and speedy automobiles to all points where difficulties arose in the corralling of the Jews for the fateful journeys.

Despite his czaristic armory of power, from which he could draw bombs of death to hurl at vast populations, Eichmann moved stealthily and even mysteriously. Not everyone in the Nazi hierarchy was aware of his absolutism in the field of Jewry or even knew of his relationship with the supreme command. Thus, in 1944, as the result of an investigation conducted by George Konrad Morgen into suggestions of corruption in Eichmann's activities, the SS Court in Berlin issued a warrant of arrest for Eichmann. General Heinrich Mueller, Chief of the Gestapo, upon being informed of this action, laughed at the SS judge and informed him that "an arrest was in no event to be considered, for Eichmann was carrying out a special secret task of utmost importance entrusted to him by the Fuehrer."

This episode wrapped the figure of Eichmann in further layers of mystification for me. Here was a person cloaked in a frightful sovereignty; he gathered up multitudes as a farmer binds his sheaves of wheat and sent them through the threshing machine of slaughter with agricultural unconcern; he talked to, dealt with, and received homicidal directions from no less a maharaja of murder than Heinrich Himmler; he could make fools of the SS courts, to say nothing of the civil courts; and now it was disclosed that he was operating a special guillotine for Moloch himself, Adolf Hitler! And yet—crowning enigma of all—his collar bore the insigne of a lowly lieutenant colonel.

And where was he now? Kaltenbrunner told me he was dead. The lawyers, in speaking of Eichmann in court, constantly referred to him as deceased, but no one offered the slightest clue as to how he had walked off the earth. Did he fall in an air raid, was he shot trying to escape, was he one of the unidentifiable dead in the empire of rubble and wreckage? The longer the trial continued the more certainly the grisly phantom of Adolf Eichmann stalked the courtroom. Yet, wraithlike as he may have seemed in the trial, an intangible Gorgonlike figure, all-pervasive and still elusive, the tribunal, in its final judgment, incarnated him with the bone and flesh of reality. In speaking of the program to kill off the Jews, the tribunal said: "Adolf Eichmann, who had been put in charge of this program by Hitler, has estimated that the policy pursued resulted in the killing of 6,000,000 Jews, of which 4,000,000 were killed in the extermination institutions."

While all this was enough to assign Eichmann a steel-plated niche in the Hall of Infamy, there was still not enough known, or at any rate, not enough disclosed, for the man himself to take his place next to Himmler, Goering, Kaltenbrunner, and Hans Frank. Eichmann's picture never appeared in Nuremberg and, after the hanging of the IMT defendants and the self-poisoning of Goering, his name became merely a sulphurous memory.

Following the first trial, I was appointed by President Truman as one of the judges in a series of trials which covered an endless field of Nazi criminality, encompassing use of slave labor, illegal and homicidal medical experiments, concentration camp murders and brutalities, and the whole horrid scale of atrocities. In one of these trials, Eichmann's name was singled out many times.

In the summer of 1947 I became President Judge of Tribunal II, which tried the Einsatzgruppen case, described by the Associated Press as the "biggest murder trial in history." Here there were twenty-three defendants and they were collectively charged with one million murders. They had commanded four battalions of expert riflemen (some 3,500 men) which followed the Nazi armies into conquered territory where, seizing Jews in their homes, on the streets, in public squares, in the fields, and at their places of employment, they transported them by trucks to the nearest woods and shot them in the back so that their bodies toppled into deep ditches already dug for their instant interment.

Before taking their places in front of the graves, the victims were relieved of all their possessions, including their shoes, so that they stood barefoot in the mud to receive bullets in their spines. The shoes, with the other garments and all other seized belongings, were shipped to Nazi headquarters in Berlin. At the end of each day the leaders reported to the Reich Security Main Office the numbers killed and the plunder reaped.

The IMB Judgment, in discussing the activities of the RSHA in exterminating the Jews, said that: "A special section, under the AMT IV of the RSHA, was established to supervise this program." On the platform of this "special section," supervising the Einsatzgruppen killings, stood Adolf Eichmann.

How did the Einsatzgruppen come into being? Several weeks before Hitler launched his attack on Russia, Walter Schellenberg, Heydrich's deputy, and General Wagner, Quartermaster General to Field Marshal Brauchitsch, commanding the invasion forces, conferred and reached a written agreement wherein the army promised to supply food and other essentials to the Einsatzgruppen personnel, in return for which the Einsatz men were to protect the rear command of the invasion forces. This agreement was an attempt to camouflage Brauchitsch's honor so that it would not be sullied with connivance at murder. The objective of the Einsatzgruppen was not to protect the rear of the armed forces but to kill all Jews in all territory to be conquered by Brauchitsch. . . .

The Einsatzgruppen trial ended with twenty-one convictions and one acquittal. I sentenced fourteen defendants to death and seven to varying degrees of imprisonment. The remaining defendant had been severed from the trial because of mortal illness. . . .

I returned to America in September, 1948, and heard nothing more about Adolf Eichmann until May, 1960, when the newspapers announced that the Prime Minister of Israel, David Ben-Gurion, had declared to the Israel Parliament that Adolf Eichmann had been apprehended in Argentina and flown to Israel where he was to be formally indicted for the crime of having directed, supervised, and effectuated the program which resulted in the murder of (six million) Jews during World War II. The newspaper stories that broke, as well as radio and television newscasts, devoted considerable space and time to explaining who Eichmann was. Up until that time, he had received no attention in the American press, and, with but a scarce item or two in European newspapers, he was almost totally unknown to the world. . . .

Although there was strong evidence that Martin Bormann

had perished during the last days of the Nazi collapse, there was still a scant possibility that he might be alive and he was accordingly tried in absentia. Eichmann's death, however, was so conclusively accepted as a vital statistic that he was practically ignored in postwar historical literature. But now the Israeli sleuths had dredged him out of the swamps of his imposture and showed him to be very much alive; and, from all the documents, records, and statements which heretofore seemed destined only for the archives, rose live accusatory evidence to face him.

Before, however, humanity in general could breathe a sigh of relief that this colossal figure of evil would be hailed before a tribunal of reckoning, a furious storm of criticism broke over Israel. Argentina charged Israel with violating Argentina's sovereignty in having abducted Eichmann out of that country, and filed a formal complaint against her in the United Nations. Critics throughout the world fired broadsides of censure, accusing Israel of illegal practices and violence. They angrily declared that the law under which Israel intended to indict Eichmann was not enacted until 1950, which was long after the alleged crimes had been committed. Therefore, this was ex post factoism, something condemned in every civilized country.

Argentina's complaint against Israel came on for hearing before the Security Council of the United Nations, which, after a spirited debate, voted a censure of Israel and called upon her government "to make appropriate reparation in accordance with the Charter of the United Nations and the rules of international law." Israel apologized to Argentina. The apology was accepted. But Eichmann remained in Israel. Despite the resolution of censure, the Security Council did acknowledge the historical reality of Jewish persecution under the Nazi regime and resolved that: "Mindful of the universal condemnation of the persecution of the Jews under the Nazis, and of the concern of people in all countries . . . Eichmann should be brought to appropriate justice for the crimes of which he is accused." . . .

Shortly before the trial began, I received a communication from Gideon Hausner, the attorney general of the State of Israel, asking me to be a witness for the prosecution. Mr. Hausner stated that because of my participation in the Nuremberg trials and my direct contact with persons who had known and dealt with Eichmann I could supply the tribunal with evidence which would be extremely helpful in the ascertainment of the truth.

I discussed the invitation with several judges and lawyer friends of mine. The majority of them counseled me strongly not to accept the invitation. One of them, a very prominent and successful advocate, said: "I think it will be a big mistake, Justice, for you to appear at the Eichmann trial. You hold high office. You should not demean yourself by becoming a witness."

I replied that a judge more than anyone else should contribute to the cause of justice in any way he may. The lawyer persisted: "Yes, that is true, but always in an official capacity. As a witness you may be the target of attack. You know better than anybody else that the trial has not met with favor in many parts of the world and particularly in the United States. You will be accused of taking part in a proceeding which does not measure up to the tenets of international law."

After listening to these observations, which, in one form or another, were repeated by others, I felt all the more an impelling duty to testify. If my testimony could make any contribution toward upholding the dignity and sanctity of human life, I could not, in conscience, refuse the invitation from Jerusalem. And so, early in May, 1961, in the venerable city of Jerusalem, with its 3,000 years of pulse-throbbing history, I entered into the Beit Ha'am, which must forever remain one of the most notable courtrooms in all the annals of the law. Here evidence was being heard on a crime which no fiction writer, with the most boundless, lurid imagination and the most macabre invention, could ever conjure up to astound and horrify his readers. And the man charged with perpetrating this ungraspable crime of planning, devising, and working the machinery which in eighteen different nations snuffed out the lives of six million men, women, and children was here before his judges to respond to the unprecedented indictment which spelled out the sanguinary offense in all its intolerable magnitude.

I study him as he sits in a bullet-proof glass enclosure, so he may be safe from any possible act of vengeance attempted by some grief-crazed survivor of the crimes attributed to him. Many of the newspaper, radio, and televison commentators covering the trial see nothing extraordinary in Eichmann's appearance. Some have described him as looking "like a bank clerk." It is true that character is not always portrayed in physiognomy and that Hollywood characterizations of bad men do not generally coincide with the realities of life, but Eichmann does not fit into any ordinary mold as I watch him.

Under the bright lights which flood the dais, his features, contour, and minutest expression are as vivid as if the crystal walls and ceiling which enclose him had become a gigantic magnifying glass, emphasizing every lineament of facial contour and expression. His beady, snakelike eyes sink into a startling skull, over which the yellowish parchment of his skin crinkles and almost crackles as his tongue, in apparently continuous movement, bulges here and there the enveloping, cadaverous cheeks. His thin lips curl, twitch, and bunch at either side of a mouth which any fox could call its own. All the cunning and craft proverbially ascribed to the fox can be observed there in that cage.

I say "cage" because it has been so designated by many newspaper men, but it could perhaps better be compared to the glass-enclosed front of a bus. It accommodates three persons comfortably—Eichmann and two guards.

I am now in the witness chair facing him. A portentous glint from his cavernous eyes persuades me that if he were really operating a bus and I were directly in his path, as I am here, I would hear no warning gong and there would be no swerving—only a deliberate, murderous acceleration. . . .

And now, with my words being translated into Hebrew, German, and French, I testify to the conversations I had with Goering, von Ribbentrop, Hans Frank, Kaltenbrunner, Schellenberg, General Koller, all of whom had had immediate contact with Eichmann and knew of their own personal knowledge of his strategic position in the Nazi blood cellar, standing at the spigot of slaughter, turning it on and off, as he, Himmler, and Hitler desired.

Eichmann's main defense is that he was a a subordinate official without any authority to issue orders. I point out that from what I learned at Nuremberg he was in fact next only to Himmler in authority to kill Jews. I emphasize: "The fact that Eichmann's rank was only that of a lieutenant colonel did not impede him at all in the fulfillment of his commitments and plans, because he had the approval at all times of Himmler; and when it became necessary he could use the name of Hitler." I relate the episode of the Gestapo chief informing the SS court that it could "have no jurisdiction over Eichmann because he was engaged in fulfilling a special mission for Hitler."

Under questioning by Attorney General Hausner I testify to the agreement made by Schellenberg representing the RSHA, and General Wagner, representing the Army, wherein it was stated that the Einsatzgruppen forces were intended to protect the rear of the Army. I point out in my testimony that "This agreement was a false facade because the Einsatzgruppen organization was not a combat outfit. Hardly anyone of the officers had any military training. The Einsatzgruppen organization, in point of fact, was a slaughterhouse on wheels."

> ATTORNEY GENERAL: Who staffed the Einsatzgruppen, Judge? WITNESS MUSMANNO: The Einsatzgruppen was staffed, of course, by Himmler. That is, he made the appointments very largely on the recommendation of Eichmann. Stahleeker, who was a friend of Eichmann's, was appointed as commander of Einsatzgruppe A, Nebe went to Einsatzgruppe B. . . .
>
> Q.: Was Schellenberg familiar with the Einsatzgruppen, sir?
>
> A.: He was, because he not only conducted these negotiations with General Wagner, to which I referred, but he was present in Berlin when Heydrich and Streckenbach, who was chief of the personnel of the RSHA, gave directions and instructions to the Einsatzgruppen personnel as to what they were to do in the East, and Schellenberg saw Eichmann at these conferences.
>
> Q.: Did Schellenberg have any further connection with the Einsatzgruppen?
>
> A.: Yes, during the Russian campaign many hundreds of thousands of Russians were captured as prisoners of war. Schellenberg, as the head of the German Foreign Secret Service, initiated a project which was entitled "Operation Zeppelin."
>
> Q.: The purpose of which was to get Russian prisoners to spy on their fellow Russians?

A.: That is correct.

Q.: Now, in this operation, headed by Schellenberg, did he have any contact with Eichmann?

A.: This operation was partially successful, but some of the Russian prisoners of war who became spies for the German forces were themselves executed by the Germans. The executions were conducted by the Einsatzgruppen, and several of the Russian prisoners were done to death under the direction of Brigadier General Naumann, who was the chief of Einsatzgruppe B. In this "Operation Zeppelin," AMT VI, headed by Schellenberg, Schellenberg worked hand in glove with AMT IV, the Gestapo, and because of that association, aside from the usual routine office camaraderie between individuals in the same organization, Schellenberg came into contact with Eichmann, who of course was heading IVB in the Gestapo. . . .

Q.: With regard to the Jewish affairs, what was the principal purpose of the Einsatzgruppen?

A.: The main and principal objective of the Einsatzgruppen was to kill Jews and rob them of their property. . . .

Q.: Did any of the Einsatz leaders complain about the work they were doing?

A.: Yes. Some of them complained because they had to travel over bad roads in order to reach the Jews whom they were going to kill. And they also complained when bad weather set in, and mud made their transportation all the more difficult. In very cold weather, when the ground was frozen and it was impossible to dig graves, they complained because the executions had to be postponed until fair weather arrived. Sometimes, they shot

> their victims in the snow and let their bodies lie in the snow.

Attorney General Hausner asks me whether, in my conversations with Schellenberg, we discussed the question as to whether one could avoid superior orders which commanded the killing of unarmed civilians. I reply that Schellenberg emphasized that if any person in the Einsatzgruppen organization did not have the callousness of heart to kill in cold blood, he would be relieved of that duty: "He stated very clearly that those who were incapable of performing these executions would be released and sent home, because they were in the way of others who were perfectly ready, willing, and able to carry out Hitler's orders for the extermination of the Jews. He pointed out that the Nazi leaders couldn't generally be accused of great human sympathy, but he said he had to admit that they were men of efficiency, and if a man couldn't go along with this type of an order then he should be sent back home. And many were sent back home."

I testify to the fact that I acquitted one defendant in the Einsatzgruppen trial because he proved to me that he had evaded the killing of unarmed civilians at every opportunity. I relate how I mitigated the sentences of other defendants because, although they had originally gone along willingly with Hitler's orders to kill noncombatant Jews, they had later had a change of heart and, to a certain extent, had sabotaged the order.

Before I took the witness stand, Dr. Servatius had objected strenuously and at great length to my testifying. The three judges declared a recess to consider the objection and then ruled that my testimony was in order. The United Press International, describing the day's session, reported: "As soon as Musmanno began to testify it became obvious why the defense had fought so hard to keep him off the stand. It was the most damaging testimony to the defense in the five-week-long trial. He said he had heard from the lips of Hermann Goering that Eichmann was a member of the high command that decided to destroy the Jews of Europe. Goering, he said, told him the others were Hitler, Martin Bormann, Joseph Goebbels, Himmler, and Reinhard Heydrich. 'I believe beyond doubt,' he said on cross-examination, 'that Hitler had the utmost faith in Eichmann and put into his hands, through Himmler, the extermination of the Jewish people.' "

Part of Dr. Servatius's cross-examination of me was reported by the UPI:

Q.: Did Reich Marshal Goering say Eichmann was responsible for the destruction of the Jews?

A.: He did.

Q.: Did Goering say he himself was not responsible?

A.: Goering said he did not realize the extent of the annihilation of the Jews that was reported in the press. He said those directly responsible were Hitler, Bormann, Goebbels, Himmler, Heydrich, and Eichmann.

Q.: Did Goering only want to avoid the responsibility for the dimensions of the killing of the Jews?

A.: I don't know what was in his mind. I only know what he said.

Q.: Did Goering try to excuse himself, to inculpate a smaller official?

A.: Goering did not consider Eichmann a small official. He said Eichmann had unlimited power to decide what Jews were to be killed, when, and in what country.

Q.: Did he try to deny personal responsibility?

A.: Goering obviously tried, and in vain, to clear himself. He was sentenced to hang and took poison.

Q.: Did you speak to von Ribbentrop?

A.: Yes.

Q.: You said this morning that Ribbentrop said Eichmann pressured him and was responsible.

A.: More than that. Ribbentrop said Eichmann influenced Hitler. I might say I did not accept that. You could not influence Hitler any more than you could a belching volcano. Ribbentrop was Hitler's sycophant. He regretted that Hitler put so much power in Eichmann's hands.

Q.: Did you believe von Ribbentrop?

A.: I disbelieved that Eichmann influenced Hitler. I believe beyond doubt that Hitler had the utmost faith in Eichmann and put into his hands, through Himmler, the extermination of the Jewish people.

Eichmann's defense, from beginning to end, was that he was under orders to kill Jews and that, had he refused to obey the orders, he would have suffered serious consequences. Attorney General Hausner dwelt at some length on this point because it was crucial. I related that, aside from Schellenberg's observations on this subject, the evidence at Nuremberg demonstrated conclusively that anyone who was "tenderhearted" about shooting down old men, women, and children was assumed to be in the way of those who killed with a sense of eager gratification. Therefore, such a reluctant soldier or officer would be given another assignment, and the tough-minded killer—one who could dash a child's brains against a wall and then light a cigarette without a trembling hand—took over. I made the inference plain that Eichmann could have stepped aside, if he wanted to.

However, aside from all this, Eichmann was not, as he insisted, a "small cog" in the Nazi machinery. He was, quite to the contrary, the engineer; he sat at the controls; he was the one who decided, so far as Jews were concerned, who was to die, when he was to die, and where he was to die. Joseph W. Grigg, UPI correspondent, described Eichmann's appearance and actions as this testimony came from the witness stand: "Eichmann grew pale and squirmed in his chair as the Pittsburgh jurist struck a severe blow at the defense story that the defendant was an obscure lieutenant-colonel who headed a minor department and blindly obeyed orders that filtered down from the Nazi high command." . . .

As I related events and dialogues which involved the defendant quite adversely, he would stare at me with obviously hostile concentration for ten or fifteen minutes, and then stab at his notebook, scribbling furiously as if he were annihilating me with daggers of refutation. Yet, when he took the witness stand later and occupied it from June 20 to July 24, 1961, he did not refute or deny one word of my directly accusing testimony.

As I testified, he seemed particularly incensed that his brother Nazis should have informed on him and he dispatched hurried notes to his attorney, apparently recommending certain lines of fierce cross-examination. It was obvious that he was the stage manager of his own defense and unquestionably knew volumes more about the case than his attorney, able and astute as the latter undoubtedly was.

Whether spurred on to the subject by Eichmann's notes or spontaneously moved to it on his own initiative, Dr. Servatius expostulated with me that Goering, Ribbentrop, and the others blamed Eichmann for the Jewish exterminations because they thought he was dead and, therefore, could easily use him as a scapegoat. But I replied that if Goering and his codefendants at the IMT trial were seeking a scapegoat they could have found a far more adaptable one in General Heinrich Mueller, chief of the Gestapo, and who was at the time also missing from the survivors, as much as was Eichmann. I specified: "What gave verisimilitude to the reply of Ribbentrop and the reply of Goering and the reply of Hans Frank and all the others that I mentioned this morning, in which they said that Eichmann was the man who headed the extermination program of the Jews, was the fact that they didn't select the man who might have been more obviously acceptable as the culprit, and that was General Mueller who headed the Gestapo."

I said further: "It doesn't follow that, just because a person is accused and even convicted, everything he states must be erroneous and a falsehood because—as you well know, Dr. Servatius—in Nuremberg practically all of the defendants who were convicted were convicted by their own words, on their own statements, on their own confessions!" . . .

Throughout the trial Eichmann remained as rigid and aloof as a slab of stone. Even when a man in the balcony hurled insults at him he did not react. He could not be bothered with people who came to look at him and ask themselves why this man, with the protruding ears, could not have heard the cries of screaming mankind and heeded its plea to cease the mad slaughter.

From time to time Eichmann licked his lips as if to suck from them a moisture which his whole body craved. The dryness was probably due to the thoughts of the barren desert ahead of him, for gone were the days of the dashing black uniform, the glittering boots, the luxurious living, the parades, the military bands, the prospect of world domination—Heil Hitler!

During all the time I watched Eichmann I kept asking myself how could this man have continued to kill—day after day, month after month, and year after year—people he did not know, with whom he had no personal quarrel, and who in no way endangered the security of his country? How could he force children into boxcars in the dead of winter without adequate clothing or food, and no fuel, and send them off to their doom, with as many as half of them perishing on the way from exposure and starvation?

Anyone who attempts to answer these questions on repetitive savagery might easily be inclined to find an explanation in simply concluding that Eichmann was crazy. Would that he had been! The stark tragedy was that he had full possession of his faculties. Had he been deranged or weak-minded he could never have worked out, almost with organizational genius, the complicated, vast, interlocking machinery which involved railroad cars, locomotives, supplies for lethal operations, movements of field forces rounding up the victims, schedules for the mobile assassins who shot their way through a continent, so that in the end a grim total of six million men, women, and children was harvested in death.

Eichmann was not crazy when he was operating his extermination factory and he was not crazy at the trial. His performance on the witness stand in Jerusalem disclosed an ingenuity, memory (for the things he wanted to remember), cunning, resourcefulness, and articulateness which could never be attributed to one crippled psychopathically.

Even so, hatred was so much a part of his being that on occasion it got the better of his otherwise shrewd sense of strategy, and this lapse disclosed him unchangingly the unrepentant killer. The following occurrence illustrates this observation. Perhaps nothing more revealed the unlimited scope of Nazi greed than the attempt, during the latter months of the war, to exchange "blood for goods." The phrase was uttered by Eichmann, who told Jewish representatives in Budapest that if they would obtain and turn over to him 10,000 trucks, he would release one million Jews. He explained that the trucks would be used on the eastern front against Russia and not against the Western allies. Dr. Servatius was particularly happy about this evidence because he felt it demonstrated that Eichmann was considerate of the Jews. In order to get this idea over to the court, Servatius asked Eichmann: "When you were negotiating with your superiors, did you give expression to your feeling of mercy and pity? Did you say they [the Jews] should be helped?"

It is easy to imagine Servatius's discomfiture when Eichmann coldly replied: "I am testifying under oath and I must tell the truth. It was not because I was moved by pity that I involved myself."

Did this signify that Eichmann was incapable of feeling or appreciating sentiment? I do not believe so. Although it was beyond the extremest periphery of his thinking to entertain sympathy for a million Jews who were for him simply chattels to be exchanged for trucks, he did understand natural emotions and the bonds of family attachment. A cousin of Eichmann's stepmother was married to a Jewess. He came to Eichmann one day and pleaded with him to allow his daughter (who was regarded as half-Jew) and a Jewish couple, friends of his, to escape to Switzerland. Eichmann made the necessary arrangements so that these three avoided the clutches of the Gestapo. With this act Eichmann revealed that he was not unaware of the value of human life and what it meant to the person involved and those whom that person loved. Later on Eichmann regretted what he had done. He called his eye-blinking a "sin," confessed it to his superiors, and begged forgiveness for this one momentary spark of charity in the night of his homicidal course.

Up to the very end, Eichmann insisted that all the deeds he performed as head of the Jewish extermination program were legal since he was simply obeying orders. Even in his final statement to the Court he said: "These misdeeds were committed against my will. I did not will the murder of human beings. . . . It is not I who persecuted Jews with avidity and fervor; this was done by the Government."

The brilliant prosecutor, Attorney General Gideon Hausner, commented on Eichmann's posture: "You might have expected that today, sixteen years after the limbs of the Nazi Hydra have been cut, the accused would utter one word of regret and repentance, one syllable of remorse. But Adolf Eichmann was cold and unyielding even toward his own countrymen. He was a gaping chasm of hatred, and truth and honor alike mean little to him."

The tribunal adjudicated Eichmann: "The dispatch by the accused of every train carrying a thousand souls to Auschwitz or to any of the other places of extermination amounted to direct participation by the accused in one thousand acts of premeditated murder, and his legal and moral responsibility for those murders is in no way less than the measure of liablity of him who put those persons with his own hands into the gas chambers. . . . Even had we found that the accused acted out of blind obedience, as he alleges, yet we would have said that one who had participated in crimes of such dimensions for years on end has to undergo the greatest punishment known to the Law, and no order given to him could be a ground even for mitigating his punishment. But in fact we have found that in acting as he did, the accused identified himself in his heart with the orders received by him and was actuated by an ardent desire to attain the criminal object."

Robert S. Bird, correspondent of the *New York Herald-Tribune,* who covered the entire trial, summed it up well when he said the Tribunal found in Eichmann "no desire to alleviate matters in this trial and no remorse." . . .

MYLAI: THE COURT-MARTIAL OF LT. CALLEY

Aubrey M. Daniel
for the prosecution

vs.

George Latimer
for the defense

by Joseph Di Mona

This second court-martial described by Joseph Di Mona must rank as one of the most controversial and shattering courtroom dramas of all time. The names of the men involved—Calley, Medina, Ridenhour, Meadlo—already belong to our history. The verdict itself polarized the American people into conflicting groups as few verdicts have, and the president of the United States, in a decision later criticized by the prosecutor in this case, was moved to intervene on the defendant's behalf. The Calley trial raises issues of moral, legal and military responsibility which will be debated for generations to come. Few have had the opportunity to read an account of the court-martial as engrossing, objective and judicious as this one.

March 16, 1968. The day began with nine black helicopters waiting in the chill dawn at Landing Zone Dotti, home of the American Army's Task Force Barker in South Vietnam. Their rotor blades gleamed in the sun as Lieutenant William L. Calley, Jr., an extra belt of M-16 bullets slung over his shoulder, led the First Platoon of Charlie Company aboard.

Charlie Company had been briefed on its mission the day before by its commander, Captain Ernest Medina, after funeral services for members of the company killed on a routine patrol by booby traps. Already decimated by such incidents, the men of the company were in a mood for revenge.

But the men knew fear, too. For, as Medina had outlined at the briefing, this would be their first pitched battle with the Vietcong. One of the enemy's crack units, composed of elements of the 48th Vietcong Battalion, was encamped in the village complex known as Mylai. Intelligence reported that by 7 A.M. women and children would be gone to the nearby market in Quang Nai City. No civilians would be left to get in the way. The orders given Medina by higher headquarters reportedly were simple: kill the Vietcong; destroy the village.

But because Medina's orders to his men at the briefing were not that simple, an enduring controversy would develop over just what, in fact, he did say. One point everyone agreed on: Medina had told them to expect a real battle, a tough fight in which men would be killed.

As Calley's men filled the helicopters, gunships already circled over Mylai 4, one of several hamlets clustered on the east coast of Vietnam in an area long known as a Vietcong stronghold. Repeated attempts to "neutralize" or "pacify" the area had failed. Minefields and booby traps still cropped up, snipers still laid ambushes, American casualties mounted. Now that rarest experience in Vietnam—an open battle—seemed about to take place.

7:30 A.M. The first helicopter took off. To the west and the north the men could hear artillery smashing into the hamlet area. Gunships crackled automatic fire as Lieutenant Calley's helicopter landed in a rice paddy just west of the hamlet and his men rushed out, threw themselves down, and began firing into the village.

Other helicopters came in gently, the downdraft from their rotor blades flattening the brush, and more men piled out until the whole platoon was assembled. Their assignment was to enter the village from the south while the Second Platoon entered from the north. The Third Platoon was in reserve.

Overhead was a command galaxy of helicopters. The task force commander, Colonel Frank Barker, was at 1,000 feet. Major General Samuel Koster, commander of the parent American Division, was at 2,000 feet. Colonel Oran Henderson, commander of the Eleventh Brigade, was on top at 2,500 feet. So certain was the Army that this was to be a major battle that a photographer, Ronald Haeberle, and a reporter, Jay Roberts, were assigned to document the battle for public information. Haeberle, the Army would eventually admit, did just that in spades.

Walking in line toward Mylai 4, firing from time to time, Calley's platoon disappeared into the heavy brush and foliage surrounding the village. Some ninety minutes later Chief Warrant Officer Hugh Thompson arrived over the area in an observation helicopter to help locate the Vietcong. Instead of enemy soldiers, he saw dead women and children lying all over the village, other civilians running, and American troops cutting them down. Infuriated, Thompson radioed a report of the "wild" firing to brigade headquarters. But before the firing could be stopped, he saw the most horrifying sight of all —a ditch with bleeding corpses, and Americans firing into it.

In one of the most ironic battlefield incidents ever, Thompson landed his helicoptor and rescued civilians from his own troops, taking two old men, five children, and two women to safety. When he turned, the carnage was still going on. This time he could find only one baby alive in the ditch, buried under its mother. Thompson took it away. Thompson was later awarded the Distinguished Flying Cross for heroism. The citation credited him with rescuing fifteen children hiding in a bunker between Vietcong positions and "advancing friendly forces."

Captain Medina eventually told Lieutenant Calley to stop the shooting, and the men took a break for lunch, sprawling about in the sun among the corpses. During the whole morning, not a single enemy shot had been fired. The Vietcong had once again melted away, leaving a frustrated American force with no enemy to confront. But this time, the frustration culminated in tragedy.

Was the Mylai massacre "an aberration of the system" as General William Westmoreland was later to call it? Was it "standard operating procedure," as many Army men would later claim? Some support of the "aberration" theory may be determined by the visit two days later of Colonel Henderson to Captain Medina to tell him an investigation was under way. (Medina later told his troops, "It looks like I'm going to get twenty years.") Why an investigation if these things happened every day? And why did Medina caution his troops to say nothing about the incident?

But the investigation mysteriously petered out; none of the scores of reporters in Vietnam even heard a rumor of the incident. It was not until a year and a half later that Robert Ridenhour, a former soldier who had not even been attached to Charlie Company, started the process of exposure. Rumors of the massacre had reached him in Vietnam. They had so shocked him that he had interviewed some of the participants on his return home. Now he wrote twenty-five letters to the White House and Congress. One of the two men who responded—Congressman L. Mendel Rivers, of South Carolina, Chairman of the House Armed Service Committee—swiftly called it to the attention of the Pentagon.

The Army began a secret investigation, and found that twenty-four officers and enlisted men should be tried by court-martial, either for "covering up" the incident, or participating in it. Subsequently, charges were dropped against everyone except Colonel Oran Henderson for the cover-up, and Captain Medina, Lieutenant Calley, and two enlisted men, Sergeant David Mitchell and Sergeant Charles Hutto, for the killing.

By now the press, at last, was onto the story. Pulitzer Prize-winning journalist Seymour Hersh journeyed to Fort Benning and interviewed Lieutenant Calley. The Columbia Broadcasting System managed to find Sergeant Paul Meadlo. His anguished story, told on television, brought angry Congressional demands for the punishment of the men of Charlie Company. President Nixon gave his own opinion, and as commander in chief it was not to be taken lightly by the Army. "What appears was certainly a massacre, and under no circumstances was it justified. We cannot ever condone or use atrocities against civilians."

On November 12, 1970, the eyes of the nation turned to Fort Benning where Lieutenant Calley stood to hear the charges against him: Murder with premeditation of no less than thirty Oriental human beings at a trial intersection in the south of the village; murder with premeditation of not less than seventy at a ditch on the east side of the village; and murder with premeditation of a monk and a two-year-old boy.

Captain Aubrey M. Daniel 3rd, the brilliant young prosecutor assigned by the Army, stood up to make his opening statement to support these charges.

"I want you to know Mylai 4. I want you to be there. We will try to put you there."

When Calley's platoon entered the village they found it to be undefended. "They found old men, women and children. None of them was armed. Some of them were still eating their breakfast."

In staccato style, Daniel told how one group of people were rounded up at an intersection of the two main trails that crossed through the village. Calley told Private First Class Dennis I. Conti and Sergeant Paul Meadlo: " 'Take care of these people.' So Conti and Meadlo had these people sit down on the north-south trail and started to guard them. That's what they thought they were to do."

But a few minutes later, according to the prosecutor, Calley was back, demanding " 'Why haven't you taken care of these people?' . . . 'Take care of them? We have taken care of them.' . . . 'I mean kill 'em—waste 'em.' The people were sitting there unarmed, unresisting, sitting on the trail. Conti stepped back. With full bursts of automatic fire, Meadlo and Calley shot these people. Haeberle [the Army photographer] saw people trying to run—they didn't make it. They were shot down dead in cold blood on that trail. Meadlo was crying he was so repulsed at what he had to do at the direction of Lieutenant Calley."

At this point in the prosecutor's statement, Calley suddenly looked at Daniel and grinned, broadly. Daniel never faltered. The story emerged as if in machine-gun bursts from his lips. He told of James Dursi, Sergeants Meadlo and Mitchell, rounding up another group of civilians. "Calley orders his men, 'Put these people in that irrigation ditch.' And they were pushed and shoved into the ditch and Calley ordered them executed—men, women, and children—and they were. But James Dursi refuses. He won't. And Meadlo cries and he fires. Conti wanders off in shock."

Helicopter pilot Hugh Thompson arrived over the ditch and couldn't believe it. He landed and spoke to Lietenant Calley, but after he left, Calley went to Sergeant Mitchell and ordered him to finish them off in the ditch. "So Mitchell with single shots proceeds to finish off any survivors of the initial burst of fire. Over seventy people were killed in that ditch."

Daniel then told of an old man by a tree. "The man began to plead for his life. Calley butt-stroked him in the face with a rifle . . . at that point, someone yelled 'There's a child getting away. There's a child.' A child somehow had miraculously survived that fire into the ditch. Calley went back and picked up the child, threw him into the ditch and shot him—killed him."

Daniel paused, looked at Calley, then turned to the jury.

"At the conclusion of the evidence, I'm going to ask you in the name of the United States Government and in the name of justice to convict the accused of all charges and specifications." . . .

After seven days of prosecution witnesses, no one had yet testified that Lieutenant Calley had shot anyone. Then Daniel brought the first members of Calley's platoon to the stand. Three of them, all civilians now, all blacks wearing Afro hairstyles, implicated Calley in the incident. The most damaging witness was former Specialist Fourth Class Robert Maples, who had been a machine gunner in Lieutenant Calley's platoon. Maples testified:

"Lieutenant Calley herded the rest of the people down into the hole. Him and Meadlo was firing into the hole and Meadlo was crying. . . . It was women, babies, a couple of old men."

"How do you know Meadlo was crying?"

"I saw him."

"Did you have any conversation with Lieutenant Calley at the ditch?"

"All I can remember is him asking me to use my machine gun."

"What was your response?"

"I refused."

On cross-examination Latimer brought out that Maples was "three-fourths the length of a football field" from Calley and Mitchell, and ridiculed his testimony.

"At seventy-five yards you saw tears in his eyes?"

But the witness was steadfast. "Meadlo was crying as he fired into the hole."

The next day, however, the prosecution suffered a major setback. The most important witness against Calley was Sergeant Paul Meadlo, whose nationwide television broadcast had done more than anything else to bring the incident to the country's attention. Now Meadlo was frightened. Calley was on trial. Perhaps the government could find some way of bringing *him* to trial even though he was now a civilian. Meadlo appeared in court and stunned everyone by refusing to testify, claiming his constitutional protection against self-incrimination.

Judge Kennedy was bitter. Looking down at Meadlo, he asked, mockingly, "Is this the man who granted the interview on TV? I didn't notice he had any great reticence to tell everything he knew about Mylai in great and nauseous detail on television."

When Meadlo stubbornly refused to testify, Kennedy turned him over to the local United States marshal "for whatever action he deems necessary—with my recommendation that you be prosecuted." (The legal basis for this move was certainly not clear—but in the end, it worked. Meadlo returned to the stand later in the trial.)

But meanwhile the parade of First Platoon members was

bringing home the prosecution's case. Dennis Conti had been a minesweeper attached to the platoon. He told of rounding up prisoners at a trailside intersection with Sergeant Meadlo. Calley ordered them to "take care of them."

" 'We are,' we told him."

" 'No,' he said, 'I mean, kill them.' "

Conti said that he then watched Calley and Meadlo fire into the people. "They were pretty well messed up. Lots of heads were shot off and pieces of heads. Pieces of flesh flew off the sides and arms. They was all messed up. Meadlo was crying. He stuck his weapon into my hands and said, 'Here you do it.'

"I said: 'If they're going to be killed, I'm not going to do it. Let Lieutenant Calley do it.' Meadlo took back his weapon. At that time there was only a few kids standing. Lieutenant Calley killed them one by one."

Later, Conti testified, he found his commander once more, this time standing on top of a dike just east of the village with Sergeant Mitchell. They were firing their rifles downward.

"I went over to see what they were firing at. It was a ditch and there were people down in it. Calley and Mitchell were firing down on them . . . automatic bursts and single shots. As I looked down, I saw a woman try to get up and, as she tried to get up, I saw Lieutenant Calley fire and hit the side of her head and blow it off. So I left."

Charles Sledge had been a radio operator with Lieutenant Calley throughout that morning at Mylai 4. His testimony of the massacre at the trial intersection differed from previous reports. Sledge said that Calley gave the order to Meadlo to "waste them" but that he then walked off, and Meadlo shot them himself.

But Sledge helped the government's case with his testimony about events at the ditch. He said that Calley and Mitchell with their rifles outstretched were pushing people into the ditch.

Then they fired into the ditch with automatic bursts. "People started falling and screaming," he added.

Sledge identified the old man whom Calley had butt-stroked as a priest because he was wearing white robes. Calley had asked the priest if any Vietcong were in the village.

"No Viet," the priest had said, and then started begging for mercy.

"Lieutenant Calley asked him a few questions, then hit him in the mouth with the butt of his rifle. The priest fell back a little, bleeding from the mouth. He stood there, sort of pleading. Lieutenant Calley pointed his rifle point-blank, pulled the trigger and fired right into the priest's face. The priest fell. Half his head was blown away."

The next witness, Thomas Turner, startled the defense when he testified that the shooting at the ditch went on for an *hour.* Turner said that several small groups had been brought to the ditch "some screaming and crying" and told of Calley "pausing between groups of victims to insert a fresh clip in his M-16 rifle."

And once again there was an incongruous touch as Turner left the stand. He touched Calley's shoulder and said, "Good luck."

The key witness, Paul Meadlo, was still missing as the government concluded its case.

On the day the defense was to begin its case, George Latimer, Calley's chief defense counsel, stood waiting for the court to be called to session. Apparently nervous, he did not sit while the jury filed into its seats. Instead he stood fiddling with the microphone, blowing into it, clearing his throat.

Then he began his opening statement. At the outset of his opening remarks for the defense, he said, his statement would be brief because "I am purposely not relating Lieutenant Calley's testimony at this time, for the very reason that his life is at stake and I prefer him to tell you first from the witness stand, rather than have it diluted by me."

Then Latimer went on to call Mylai "a death trap for American servicemen" where the young riflemen of Charlie Company really believed they would be killed, or at least lose their arms and legs to mines. Lieutenant Calley and his men, said Latimer, "were inadequately trained and instructed for this type of combat. The unit was under strength, and it was the first time some of the men were tested in an assault operation —which they were led to believe would be bitterly contested."

He pointed out that Captain Medina's briefing had come right after a funeral for three of their comrades. "The nature of the services was such that a feeling of revenge and reprisal was created in the minds of all the men. . . . The company commander stated that . . . every living thing in that hamlet should be killed. No instructions were given on the handling of civilians."

And then Latimer tried to implicate the Army hierarchy in the massacre. The whole episode, he said, was observed by higher commanders on the ground or in the air. These higher commanders knew or could see what was transpiring on the ground. But it was not until after *four hours* that an order to cease fire was given. And that was given during a lunch break.

With that, Latimer sat down. His opening statement had taken only nine minutes. But the direction of the defense was clear: untrained men, angry at the loss of their comrades, had been told that they must destroy every living thing. Calley had been acting under orders. If not, why hadn't the superior commanders on the spot stopped him right away?

One of the first defense witnesses helped bolster the defense's case. Chief Warrant Officer Scott Baker, a former helicopter pilot, testified that a large group of dead Vietnamese along a trail in the southern part of the village had been killed by fire from gunships or artillery *before* American troops reached the spot. This testimony conflicted sharply with witnesses who had related that Meadlo and Calley had shot the civilians. Baker further said that American troops were only about one-third through the village when he observed the corpses.

The next witness did much to change the picture of Mylai as an undefended area. Captain George White had been leader of a platoon in Alpha Company, part of Task Force Barker as was Charlie Company. White testified that the whole area, known as "Pinkville," was a murderous enclave before the incident. In the weeks preceding, White's company had swept through the area—and been decimated. Only one-third of his company was left. And White testified that on these operations his unit had allowed Mylai civilians to pass through their lines, only to find themselves trapped by the enemy. "When time of contact came, our back door was closed with sniper fire. We don't say these people did it, but they had something to do with it. There were times you could see bullets sweeping across the field like a gray shadow, a cloud —it was that thick."

White stood up and pointed to the map as he spoke. "I can see it like it was right today," he said, referring to an earlier battle at Pinkville. "Our machine gunner ran up to a hole and started firing his M-60 into it. A burst of fire from the hole ran up this man's leg and at about the same time a grenade or mine went off right next to him. The man didn't die, but it tore his body apart.

"The assistant machine gunner dropped his weapon. He turned into a complete vegetable. It was the first time I'd seen battle fatigue or shock. He didn't say anything. He couldn't walk or move a muscle. He had to be dragged out of there."

Having established that Mylai was a hostile area, and implied that gunships and artillery might have been responsible for the dead civilians, the defense introduced its main theme:

if anyone was to blame, it was Captain Medina, who had ordered Lieutenant Calley to kill the civilians. . . .

January 11th brought an important development for the prosecution. Paul Meadlo now was willing to testify. Judge Kennedy allowed the prosecution to bring him to the stand, interrupting the defense case. But the defense was not to be entirely displeased with the witness. Meadlo said that Medina had ordered them to search and destroy the village, "and that includes women, children, and livestock. We took it for granted that the people were Vietcong and I still believe they were Vietcong," he added, angrily.

But Meadlo did confirm the shootings at the trail intersection and the ditch. At the trail, "Calley backed off and started shooting automatic into the people, the Vietcong. He told me to help him shoot. He burned off four or five magazines [a magazine for an M-16 rifle usually contains about seventeen bullets]. I burned off a few, about three."

Later, Meadlo had gathered a group of seven or eight persons and was marching them past a drainage ditch when someone shouted to bring his prisoners to the edge of the ditch. There were about seventy-five to a hundred civilians standing at the edge of the ditch. Calley told him, " 'We got another job to do, Meadlo.' Then he started shoving them off and shooting them in the ravine. He ordered me to help kill the people, too. I started shoving them off and shooting them."

He estimated that Calley reloaded his rifle ten to fifteen times—a total of more than 170 bullets poured into the ditch.

Defense counsel Latimer than asked, "Did you form any impression of Lieutenant Calley?"

"I thought Calley was doing his duty and doing his job."

Captain Daniel was angry at this statement, particularly since Meadlo had once proclaimed on television his horror at Mylai. Bitterly, he forced Meadlo to admit that he shot some babies in their mothers' arms.

"Were you afraid the babies might attack you?"

"Yes. Any baby might have been loaded with grenades that the mother could have throwed."

"Were they making any move to attack?"

"Not at that time, no."

"What were the mothers doing?"

"They were just squatting there."

"What were the babies doing?"

"They were in their mothers' arms."

"Is it true that you cried when you were shooting?"

"I could have. I was upset."

"Why?"

"Nobody really wants to take a human being's life."

With this answer (which brought a loud burst of laughter from an anteroom where Army personnel were recording the testimony on electronic tape) Meadlo was excused. Reluctantly or not, he had proved to be the prosecution's most damaging witness. He was the only man from Charlie Company's First Platoon who admitted killing people under Lieutenant Calley's direction—the same people who were specified in the Army's murder charge against Lieutenant Calley. . . .

At 2:10 in the afternoon of February 23, 1971, Lieutenant William L. Calley, Jr., took the stand. He looked smart but tense in his green uniform, and although he held the Bronze Medal and a Purple Heart, he wore only his modest Combat Infantryman's Badge. His defense counsel led him gently through a narrative of his early life. It too was modest. He had been in some trouble in the Seventh Grade—"for cheating, basically, sir"—and had received poor marks through military school and junior college. His father had lost his business, his mother died of cancer, and Calley was forced to take a series of menial jobs ranging from dishwasher, short-order cook ("not that I know how to cook," he said with a chuckle), to car drier in a minute car-wash. After brief stints as a strike-breaking freight conductor on a Florida railway and an insurance claims investigator, he ended up jobless in San Francisco and began driving east with no goal in mind. His car broke down in Albuquerque and there he wandered into a recruiting station.

As the friendly interrogation continued Calley became more relaxed, without losing his military bearing. He told of his officer training and, asked of Army classes on the Geneva Convention, asserted, "I can't remember anything of it, sir."

Referring again to this training, Latimer asked, "If you had a doubt about an order what were you supposed to do?"

"If you were given a mission to attack, you were to carry it out immediately and if you had some discrepancy with an order you would carry out the task and the mission first."

"What if you refused an order?"

"You could be court-martialed for refusing an order, and for refusing an order in the face of the enemy, you could be sent to death."

The defense counsel prompted him to tell of the eve of the Mylai operation. Much of the attention of the defense had been devoted to Captain Medina; now Calley began to bring home in person the responsibility the defense accorded to Medina for the killings.

In the first briefing, according to Calley, "he started off and listed how many men we had lost. Everyone was quite surprised. I was quite surprised. We were getting low, fifty percent down. The only way we could survive in Vietnam was to be aggressive, we couldn't take any more casualties, and it was the people in the area who were causing the casualties, and we should look on them as the enemy."

Medina had shown them a map of the area. The main target that day was Mylai I on the coast. But to get to it, four other hamlets which surrounded it had to be neutralized or the unit would be exposed to fire from the rear.

"Was anything said about civilians?"

"Yes, sir. There were no civilians in the area. Anybody there was enemy."

"Did you have a second briefing?"

"Yes, sir, for the platoon leaders."

"What was the substance of his remarks at that briefing?"

"He re-emphasized that under no condition should we let anyone get behind us. We leave no one standing in these areas."

"Going back to the first briefing, did anyone *ask* about civilians?"

"I believe there was a question."

"Did he respond?"

"He said he meant *everyone.*"

Calley went on to add another point. Mylai was in a free-fire zone. That meant "We had political clearance to burn and destroy everything in the area. We could engage any target of opportunity.". . .

Calley found Meadlo with a group of Vietnamese civilians. "I asked him if he knew what he was doing with those people. Get them on the other side of the ditch."

Then Medina called again.

"What was the substance of the next conversation between you and Captain Medina?"

"He asked me why I was disobeying his orders."

"All right. Was anything else said by him?"

"Well, I explained to him why—what was slowing me down, and at that time he told me to waste the Vietnamese and get my people . . . in the position they were supposed to be."

"What did you do?"

"I started over to Mitchell's location. I came back out. Meadlo was still standing there with a group of Vietnamese and I yelled at Meadlo and asked him—I told him: if he couldn't move all those people, to get rid of them."

"Did you fire into the group of people?"

"No, sir, I did not."

And so Calley, for the first time, denied a specific charge: the murders at the trail intersection, which Sergeant Meadlo, among others, had testified to.

"What happened next?"

"I heard a considerable volume of firing to my north, and I moved up along the edge of the ditch and around a hooch and I broke out into a clearing and my men had a number of Vietnamese in the ditch and were firing, sir."

"What is your impression of how many of your men were there at the ditch?"

"Four or five, sir. . . ."

"What did you do after you saw them shooting in the ditch?"

"Well, I fired into the ditch also, sir."

The words hung heavy in the court. The answer was a crucial one, and one of the jurors would later say that if he hadn't *admitted* the killings, they might have found some way to let him off.

"What did you see in the ditch?"

"Dead people, sir."

"Let me ask you, did you help anybody push people into the ditch?"

"Yes and no, sir. I came up as the last man was going into the ditch. . . . But, like I said, I gave the order to take those people through the ditch and had also told Meadlo, if he couldn't move them to waste them. It was my order."

"Now why did you give Meadlo a message or the order that if you couldn't get rid of them to waste them?"

"Because that was my order, sir. That was the order of the day, sir."

"Who gave you that order?"

"Captain Medina, sir."

"All right, now aside from what you have said about the shooting into the ditch, was there any other shooting you did in that general vicinity?"

"Yes, sir. I just saw a head moving through the rice and I fired. It turned out to be a small boy. I didn't know it at the time."

"Did you have an incident with a monk?"

"A man was brought to me for interrogation. I hit him in the mouth . . . knocked him down. . . . I did not shoot him. I don't know if the blow knocked him into the ditch."

"What propelled him into the ditch?"

"Maybe somebody's foot."

"Was it yours?"

"No, sir."

"There is testimony on the record that a child ran from the ditch, and you threw him back."

"No, sir. The only child was the one I mentioned before."

Latimer once again brought up the trail intersection.

"Did you see any dead bodies at the trail?"

"No, sir. I didn't."

This flat contradiction of previous testimony led Judge Kennedy to ask: "What's the answer? That you were never down there?"

"I was never down there."

Latimer asked him whether he ever formed any specific intent to kill any Vietnamese civilian, and Calley said no. Latimer drew from Lieutenant Calley his most ringing statement:

"I felt then—and I still do—that I acted as directed, I carried out my orders, and I did not feel wrong in doing so."

Lieutenant Calley's testimony had so far been impressive. In addition to his good appearance, he had managed to implicate

Captain Medina as the real villain. But now Captain Daniel stepped forward to start his cross-examination and, in his soft, hammering voice, began to drill the lieutenant with questions. Within minutes, with Lieutenant Calley shifting nervously in the witness chair, they reviewed the events when the First Platoon entered the village.

"What were your troops doing?"

"They were on line moving through the village."

"Were they firing?"

"Yes, sir."

"What were they firing at?"

"At the enemy, sir."

"At *people?"*

"At the enemy, sir."

"They weren't *human beings?"*

Pause, then reluctantly, "Yes, sir."

"They *were* human beings."

"Yes, sir."

"Did you see women?"

"I don't know, sir."

"Did you see children?"

"I wasn't discriminating."

"What do you mean you weren't discriminating?"

"I didn't discriminate between individuals in the village, sir. They were all the enemy, they were all to be destroyed, sir."

But later in his testimony Calley spoke of children rescued by a U.S. helicopter pilot and called them "definitely noncombatants." Daniel asked how he could recognize children as noncombatants at that point when previously he hadn't been discriminating.

Calley squirmed and answered, confusedly: "I had a means to discrimate and we were no longer firing—I had been given a no-fire order."

Then Lieutenant Calley admitted for the first time that Captain Medina hadn't wanted *all* civilians killed. This came when Calley testified he had intended to kill all the civilians except for the few Medina "told me to hang onto in case we hit a minefield."

"Did he elaborate or was that just understood by you?"

"Yes, just have them go ahead of us, that was understood. He didn't have to go into detail."

"How many civilians would you normally take to a minefield?"

"Never any larger than the front I was covering, sir. If I had five men on the front, I wouldn't use more than five, sir. If I had a twenty-man front, I would use no more than twenty, sir."

But, Calley continued, sensing the contradiction between killing *all* the civilians and saving some as minefield human detonators, "Captain Medina rescinded that order and told me to waste them, sir."

"Did he specifically tell you to disregard the previous order?"

"No, sir, he said those people were slowing me down, waste them, sir.". . .

The following day the long-awaited confrontation took place. Into the court strode Medina, wearing the Silver Star among many other decorations on his chest. Relaxing in the witness chair with his knees crossed, turning his lined face to the jurors for most of his testimony, he was the image of an officer engaged in combat chatter with fellow veterans. He told of the horror of minefields in Vietnam. In the weeks before Mylai his company had stumbled into such a field. It had cost three killed and sixteen wounded.

One of the casualties "was split as if somebody had taken a cleaver right up from his crotch all the way up to his chest cavity. I have never seen anything that looked so unreal in my entire life: the intestines, the liver and the stomach and the blood looked just like plastic. . . . The medic started to pick him up by the legs. I reached underneath his arms to place him under the poncho and we set him on top of *another mine!*

"The concussion blew me back. I fell backwards. As I got up the medic was starting to go to pieces on me. He was—he had blood all over him. I grabbed him as he started to pass me and I shook him and I said, 'My God, don't go to pieces on me. You are the only medic that I have got. I have got people that are hurt!' I hit him. I slapped him. I knocked him to the ground and I helped get him back up and I seen on his religious medal a piece of liver and I tried to get it off the individual before he seen it. The individual was very shook up."

With this bloody prelude, Captain Medina went on to tell of the untrained troops in his command, part of "McNamara's 100,000" referring to what many military officers felt was a below-normal standard of draftees while Robert McNamara was defense secretary. Charlie Company's training in Hawaii had not been very thorough, and its training in Vietnam wasn't much better. "The men affectionately called themselves 'Barker's Bastards.' We were illegitimate. Nobody wanted us."

A slight smile crossed Calley's face as he sat there, his left fist clenched near his mouth.

Medina's testimony moved to his briefing on the eve of the Mylai operation.

"All right. Were any questions asked of you at that briefing?"

"Yes, sir."

"Do you recall what they were?"

"Yes, sir. One of the questions that was asked me at the briefing was, do we kill women and children?"

"What was your reply?"

"My reply to that question was 'No, you do not kill women

and children.' " (Medina looked straight at Calley.) "You must use common sense. If they have a weapon and are trying to engage you, then you can shoot back. But you must use common sense."

"Were any provisions made for the capture and collection of Vietnamese in that village?"

". . . It was standard operating procedure in other operations that we had conducted that the sweep elements, when they moved through the village . . . would push any of the inhabitants to the far side of the village, collecting them in an open area."

On cross-examination Latimer drew several admissions from the captain, who candidly admitted trying to cover up the incident. He gave four reasons for this. First, what took place at Mylai "was a disgrace upon the Army uniform I am very proud to wear. Number two, I also realized the repercussions it would have against the United States of America. Number three, my family. And Number four, lastly, myself, sir."

Medina also admitted that, even though he had not told Lieutenant Calley to kill civilians, he had authorized him to "utilize prisoners to help lead his unit through the minefield." He also conceded that he had shot a Vietnamese woman, explaining that he thought she was reaching for a rifle. He denied however that he had killed a wounded little boy who came running up the trail. But he said he was so confused that he might have commanded the shooting by others.

"When the child was shot I became very emotional. I felt very bad about this and I grabbed the radio and I says: Be sure you inform all your personnel that they don't shoot innocent civilians."

Then Medina, military to the end, stepped down from the witness box, turned, gave a smart salute to a rather startled military judge, and marched past Calley's table without glancing at him.

So ended the testimony. The judge announced that he would be prepared to hear summations on both sides, after a weekend recess.

Daniel's summation first established that there had been a massacre at Mylai. Not less than twenty witnesses told of seeing some thirty dead at a trail intersection south of the village; another dozen witnesses remembered some seventy dead in an irrigation ditch east of Mylai.

Daniel then attacked the main defense argument: that Calley had been acting on orders from his captain, and that he had been under too much emotional stress to know the orders were illegal. "We submit to you the accused in fact received no order. . . . Even if such an order had been given, it would not constitute a defense if a reasonable man in similar circumstances would know it was illegal. . . . He put over seventy people into a ditch like a bunch of cattle—men, women, children, and babies. Is that a reasonable order?"

When it came the defense's turn, counsel Latimer rose wearily to his feet. Exhaustion was in his voice as he began his closing remarks. It was an emotional speech, and it hammered over and over again at the role in the massacre played by Captain Medina, whose testimony had so damaged the defense case.

Latimer referred to the reasons Captain Medina had given for his failure to report the deaths of civilians at Mylai and told the jury, "I am sorry, gentlemen, but those reasons seemed very hollow to me. . . . I do not believe there was an area in that village where a shot could be fired that Medina couldn't hear. Gentlemen, if you believer that story, well, you can believe that the man was not fit to be company commander. But between him and Lieutenant Calley, they are both running the last yards to a life-or-death sentence, and when the stakes are that high, somebody has got to try to escape the responsibility."

With this implication that Captain Medina was lying, Latimer continued: "Gentlemen, I don't see how you could take a group of twenty-thirty men—all good soldiers, all good men —and put them over there and have an incident like this, unless it was suggested, ordered, or commanded by someone upstairs. And I need go no further than Captain Medina."

During the investigation of Mylai, immediately after the massacre, Latimer pointed out, the "finger was pointing at Captain Medina, who himself said he would 'probably get twenty years.' And all of a sudden things changed. Who becomes the pigeon? Lieutenant Calley, the lowest officer on the totem pole in this entire business."

His voice rising to an emotional peak, the seventy-year-old attorney announced that in the course of the long trial he had come to regard the twenty-seven-year-old lieutenant as an adopted son—"and I would not adopt a murderer." He then turned to the jury and cried: "I ask that you let this boy go free."

With this emotional appeal ringing in the court, Daniel jumped to his feet. "There has been talk of the accused as a poor kid sent over there, but there hasn't been anything said for the victims. Who will speak for them? . . . Would any tribunal in this world have found one of those children guilty of any offense and then ordered his execution? . . . When the accused took the oath of a United States officer, he was not given a license to slaughter unarmed, innocent, men, women, and children." To condone Calley's action, Daniel charged, is "to make us no better than our enemy, to legalize murder."

Lieutenant Calley, he said, "assumed responsibility for their deaths so now he must assume responsibility for this unlawful act." Daniel faced the jury directly. "You gentlemen are the conscience of the United States Army. You are the conscience of this country. Your duty is clear . . . to find the accused guilty as charged."

Three years to the day after American troops walked into Mylai 4 the Calley case went to jury.

The judge instructed the jury that they must decide these issues:

1) Did Calley actually order or particpate in the killing of any civilians at Mylai?
2) If he did kill, did he act with premeditation?
3) How many people were killed?
4) The Nuremberg dicta—was he acting under orders, and if so, did he know as a reasonable man in such circumstances that such orders were illegal?

. . . As the days went on, Calley became noticeably more nervous and Latimer louder in his impatience. At one point he heard that the jurors had had two cocktails one evening, and complained to Judge Kennedy that they were "wining and dining." By the time the jurors filed back into the courtroom to announce their verdict, nerves were at the cracking point. Lieutenant Calley was escorted before the jury box as the courtroom fell silent. The jury had deliberated thirteen days, a conclusion that befitted what was already the longest court-martial in the history of America. Lieutenant Calley saluted the President of the Court, stout, graying Colonel Clifford Ford, a fifty-three-year-old veteran of World War II and the Korean War, with three rows of ribbons on his chest.

In a surprisingly gentle voice, the Colonel began reading the verdict:

"Lieutenant Calley, it is my duty as President of this Court to inform you that the court, in closed session, and upon secret written ballot, two-thirds of the members present at the time the vote was taken concurring in each finding of guilty, finds you:

"Of specification one of the charge: guilty."

Specification one referred to the trailside killings, which Calley had denied. But because the exact number of victims was not known, the jury had convicted Calley of premeditated murder of "an unknown number, no less than one."

Calley visibly sagged.

On specification two, referring to the alleged killings at the ditch, Calley was judged guilty of premeditated murder "of no less than twenty." On the additional charges of murdering the monk, he was found guilty, and of the small child, guilty of assualt with intent to murder.

Calley listened to the verdict, standing stiffly, his face flushed, staring at Colonel Ford. When the Colonel finished, Calley saluted crookedly, turned, and walked stiffly back to the defense table. . . .

About the Editor

Richard Rubenstein is a graduate of Harvard College, Oxford University, where he was a Rhodes Scholar, and Harvard Law School.

Mr. Rubenstein practiced law in Washington, D.C., for four years and was formerly assistant director of The Adlai Stevenson Institute in Chicago. He lives in Chicago with his wife and two children, and is presently associate professor of political science at Roosevelt University in Chicago.